# Gender in Political Theory

## Judith Squires

Polity Press

The right of Judith Squires to be identified as author of this work has been asserted in accordance with the Copyright, Designs and Patents Act 1988.

First published in 2000 by Polity Press in association with Blackwell Publishers Ltd.

*Editorial office:*
Polity Press
65 Bridge Street
Cambridge CB2 1UR, UK

*Marketing and production:*
Blackwell Publishers Ltd
108 Cowley Road
Oxford OX4 1JF, UK

*Published in the USA by*
Blackwell Publishers Inc.
Commerce Place
350 Main Street
Malden, MA 02148, USA

A catalogue record for this book is available from the British Library.

**Library of Congress Cataloging-in-Publication Data**
Squires, Judith.
    Gender in political theory / Judith Squires.
        p.  cm.
    Includes bibliographical references.
    ISBN 0–7456–1500–7 (hardbound). — ISBN 0–7456–1501–5 (pbk.)
    1. Feminist theory—Political aspects.   2. Political science.
I. Title.
HQ1190.S685   1999
305.42′01—dc21                                                    99–25390
                                                                      CIP

Typeset in 10 on 12 pt Sabon
by Graphicraft Limited, Hong Kong
Printed in Great Britain by T. J. International, Padstow, Cornwall

This book is printed on acid-free paper.

# Contents

# Introduction

## *Gendering Political Theory*

### Introduction

Gender theory, in all its complex forms, has worked to unsettle established conventions about the nature and boundaries of the political. Until the emergence of feminist theory as a recognized academic perspective, contemporary political theory was largely assumed to be gender-neutral in focus. This assumption has now been subject to extensive critique. To look at gendered perspectives in political theory is not to engender that which was gender-neutral: it is to reveal the highly gendered nature of mainstream political theorizing. This entails outlining alternative gendered perspectives that are silenced by mistaking a particular perspective for impartiality. It is to create space for more heterogeneous gendered perspectives within political theory.

There is an oddly paradoxical relation between politics and gender. On the one hand issues of gender are clearly central to any understanding of the political. Both the practice and the study of politics have long been notoriously masculine endeavours. So much so that many commentators have argued that politics has historically been the most explicitly masculine human activity of all. It has been more exclusively limited to men and more self-consciously masculine than any other social practice (Brown 1988: 4). The institutional manifestations of politics located in government have been notoriously resistant to the incorporation of women, their interests or perspectives. Women have by and large been excluded from traditional political activity and discouraged from defining their activities as political. In this sense issues of gender have long been constitutive of the definition and operation of politics. On the other hand issues of gender are largely assumed to be irrelevant to the political. If gender is understood, as it frequently has been, as synonymous with women, then women's absence from the political sphere can be taken to imply that gender issues are simply not relevant to politics.

In the light of this apparent paradox, explorations of gender in political theory have to date been undertaken primarily by those pursuing a feminist agenda. For it is feminists who have been most sensitive to the fallacy involved in conflating men with individuals and masculinity with neutrality. So, while it is feminist political theory that has explicitly theorized gender in recent times, it is entirely possible to consider gender in political theory from perspectives other than feminist. There is, for instance, a growing body of literature exploring men and masculinity, which might usefully inform considerations of gender in political theory, and which is distinct (in its intellectual and political focus) from the extensive feminist literature that has developed. Nonetheless, given the overwhelmingly masculine nature of politics up to the present time, it has been feminists who have had the strongest political motivation and intellectual ambition to explore gender in political theory. And it is for this reason that I draw on feminist political theory in the following reflections on gender in political theory. It should become clear by the end of the book, though, that future explorations of gender in political theory are far less likely to be so dependent on an exclusively feminist literature. The feminist debates considered in this book have opened up the space for rethinking gender in more multiple ways, allowing us to move beyond the male–female dichotomy as it has operated within political (and also much feminist) theory to date.

It still makes sense to approach the issue of gender in political theory via feminist theory, not least because the literature that engages with this topic is either focused on, or has emerged from, 'the woman question'. Nonetheless, I accept that to focus exclusively on the woman question is to make men and masculinity the unnamed norm and to silence gender (in its fullest sense) as an analytic category (Ferguson 1993: 2). My aim is to show how feminist theorizing has transformed the terms of debate within political theory such that it becomes possible to theorize not only female subjectivity but also female and male subjectivities (in pluralized forms), and ultimately corporeal subjectivities more generally. The implicit presumption that the discipline was concerned with 'the man question' was challenged by the demand that it overtly consider 'the woman question'. This demand is itself now challenged by the proposal that the more important task is to consider the complexities of gender questions beyond the confines of the dichotomous construction of masculinity and femininity.

Not only is the relation between politics and gender paradoxical, and the relation between gender and feminism shifting; intriguingly the relation between feminism and politics is also paradoxical. Feminists routinely claim that politics has consistently excluded women. They also claim that feminism is explicitly political. Feminism, as Anne Phillips tells us, 'is politics' (Phillips 1998: 1). Its project, to realize fundamental transformations in gender relations, is overtly political in the sense that it seeks to shift existing power relations in favour of women. The apparent tension between the claim that 'feminism is politics' and that politics has been exclusively limited to men lies in the different notions of politics employed here. Women have largely been excluded from the political, where politics is defined as the institutional forum of government. But, when defined primarily as a process of negotiation or struggle over the distribution of power, it becomes evident that, far from being excluded from politics, women have both shaped and been shaped by its operation. In other words, the apparently paradoxical nature of these two statements subjects the political itself to scrutiny. It also raises questions about the nature of feminist objectives in relation to the political: is the ambition to include women in a political from which they are currently excluded, or to reconfigure a political by which they are currently oppressed? Or is it to displace the apparent opposition between these two options? The centrality of these three strategies will become apparent in the course of this book.

I shall be using a typology of 'inclusion', 'reversal' and 'displacement' to map out three importantly distinct approaches to gender in political theory. Those pursuing a strategy of inclusion aim to include women in a political from which they are currently excluded. They usually aspire to impartiality, conceive of people as autonomous and espouse an equality politics. They are often labelled liberal feminists. Those pursuing a strategy of reversal aim to reconfigure the political as currently conceived such that it becomes more open to their gendered specificity. They usually adopt an interpretative methodology, talk of 'Woman' or 'women' and espouse a difference politics. They are often labelled radical, maternal or cultural feminists. Those pursuing a strategy of displacement aim to destabilize the apparent opposition between the strategies of inclusion and reversal. They usually adopt a genealogical methodology, speak of subject positions and of gendering (as a verb) rather than gender (as a noun) and espouse a diversity politics. They are often labelled postmodern or post-structuralist feminists. The strategy of inclusion seeks gender-neutrality; the strategy of reversal seeks recognition for a specifically female gendered identity; and the strategy of displacement seeks to deconstruct those discursive regimes that engender the subject.

Kathy Ferguson neatly summarizes the distinction between the three archetypal strategies. In the first, she argues, women's exclusion is problematized, in the second, men are problematized, and in the third 'the gendered world itself becomes a problem' (Ferguson 1993: 3). Christine Di Stefano offers a similar tripartite distinction (which she labels rationalist, anti-rationalist and post-rationalist respectively). In the first frame '*she* dissolves into *he* as gender differences are collapsed into the (masculine) figure of the Everyman.' In the second, '*she* is preserved at the expense of her transformation and liberation from the conventions of femininity.' In the third, '*she* dissolves into a perplexing plurality of difference, none of which can be theoretically or politically privileged over others' (Di Stefano 1990: 77).

This last strategy of displacement has had profound implications for the nature of debate within gender theory. Before its impact it was common to find feminist theory characterized by a clear opposition between those who would endorse and extend dominant values to all irrespective of gender, and those who would challenge and reverse dominant values from a specifically female perspective. The advocate of displacement, by contrast, argues that, whether gender justice was thought to entail the extension or reversal of dominant norms, it actually manifests a tendency to echo that which it sought to oppose. Both operate, in different ways, within a dichotomous framework generated by established power networks. The truly radical project is here understood to entail recasting rather than sustaining or rejecting masculinist binary thought (Brown 1995: 20).

The normative task for the theorist aiming at inclusion is to argue that gender ought to be non-pertinent to politics. The normative task for the theorist aiming at reversal is to argue that politics ought to be reconstructed to manifest the distinctive perspective of non-hegemonic gender identities (usually female). The normative task for the theorist aiming at displacement is to reveal the extent to which gendered identities are themselves products of particular political discourses (although – it should be noted – there is some uncertainty as to whether this is actually a normative project at all). Understanding the nature of, and interplay between, these three strategies is vital to understanding current debates about gender in political theory. Between them, they map the current preoccupations of gender theorists.

These strategies of inclusion, reversal and displacement are, though, only archetypes. They are rarely manifest in their pure form in practice. They should not be taken to delimit the range of political perspectives possible. To get too bogged down in a dispute between them is to confuse archetypal purity for actual complexity. It is, if you like, to confuse characters with characteristics. As each character embraces a multitude of complex (and often conflicting) characteristics, so too individual theorists and activists inevitably oscillate between and within the three political perspectives delineated. There will always be some who adopt one perspective unambiguously. But it does not lessen the significance or pertinence of the archetypes to recognize that one can (and most do) adopt a more fluid relation to them than this.

It is also worth noting that, although my intention is to convey the diversity of opinion within current writing on gender in political theory without oversimplifying the literature, by imposing a typology on what is actually a very complex field I shall inevitably be creating my own frame of analysis. The creation of frames from which one can view the literature is a political act in itself, and one that the reader might usefully reflect upon. Though these three strategies have come of late to be seen as central to gender theory, they do, notwithstanding their complexity and diversity, occlude many of the concerns central to socialist and Marxist feminists. Significant exclusions, which are themselves revealing, arise from constructing the focus of gender theory in this way. Notably, the inclusion, reversal, displacement schema focuses attention on, as it is largely shaped by, questions of subjectivity.

A real achievement of the gender in political theory literature has been to focus attention squarely on the ontological presumptions underpinning existing political debates. Those theories that did not explicitly address the ontological relied on an implicit and unexamined view of these issues. If dominant debates in political theory rarely explicitly addressed questions of gender identity, it was because these were presumed rather than absent. Feminist political theory has challenged this presumption in a three-stage project. It has first of all uncovered and made explicit the ontological assumptions implicit in existing advocacy debates about justice. It has then engaged directly in ontological questions and critically evaluated implicit ontological assumptions. Finally, it has returned to and reconceptualized the advocacy debates in the context of this new ontological 'background'.

The obvious focus of much of the early feminist political theory was directed towards the first of these tasks: engaging in detailed and thorough critique of the ontological presumptions within mainstream texts and making explicit the gendered nature of the canon of political theory. More recent feminist political theory, the focus of this book, has moved on to address the second and third tasks: the direct reconceptualization of the ontological background framing future advocacy debates; and the subsequent 'revisioning of the political' itself (see Yeatman 1994b and Hirschmann and Di Stefano 1996). The second of these tasks has generated extensive and, at times, heated debates. These are outlined in Part I.

The third task, that of revisioning the political in the light of the new ontological background, is still underway and will be considered in Part II. The chapters in this section focus on the issues of equality, justice, citizenship and representation respectively – central categories of mainstream political theory and therefore equally central sites of the revisioning of the political from gendered perspectives. These attempts to elaborate a reconceived conception of politics are clearly a part of the third phase of feminist theory. They have been and will continue to be hugely invigorating and beneficial for political theory.

Although the fractious frames delineated in Part I correlate to the political strategies of inclusion, reversal and displacement surveyed in relation to specific political issues in Part II, they are not synonymous. I have distinguished between ontological debates in Part I and advocacy debates in Part II in order to focus attention on the different order of debate at play in each, and to encourage reflection on the appropriate relation between the two. As Charles Taylor has argued, ontological and advocacy issues are distinct 'in the sense that taking a position on one does not force your hand on the other. On the other hand, they are not completely independent, in that the stand one takes on the ontological level can be part of the essential background of the view one advocates' (Taylor 1991: 160). It is, Taylor argues, the inadequate appreciation of the distinctness and the connection that confuses debate. The distinction between these two orders of debate is signalled in this book by the division between Parts I and II. Part I outlines the ontological and methodological background disputes that frame more particular advocacy debates. The stance adopted in relation to the ontological and methodological debates of Part I provides the 'essential background' to the distinctive strategies of inclusion, reversal and displacement that are evident in Part II, but does not itself do all the work. The project of reconceptualizing the political will also require a direct engagement with issues of advocacy.

The chapters in Part II address specific debates within political theory. The debates considered are those which address the core political concepts of equality, justice, citizenship and representation. Each debate is structured around the three strategies outlined above. The first perspective in each of the chapters in Part II represents the position from which gender is to be transcended to allow political theory to be neutral. The task of the theorist concerned with gender and political theory is to rid political theory of an inappropriate intrusion of gendered identities where they ought properly to be non-pertinent. The second perspective is characterized by the belief that gender identities are to be asserted as the basis for a reconceptualized, but inherently gendered, political theory. The task of the theorist concerned with gender and political theory here is to reverse political theory's masculine presumptions and articulate a distinctively feminine or feminist political theory. The third perspective holds the concept of gender to be partly constituted by the discourses of political theory itself. The task of the theorist concerned with gender and political theory here is neither to de-gender nor to re-gender political theory, but to reveal the ways in which political theory genders.

In order to grasp in more detail what the project of 'gender in political theory' entails, let us consider the nature of the discipline of politics, comprising both political science and political theory and the ways in which the issue of gender gets configured, or excluded, by these formulations of the political. We can then turn our attention to the nature of feminist theorizing outside the confines of politics, focusing on the ambivalent relation between feminism and theory and the inter-disciplinary nature of feminist theorizing. Drawing these reflections together, we can look at the way in which feminist theory relates to political theory. It should then be possible to consider how and why the project of gender in political studies is conceived of in distinct ways.

## The Discipline of Politics

The origins of the discipline of politics are commonly located with Aristotle's *The Politics*, in which he evaluates differing constitutions in search of the best method of government. Since this time there has been deep-rooted disagreement as to what constitutes the political. There is even disagreement about the status of statements about the nature of the political. With regard to definitions of the political, there are those who define politics in terms of governmental institutions and others who define it in terms of relations of power. Some focus on a narrowly defined range of power relations; others adopt a very broad range. With regard to the status of such definitions themselves, there are those who argue that there is an empirically verifiable truth as to what constitutes the political (Easton 1968). There are others who maintain that any definition will be no more than a contingent social construction, the discipline of politics being dependent upon the nature of the political arena, itself dependent upon socially constructed and historically variable forces. Definitions of the political are not therefore discoverable in nature but are rather a legacy or convention (Wolin 1961: 5).

It is this second contextualist approach that is more dominant in contemporary debates. While the positivist perspective (endorsing objectivity) was strongly articulated throughout the 1950s and 1960s, the more common approach during the 1970s and 1980s was social constructionist in relation to status (Leftwich 1984a: 4). During the 1990s, with the rise of deconstructionist methodologies, a third perspective also emerged in relation to this debate. Definitions of the political, it is now frequently argued, are neither empirically true nor simply reflections of underlying social relations, but rather active means to shape the 'real' world. Political theory does not reflect already given social relations, as Kate Nash argues, 'it is part of attempts to institute them' (Nash 1998: 50). This insight has increased the intensity of the debate concerning the substance of these definitions.

In recent times debates within political studies about the nature of the political have tended to be polarized between advocates of politics as institutions of government and as relations of power. In the former the political is equated with the juridical – issues of rights, justice and responsibility. In the latter the political is equated with the instrumental – issues of power, policy and pragmatism. Within this debate politics gets bifurcated, as William Connolly tells us, between principle and instrumentality, 'with one group of individualists (rights theorists, theorists of justice) celebrating the former and another group (utilitarians, pragmatists) insisting upon the incorrigibility of the latter' (Connolly 1991: 74). On the institutional conception of the political politics is defined as government institutions. On the instrumental conception of the political politics is defined as power and decision-making. These two different conceptions of politics generate two different sets of criteria for differentiating political life from all other aspects of society and 'thereby for isolating the subject matter of Political Science' (Easton 1968: 283).

The institutional perspective has been a dominant one within the academic study of politics in contemporary liberal states. Many people have argued that the instrumentalist perspective emerges in response to the perceived inadequacies of the principled or institutional perspective (Easton 1968, Connolly 1991). During the 1970s the instrumental conception of politics was even deemed the true definition, finally releasing political science 'from its synthetic past', thereby enabling theoretical consensus (Easton 1968: 87). Now, however, it is more common to find academics arguing that both perspectives are the partial and flawed product of an underlying, though itself socially constructed, commitment to individualism. Connolly, for example, asserts that neither faction 'comes to terms vigorously with the constructed character of both the virtuous self and the self-interested self or with the extent to which both constructions were valued by their early theoretical designers because of their calculability, predictability, and utility to sovereign power' (Connolly 1991: 74). In other words, the institutional and the instrumental conceptions of the political adopt very different understandings of people (pursuing moral reason or self-interest) but share a common focus on individuals rather than groups, structures or systems. Given this, more structuralist (and post-structuralist) critics argue, to focus only on the debate between the institutional and the instrumental definitions of politics is to work within the narrow confines of individualism.

Accordingly it is now common to find academics proposing a broader definition of politics as the study of power. This is usually an extension of the early instrumentalist definition of the political, differing in its refusal to delimit political power and political decisions from all other types of power and decisions. Whereas instrumentalist theorists of politics claimed to have objective criteria for delimiting the boundary of the political, contemporary theorists of politics commonly exhibit scepticism not only about the particular boundaries proposed, but also about the possibility of producing any objective criteria of delineation at all. As Leftwich and Held comment: 'There is, in fact, nothing *more political* than the constant attempts to exclude certain types of issues from politics' (Leftwich and Held 1984: 144). Far from being neutral clarifications of empirical fact, these delimitations are 'strategies of depoliticization' whereby issues are kept off the political agenda. The achievement of such a delimitation, and erection of particular boundaries around the political, is itself a manifestation of power.

If one accepts this challenge, one is then required to consider whether there can be any convincing boundary to the political at all. Focusing attention on politics as power, in all its manifestations, reduces the significance of the precise boundaries of the institutional form of politics (Leftwich 1984a: 10). Indeed it runs the risk of generating a definition of politics that is so wide as to lose its specificity and usefulness. Politics, Leftwich and Held tell us, 'is a phenomenon found in and between all groups, institutions (formal and informal) and societies, cutting across public and private life. It is involved in all the relations, institutions and structures which are implicated in the activities of production and re-production in the life of societies. It is expressed in all the activities of co-operation, negotiation and struggle over the use, production and distribution of resources which this entails' (Leftwich and Held 1984: 144).

Although this broad conception of the political has its weaknesses, it is nonetheless the one that – more than any other – has created the disciplinary space for considering issues of gender as central to the study of politics. It is the adoption of the narrow institutional or instrumental conception of the political within most dominant renderings of the discipline that accounts for the fact that the study of politics has been one of the last to take up the challenge of feminist scholarship, and more recently men's studies, and modify the canon. The more extensive power-based conception of the political both emerges from, and makes possible, the feminist challenge to the orthodoxy of politics.

## Gender and Political Studies

There is, Pateman has influentially proposed, something about the discipline of politics and the orthodox understanding of the subject matter of political inquiry that makes it particularly resistant to feminist argument. She claims that the power of men over women 'is excluded from scrutiny and deemed irrelevant to political life and democracy by the patriarchal construction of the categories with which political theorists work' (Pateman 1989: 13–14). Joni Lovenduski makes a similar claim. The dominant conception of political studies is bound to exclude women, she tells us, 'largely because women usually do not dispose of public power, belong to political elites or hold influential positions in government institutions' (Lovenduski 1981: 88).

What is intriguing here is that Lovenduski and Pateman make the same claim in regard to the 'orthodox' study of politics, even though they have significantly distinct conceptions of which orthodoxy they have in mind. The discipline of politics has been bifurcated into political science and political theory, which have tended to operate with instrumental and institutional conceptions of the political respectively. The former largely fails to theorize power; the latter adopts narrow, one- and two-dimensional conceptions of power. Each has been overtly and inherently exclusionary regarding issues of gender. They represent distinct – but equally inhospitable – traditions.

Pateman criticizes the primarily institutional focus of liberal political theory, while Lovenduski criticizes the primarily instrumentalist focus of positivist political science. Both the instrumental and the institutional conceptions of politics focus attention on a public sphere of decision-making. Both exclude from the proper remit of political study the social relations that characterize the private sphere. As a result, Pateman argues, 'both women's exclusion from the public world and the manner of our inclusion have escaped the notice of political theorists' (Pateman 1989: 4).

With regard to political science, Lovenduski argues that, if gender is considered from the instrumentalist conception of the political, it is as a background variable, rarely surfacing as significant. Work has been done by female political scientists within this framework to identify bias in the standard literature on political participation and voting behaviour and to collect new research material (see Bourque and Grossholtz 1998). But many feel that a more substantial understanding of women's political behaviour would require a critical questioning of the definition of what is political itself.

Lovenduski locates the primary source of women's apparent exclusion from the study of politics with post-war positivism and its construction of American political science. Virginia Sapiro argues that the legacy of positivism has been more ambivalent than this in relation to feminist research. While it has inhibited research (as Lovenduski points out), it has also promoted the study of women in that the rigorous conventions of objectivity adopted by positivist political science enabled women to subject the statements made by political scientists to empirical tests (Sapiro 1998a: 72). In other words, women were able to break into the field by holding the discipline accountable to its own professed ideals of objectivity.

Yet the political theory half of the discipline of politics has been perhaps more resistant to the question of gender. Indeed, Susan Moller Okin, herself a prominent political theorist, argues that, 'compared with some other academic disciplines, contemporary political theory is in one significant respect in the Dark Ages . . . most political theorists have yet to take gender – by which I mean the social institutionalization of sexual difference – seriously' (Okin 1991: 39). One of the first and most influential theorists to attempt to challenge this state of affairs was Pateman. The object of her critique is not 1950s positivism but seventeenth-century social contract theory.

Pateman claims that sexual difference and the subordination of women are central to the construction of modern political theory. This means that contemporary political theorists, whatever their personal commitments, are able to admit the relevance or significance of feminist questions and criticisms only with great difficulty. This is not because of individual bias, but because 'such matters are systematically excluded from their theorizing by the modern patriarchal construction of the object of their studies, "political" theory itself' (Pateman 1989: 3). The central mechanism by which this exclusion is realized is the assumption that the political is public and that the private realm of the domestic, of familial and sexual relations, lies outside the proper concern of the study of the political (see Chapter 1).

Pateman's distinctive contribution has been to reveal the significant role played by the seventeenth-century social contract theorists in the creation of this exclusion. Such is the continued influence of these theorists that contemporary theorists now work within their parameters without subjecting them to explicit scrutiny. This means that the political implications of a social order divided between public and private arenas have come to be precluded from critical investigation. If definitions of the political are themselves political acts entailing the exercise of power, the power of this particular discourse is so great as to have achieved hegemonic status. We need, Pateman tells us, to understand what is excluded in the classic social contract definition of the political, and why. The original social contract is conventionally depicted as a contract between equals which ensured people's political freedom. What has been systematically forgotten is that it also entailed a sexual contract, which ensured women's social subordination (Pateman 1988: 77–115).

One of the many implications of Pateman's analysis is that the continued omission of questions of gender from politics syllabuses has been a result not simply of contingent and individual acts of sexism, but rather of a fundamental partiality of the very terms of debate upon which the discipline has been based. Both Lovenduski and Pateman take what they perceive to be the dominant disciplinary paradigm to task for failing to be adequately inclusive with regard to gender. Because the study of politics has become so bifurcated between science and theory, they do so on very different terms. What they share, however, is a firm belief that the very construction of the discipline of politics needs to be recast if it is to consider the political experiences of women and allow a meaningful consideration of gender.

## Feminist Theory

The attempts to develop a political theory sensitive to the insights of feminism have clearly been significantly hindered by the essentially patriarchal assumptions underpinning the very discipline itself. But there have been other barriers too, one arising from within feminism itself. The belief that the bases of theoretical reflection need to be reconceptualized if gender is to be adequately considered stood, for a significant period, in direct conflict with a widespread feminist rejection of the very project of theoretical abstraction. Once feminists did embrace theoretical inquiry, however, the areas of study ranged from subjectivity to aesthetics, but rarely concentrated on the institutions of government.

### Anti-theoreticism

If there is a paradoxical relation between politics and feminism, there is also an ambiguous relation between feminism and theory. Within early second-wave articulations of feminism there was a pronounced hostility to theory. Misgivings about the pursuit of gender theory came not only from within the male academic establishment (worried about gender as an appropriate theoretical concern), but also from within the women's movement itself (worried about theory as an appropriate form of engagement). The feminist suspicion of theory was, at least at the beginnings of second-wave feminism, pronounced.

A significant number of feminists argued, and some continue to argue – though increasingly against the tide of both feminist and academic opinion – that the establishment of feminist theory as an academic discourse, and of women's studies as an academic discipline, entailed the exploitation and de-radicalization of feminism. The fear was, and is, that the energies that should be directed towards the transformation of social and sexual relationships would inevitably be dissipated in 'narrow scholastic battles which serve only to perpetuate those hierarchies of control and authority to which the women's movement is opposed' (Evans 1997: 17). This suspicion was based on two distinct concerns: elitism and abstraction.

The concern about the elitist, anti-democratic nature of theory can be met with the argument that theory is likely to become elitist for reasons outside itself. To assume that work which is difficult is elitist is to confuse the form with the context. The concern about abstraction, however, pertains to form itself. It has often been asserted (both by certain feminists and by their mainstream critics) that there is something distinctly masculine about the very endeavour of theory, and something particularly feminine about the reliance upon feeling and personal experience. As Mary Evans notes, this frequently served to legitimate subjective and personal reactions to subordination rather than the coherent analysis of that subordination (Evans 1997: 18).

Both essentialist and strategic arguments were deployed to justify this subjectivism. The essentialist argument asserts an essential female nature, which generates an embedded, particular and emotional form of understanding (to be discussed in Chapter 3). The strategic argument responds to the perceived role of existing theories in the perpetuation of patriarchal power relations with the inversion of the allegedly objective view of theory and the celebration of subjectivism. In the words of a much-read manifesto of early second-wave feminism: 'We regard our personal experiences and our feelings about that experience as the basis for an analysis of our common situation. We cannot rely on existing ideologies as they are all products of male supremacist culture. We question every generalization and accept none that are not confirmed by our experience' (Firestone and Koedt 1969: 55). This perception that all theory could be equated with patriarchal ideology led to an anti-theoreticism and radical subjectivism among many women active in the women's movement (Grant 1993).

It is interesting to reflect that this early hostility to theory has done little to dampen the enthusiasm with which numerous other feminists took up the challenge of developing new, distinctive feminist theories. The 'risks of anti-theoreticism' and the dangers of remaining at, what Evans refers to as, 'that stage of primitive subjectivism that is characteristic of some of the most reactionary social organizations in existence' (Evans 1997: 20) proved too compelling to ignore. Theory became something to embrace and transform. In response to the question 'why theory?' Jane Flax argues that:

> the most important characteristic of theory is that it is a *systematic, analytical* approach to everyday experience. This everybody does unconsciously. To theorise, then, is to bring this unconscious process to a conscious level so it can be developed and refined. All of us operate on theories, though most of them are implicit. We screen out certain things; we allow others to affect us; we make choices and we don't always understand why. Theory, in other words, makes those choices conscious, and enables us to use them more efficiently. (Flax 1993: 80–1)

In short, the political commitment to social change which motivated early feminist anti-theoreticism has now come to underpin the creation and application of ever-increasingly sophisticated theories. Since the early 1980s the production of feminist and gender theories has been nothing short of staggering. The initial suspicion of abstraction nonetheless remains. Many feminists emphasize the importance of experience, context and narrativity and view the desire to abstract as underpinned by discourses of power (Christian 1997: 69–78).

## *Inter-disciplinarity*

It is important to note that the development of feminist theory has been largely inter-disciplinary. It has emerged across disciplinary boundaries, drawing together ideas, methodologies and concerns that had conventionally been located within discrete disciplinary canons.

Feminist scholarship – as Barrett notes – 'has always had the ambition to transcend disciplinary boundaries' (Barrett 1992a: 211). And this has usually entailed the importing of methods and techniques from elsewhere. The analysis of gender has generated a highly eclectic approach to existing theories, with feminist theorists taking the theoretical tools of one discipline to engage with issues in another. Theorists engaging in the project of reconstructing political theory in the light of feminism have frequently drawn upon theoretical literature developed within psychology, literary theory, film theory, sociology and philosophy.

The introduction of the concerns and approaches more common to the humanities into the study of politics has not only eroded the boundaries but has also challenged the foundations of much that went before. The debates, which have generated such productive contributions to the reconceptualization of the political from various gendered perspectives, have largely drawn upon a feminist theory literature that is avowedly and self-consciously inter-disciplinary. Suspicion of dominant constructions of disciplinary boundaries among many feminist theorists has propelled most to work in an inter-disciplinary fashion, drawing upon and developing theoretical debates that seem to offer useful insights wherever they emerge.

However, this inter-disciplinarity has not taken the form of an equal flow of theoretical approaches across disciplinary boundaries. The movement has tended to be from the humanities to the social sciences and sciences, not the other way around (Sapiro 1998a: 74–6). One notable trend within recent years has been the importation of literary and aesthetic theories into social and political theory. As Barrett rightly points out, we have seen, in the last ten years, 'an extensive "turn to culture" in feminism. Academically, the social sciences have lost their purchase within feminism and the rising star lies with the arts, humanities and philosophy' (Barrett 1992a: 204). The attention of humanities feminists to social-science feminists, Sapiro notes, 'is not equivalent to the attention social-science feminists pay to the humanities' (Sapiro 1998a: 75).

Sapiro discerns four distinct reasons for this lack of two-way inter-disciplinarity: the 'science' question in feminism; the discovery of politics; the political climate; and the rise of post-structuralism (Sapiro 1998a: 76). Each of these makes humanities-based feminist theorists less likely to borrow theoretical insights from the discipline of politics than vice versa. Firstly, there is a tendency within feminist studies to be suspicious of research that invokes scientific norms (to be discussed in Chapter 3). Secondly, the impact of the feminist claim that 'the personal is political', and the rise of cultural politics generally, led many to focus on politics in disparate locations and consider their own discipline as political (to be discussed in Chapter 1). Thirdly, a negative reaction to the overly narrow institutional and instrumental conceptions of politics led many to vacate the traditional arena of government altogether in their research (also to be discussed in Chapter 1). Fourthly, the rise of post-structuralism renders problematic the contemplation, central to political studies, of responsibility, voice and intention (Sapiro 1998a: 76–82).

While not all feminist political scientists and political theorists would accept all of these four claims, Sapiro rightly highlights the uneasy relation between feminist theory and political studies, and the need to reclaim a distinctive disciplinary identity for feminist political studies. This is an important point in the context of the 'turn to culture' which has left many feminist political scientists and theorists rather unsure as to the centrality of their own project. The impact of this turn to culture on the study of gender in politics has been complex. Some simply view it as 'somewhat perplexing' (Phillips 1998: 2). Others consider it a negative refusal to engage in the important issue of government. Others again view it as a positive move, which might generate a more adequate understanding of subjective political motivation and contemporary cultural politics. There may be some truth in each of these positions. There has certainly been a turn away from theorizing material structures of oppression and institutional mechanisms of governance towards theorizing identity and knowledge, or subjectivity and epistemology (as considered in chapters 2 and 3 respectively). Whether these new theoretical insights can be brought to bear on the more traditional concerns of political studies and tied into considerations of government is the central issue facing contemporary theorists of gender in political studies.

When considered in isolation from instrumental and institutional conceptions of politics, this feminist literature can appear apolitical and certainly does little to reconstruct more orthodox discourses. As one commentator claims: 'Feminist theory and empirical gender politics research have surely not been deliberately estranged, but it seems that they have had unfortunately narrow epistemological grounds, and almost no methodological grounds, in common' (Rinehart 1992: 16). This is certainly the case if one contrasts a narrow instrumentalist view of political science with much of the recent feminist cultural theory. But happily there also exists a significant body of work that attempts to bridge these two and develop a coherent discipline that addresses gender in political science and political theory. As one political theorist notes: 'feminism – at least in its academic guise – needs a calling back to politics' (Dietz 1991: 250).

## Feminist Theories and the Discipline of Politics

There is a broad consensus among feminist commentators as to the chronological development of strategies for integrating feminist theory into the discipline of politics. Kathleen Jones offers an account of the impact of feminist theory upon the discipline, which follows distinct chronological stages (Jones 1993a: 26–30). The engagement starts with a critical exploration and articulation of what classical theorists have said (for example, Okin 1979, Eisenstein 1981). It then entails the extension of the boundaries of political theory by broadening the range of questions asked (for example, Okin 1979, Okin 1989, Sapiro 1983). It ultimately involves the production of genealogies of the central concepts of political discourse (for example, Brown 1988, Hartsock 1983, Elshtain 1981, Elshtain 1982a, O'Brien 1983).

Pateman adopts a similar schema. She argues that the development of feminist political theory follows a path that starts with feminist interpretations of the classic texts, moves on to extend the range of questions asked ('does the foetus have rights?', 'is there a form of injustice that happens to affect women in particular?'), and culminates in a distinctive feminist theory (Pateman 1989: 2).

This threefold schema of 'adding women in', 'extending the boundaries', and 'reconceptualizing the core concepts' is used in relation to political science as well as to political theory. Lovenduski argues that feminism has made a threefold contribution to political science. The first entails 'identifying and publicising sexist bias in the standard literature on political participation, political socialisation and voting behaviour'; the second involves the collection of new research material; and the third contribution is the production of works of critical theory which challenge the manner in which political studies has constructed its object of study (Lovenduski 1981: 93). Indeed this schema is not unique to the discipline of politics, but is thought to hold in relation also to other disciplines (see Walby 1997: 137).

As the relation between feminism and political studies evolves, so also the objectives of the feminist political theorists develop. Significantly, there is a shift from an integrationist project – which aims to add women into the existing framework – to a transformative project – which aims to reveal the extent to which current conceptions of gender structure the nature of politics itself. The former focuses on the ways in which politics has structured gender relations, the latter on the ways in which gender structures politics itself. The understanding of gender is distinct in these two positions. As Jones tells us, in the first 'gender' is merely a descriptive category; in the second it is also a code of meaning through which actual experiences are constructed (Jones 1993a: 29–30). In other words, the integrationist project focuses on women's exclusion from the public world, while the transformative project concentrates on the manner of their inclusion (Pateman 1989: 4).

There is a general consensus within much current feminist political theory that the integrationist project of 'adding women in' was a necessary first step that inevitably led to the adoption of the more profound transformative project of reconceptualizing the very terrain and terms of political discourse. Sapiro offers a characterization of this development that is widely held: 'In the early days defining th[e] field as *women and politics* seemed unproblematic because we were primarily interested in how women fitted into politics and what their impact was. Some of us now prefer *gender politics*, explicitly reconceptualizing the field as exploring the relationships between gender and politics more broadly defined' (Sapiro 1998a: 68).

Transformers argue that the integrationist project is essentially self-defeating in that women's exclusion from the political is not contingent on the construction of politics, but is integrally bound up with it, if not one of its central premises and preconditions. The integrationist project is therefore insufficient in that it fails to acknowledge 'that a repressed problem lies at the heart of modern political theory – the problem of patriarchal power or the government of women by men' (Pateman 1989: 2). If political theory as a discipline is itself premised on the exclusion of women and the privileging of a particular conception of masculinity, there is little to be gained from the attempt to integrate women into this paradigm. If there are structural reasons underpinning the exclusion of women from our political tradition then attempts to add women in, or even to remodel the form of hegemonic masculinity assumed, will have foundational implications for the discipline.

One of the discernible features of the movement from the integrationist to the transformative project – the shift from 'women and politics' to 'gender politics' – has been the accompanying turn to an engagement with the metatheoretical assumptions generating the framework in which political theory operates. The argument is that gender is not a variable: it is central to understanding basic power dynamics. One cannot simply add in a gender variable to a pre-existing political theoretical framework, discuss women as an addendum to one's unaltered text or simply replace 'he' with 'she' in one's narrative. The very epistemological and ontological premises of the discipline are significantly challenged. As Frazer and Lacey note: 'the invisibility of gender in political theory, an influential intellectual discourse in our culture, is symptomatic of a fundamental inadequacy of the social ontology in which that theory is based' (Frazer and Lacey 1993: 214). As a consequence, the ontological assumptions on which political theory is constructed will need to be revisited and reworked.

However, to represent the three approaches as chronological stages rather than as competing perspectives is somewhat to underplay the political nature of the battle between the three. In contrast to the evolutionary account of the integrationist and transformative projects, it is possible to view these not as moments in a maturing body of feminist thought, but rather as ideologically competing commitments.

Viewed from an ideological perspective, it is common to find theorists proposing a similar tripartite categorization relating feminist theory to political studies. These approaches are usually mapped onto the liberal, radical and postmodern schools of thought respectively. As Sandra Whitworth argues, liberal feminists seek to add women in, radical feminists assert a feminine perspective, and postmodern feminists deconstruct the fiction of the category of 'woman' (Whitworth 1994: 75–88). This typology draws attention to the differences within feminism, and therefore the differing understandings of what constitutes the appropriate relationship between feminist and political theory. It is significant that, where the first set of distinctions is presented as one of a gradual and positive progression, the second is presented as a continuing and antagonistic debate. To equate the two directly, as many do, is to make the claim (usually implicitly) that liberal, radical and postmodern feminism are not simply different and competing, but rather progressively sophisticated stages in a maturing feminist theoretical paradigm.

It is undeniably the case that the overwhelming majority of contemporary feminist political theorists do regard their central task to be one of reconceptualization, rather than simply inclusion or extension. It is also interesting to note how many theorists also explicitly refer to the need to move beyond the dichotomous thinking that would require one either to integrate into the dominant norm, or to refuse it and celebrate its other. Whether one represents these approaches as a rejection of, or a development from, the previous two approaches is a matter of debate. Whitworth argues that: 'Combining the best of each theory will help us to move from an examination of women to an analysis of gender in world politics' (Whitworth 1994: 83). Others are more critical of the integrationist and the separatist moments and see their project as analytically distinct (Brown 1995: 20). However, it is definitely the third of the threefold distinctions that currently sets the tenor of most debates within gender in political theory. The project, as Brown articulates it, is neither to sustain nor to reject, but to recast (Brown 1995: 20). Or, in the terminology adopted in this book, neither inclusion nor reversal, but displacement.

## Conclusion

The relation between gender and political theory is highly contested. Political theory has long failed to theorize gender relations. But if we proceed, as Frazer and Lacey suggest (Frazer and Lacey 1993: 37), from the assumption that political theory is concerned with power relations, and we accept the empirical basis that gender relations significantly determine the distribution of power, then political theory needs to analyse their operation. Such an analysis takes political theory into areas not conventionally demarcated as political. But it will also require us to think anew about what the boundaries of the political should be and to integrate these new insights into the established core of political theory.

# PART I
# Fractious Feminist Frames

# 1

# Framing Politics

## Introduction

Conventional conceptions of politics, whether instrumental or institutional, have presumed that politics is distinguishable from, and stands in opposition to, the personal. The feminist assertion that 'the personal is political' issued a direct challenge to this presumption. It questioned two of the central features of most conventional articulations of the political: the nature of political power and the correlation between politics and the public sphere. The force of the claim lay in the implication that politics needed a more adequate theory of power and a less patriarchal division between public and private spheres.

Both instrumental and institutional conceptions of the political were claimed to be wrongly conceived and overly restrictive. The claim that 'the personal is political' destabilized all that had previously been presumed. Indeed, Phillips reflects, ' "politics" was subjected to such devastating criticism that it threatened 'to dissolve as a distinct category of analysis' (Phillips 1998: 4). Feminists rejected the conception of the political as located only within the institutional arena of government. They adopted the instrumentalist conception of politics as power and proceeded to extend the definition of power such that power was ubiquitous and politics all-encompassing.

The idea that politics is power, coupled with the adoption of an extensive heterogeneous conception of power, encouraged many feminist theorists to consider politics as largely indistinguishable from anything else. This has generated a huge series of reflections on 'the politics of . . .' (sexuality, reproduction, identity, housework, fashion . . .) but does little to define the nature of the political itself. Politics, Fuss states, 'represents the aporia in much of our current political theorizing; that which signifies activism is least actively interrogated' (Fuss 1989: 105).

At its most extreme the feminist challenge threatens to eliminate the boundaries of the political altogether: the public/private distinction is collapsed and power is extended to all social relations. But more recent reflections by feminist political theorists on the boundaries to the political have been more restrained. While drawing on the insights of the early challenges, feminist political theorists are increasingly concerned to reconstruct the boundaries of the political, entailing rethinking the public/private dichotomy such that it no longer marginalizes women, and distinguishing between democratic power and undemocratic domination such that the constraints provided by a democratic form of power might allow individual empowerment. 'Minimally', says Elshtain, 'a political perspective requires that some activity called "politics" be differentiated from other activities, relationships and patterns of action. If all conceptual boundaries are blurred and all distinctions between public and private are eliminated no politics can exist by definition' (Elshtain 1981: 201). There have been three different approaches to reconstructing the political within recent feminist theorizing. The first seeks to modify the institutional conception of politics; the second to develop the norms of the private sphere into an ethical conception of politics; and the third to move beyond the dichotomy between these two and develop a more critical conception of politics.

In order to get a sense of what is meant by politics, and the ways in which taking gender as the first question of political theory rather than its first premise alters these meanings, let us first consider why and in what ways feminists have challenged the distinction between the public and the private spheres and proposed to replace a public institutional conception of the political with an extensive power-based conception. Let us then look at the notions of power adopted within the mainstream politics literature and at the ways in which these are reworked within feminist theory. Taken together, these debates provide an account of how and why the feminist claim that 'the personal is political' eroded the conventional boundaries of the political. We can then go on to consider the ways in which feminist political theorists are now proposing to reconstruct the boundaries of the political, institutional, ethical and critical.

## Public and Private

Liberalism has been constructed around a distinction between the public and private realms. The key significance of this distinction lies, for its liberal advocates, in its perceived role in securing individual freedom. As Judith Shklar notes, liberalism 'has only one overriding aim: to secure the political conditions that are necessary for the exercise of personal freedom' (Shklar 1991: 21). These conditions are held to require the clear demarcation of the spheres of the personal and the public. 'The limits of coercion begin', argues Shklar, '. . . with a prohibition upon invading the private realm' (Shklar 1991: 24). Freedom is secured by limiting the constraints placed upon the individual. Given this, the line between the public and the private has to be drawn, and 'must under no circumstances be ignored or forgotten' (Shklar 1991: 24).

What is meant by the public and the private here is the distinction between the state and civil society. Politics is equated with the public power of the state. Freedom is equated with the absence of constraint imposed by the state – freedom from political power. Civil society is therefore cast as that sphere of life in which individuals are allowed to pursue their own conception of the good in free association with others. Civil society is 'private' in the sense that it is not governed by the public power of the state.

Private does not here imply the personal, intimate or familial. As Nancy Rosenblum notes: 'Private life means life in civil society, not some presocial state of nature or antisocial condition of isolation and detachment' (Rosenblum 1987: 61). A social sphere freed from the constraints of the political will be more vibrant and allow for greater autonomy than will one in which the power of the state extends to all aspects of life. As politics is conceived as the state-based exertion of power over individuals, it becomes a necessary evil, to be limited and constrained such that it guarantees the framework for civil society without eroding its vitality.

However, the apparently binary division between public and private is complicated by the existence of a third sphere, also labelled private – that of personal life. This creates a tripartite, rather than a dual, division of social relations: the state, civil society and the personal. It is clear that the state is always cast as public. It is equally clear that the personal (when considered within political theory) is cast as private. Confusingly, civil society is cast as private when opposed to the state and public when opposed to the personal. This inevitably makes any discussion of a single public/private dichotomy either partial or confused, or both.

There are, Kymlicka helpfully notes, 'in fact two different concepts of the public–private distinction in liberalism: the first, which originated in Locke, is the distinction between the political and the social; the second, which arose with Romantic-influenced liberals, is the distinction between the social and the personal' (Kymlicka 1990: 250). The social/personal distinction arises later than the state/civil society distinction, and in some ways may be viewed as a response to the latter. It represents a modification of the classic liberal celebration of civil society in the light of the growing awareness of the constraints placed upon individual freedom by social and not just political manifestations of power.

Classic liberals had viewed society as the realm in which individuals could act freely. However, it has become increasingly evident that society itself places intense constraints upon individuals, and the pursuit of individual freedom may require the limitation of both state and civil society in order to create space for self-expression. The relations of power which might work to constrain the individual, it has become increasingly clear, are more extensive and pervasive than those captured by the institutional power of the state alone. Recognition of the pressures of social conformity led to a need to distinguish between the social and the personal in order that one might retreat from ordered social life into a sphere of intimacy.

Significantly, neither of these two public/private distinctions explicitly invokes the family: neither characterizes the family as paradigmatically private. Indeed the family is not necessarily private in the sense implied by either the term civil society or the personal, and the arguments for each could actually provide grounds to criticize the traditional family. Nonetheless, when the domestic or familial are considered within liberal theory, they are systematically represented as private (Okin 1998: 117). There is then a third form of the public/private distinction at work: that between the public and the domestic. Here the public comprises both the state and civil society and the private is defined institutionally as the relations and activities of domestic life, often assumed to embody the intimacy valued for self-development.

The intriguing, and politically significant, thing for feminists is the fact that contemporary liberal theory nowhere explicitly theorizes the relation between this third articulation of the public/private dichotomy in relation to either of the other two public/private dichotomies. Both civil society and the personal are highly valued conceptualizations of the private sphere: both are viewed (to differing extents in differing articulations of liberalism) as essential to the realization of individual freedom. The domestic, in striking contrast, has no place either within the accounts of the pursuit of freedom (the private) or within the necessary structural constraints which allow individual freedom to be pursued equally by all (the public). Liberals, Kymlicka notes, have 'generally neglected the role of the family in structuring both public and private life' (Kymlicka 1990: 250). For many feminist theorists this neglect renders the entire liberal project suspect.

As Pateman has argued, the separation of state and civil society is a distinction within the non-familial world. By labelling civil society private, the family remains forgotten in theoretical discussion (Pateman 1983: 286–7). Had the family been viewed as a part of civil society, liberal theorists would surely have been compelled to oppose its hierarchical form and argue for its organization on the basis of equality and consent, as they did with all other forms of civil co-operation.

Yet there were structural (historical and conceptual), rather than simply contingent, reasons why the family was not included within civil society. As Young has argued: 'Extolling a public realm of manly virtue and citizenship as independence, generality, and dispassionate reason entailed creating the private sphere of the family as the place to which emotion, sentiment, and bodily needs must be confined. The generality of the public thus depends on excluding women' (Young 1998: 405). In other words, although liberal theory does not theorize the place of the domestic, it relies upon (indeed serves to constitute and legitimize) a domestic realm which is quite distinct to those spheres that it does theorize.

Arguments vary as to why the domestic has been neglected in this way. Feminist critiques of the liberal characterization of the public/private distinction are numerous and qualitatively distinct in focus. Criticism is levelled at the premises of liberalism itself (especially its conception of the self), at liberalism's historical origins in social contract theory, and at the historical practice of liberal regimes.

The first critique focuses on the question of subjectivity. Liberalism, it is frequently charged, works with a conception of the subject as an autonomous agent: it assumes people to be equal, unattached, rational individuals. Yet many critics view this claim as an account of a particular, socially specific type of identity formation rather than as a statement of universal human nature. If people are equal, unattached, rational individuals, it is because they have been constructed as that. This liberal discourse of individual autonomy is a prescriptive rather than a descriptive account, and one that works to structure or distort, rather than simply reflect, social relations (see Di Stefano 1996: 95–116).

Recognition of this fact leads to two further insights. The first is that very particular social structures and institutions are needed to shape individuals into this mould; the second is that this conception of subjectivity may not apply equally to everyone. The first insight leads to a concern with the processes of reproduction, nurturance and socialization, the second to an exploration of the extent to which women have been understood as subordinate, dependent and emotional, and so excluded from the category of 'individuals' within liberal theorizing.

The two issues are linked in women's status as primary carers. Neither the process of caring and nurturing nor the status of carers and nurturers is theorized in liberal theory. The concern of feminist theorists is that, as a result of this omission, not only have women been denied the rights and privileges granted to the 'rational individuals' of liberal societies, but also a crucial aspect of life, associated with the caring performed by women, has been glossed over. As Okin argues, liberalism 'pays remarkably little attention to how we *become* the adults who form the subject matter of political theories' (Okin 1991: 41). If the acquisition of the characteristics deemed essential to the liberal individual occurs, not (or not solely) as a result of genetic and hormonal predetermination, but (also) as a result of parental practices (conscious or unconscious), then liberal theorists ought perhaps to pay more attention to the processes by which liberalism reproduces its subjects and secures its own future. 'Liberal theorists', argues Okin, 'who take such arguments seriously cannot continue to regard the structure and practices of family life as separate from and irrelevant to "the political"' (Okin 1991: 41). This insight has implications not only for the role of caring as a practice but also for its role as a perspective.

The sort of thinking and moral reasoning generated by and required within the social relations characteristic of familial life are quite distinct from those generated by and required within the social relations characteristic of public life. The emphasis here is on empathy, relationality and caring rather than on autonomy, individuality and justice. Many feminists explore the implications of recognizing the existence of these two distinct forms of moral reasoning, and there is an extensive literature proposing that the balance between the two should be reassessed (see Chapter 5).

This critique of the public/private distinction, which emerges from a focus on subjectivity, is complemented by a second, which focuses on contract. Here the object of concern is not the rational liberal individual, but liberalism's origins in social contract theory. This contract-based critique places the subjectivity-based critique in historical context. It concentrates attention not on abstract debates concerning agency, but on concrete investigations of political relations. The focus here is the particular social and political forces that created the situation in which women were confined to a private, domestic, care-taking role while men were presumed to be able to move freely between the private (domestic) and the public (civil society and state) spheres.

The most influential theorist here is Pateman. She claims that the social contract that generates liberal politics and establishes the political freedom of individuals simultaneously entails the sexual subordination of women in marriage. The social contract that is required to create both civil society and the state requires a sexual contract to accommodate the patriarchalism that predates liberalism. The liberal social contact therefore represents the reorganization, but not the abolition, of patriarchy. The distinction between state and civil society established in the writings of Locke rests on the separation of political and paternal power such that the 'masculine right over women is declared non-political' (Pateman 1988: 90). Patriarchy was relocated into the private domain and reformulated as complementary to civil society. It was not rejected altogether: it was entrenched rather than eradicated. Classic liberal theory assumed the (male-headed) family to be a natural, biologically determined unit. As politics was assumed to apply only to that which was socially constituted, and so amenable to change, relations within the family were deemed apolitical (Pateman 1988).

Liberal states have been able to act in this apparently contradictory manner because of an essential tension within liberal theory. The original contract, upon which contemporary liberal theory still rests, was, Pateman has claimed, not only a social contract that established freedom, but also a sexual contract that perpetuated domination. The contract established men's political right over women through conjugal right. While the contract theorists challenged the paternal rights of fathers, they incorporated into their theories the patriarchal rights of husbands over wives. As a result they created a division not only between the state and civil society, but also between the public sphere of civil freedom and the private sphere of the family.

This private sphere is then deemed politically irrelevant, and theorists focus exclusively on the relation between the state and the sphere of civil freedom. Indeed, public and private come to be understood as relating to the state and the sphere of civil freedom respectively, thereby rendering the 'private' sphere of the family invisible. Women, Pateman tells us, 'are not party to the original contract through which men transform their natural freedom into the security of civil freedom. Women are the subject of the contract' (Pateman 1988: 6). The public realm cannot be understood in isolation from the private realm, and yet there is now a refusal to admit that marital domination is politically significant.

This critique focuses on the way in which the historical origins of liberal theory rely on the incorporation of already existing patriarchal relations which, being excluded from the categories of both civil society and the state, are then rendered invisible. It then becomes possible for contemporary liberal theorists to forget (or overlook) the fact that the 'liberal individual' was explicitly argued to be the male head of household by the classic exponents of liberal theory. In this way gender is given a highly specific and structuring role within liberal theory at the same time as liberal theory presents itself as gender-neutral.

There is a third type of critique of the public/private dichotomy as articulated within liberal theory. This focuses on the historical practice of liberal regimes. The charge here is that, notwithstanding the abstract commitment to the importance of a prohibition on state intervention in the private sphere, liberal states have in practice regulated and controlled the family. Not only has this practice been contrary to the fundamental principle of liberalism, it has been adopted in pursuit of a profoundly illiberal end: the perpetuation of patriarchy. This tension, arising from the very formulation of liberalism itself (as discussed above), is the inevitable conclusion of the ambivalent role of the family in relation to the private sphere.

'For hundreds of years in Britain and the United States', notes Okin, 'the Common Law notion of coverture deprived women of legal personhood upon marriage. The state enforced the rights of husbands to their wives' property and persons and made it virtually impossible for women to divorce or even to live separately from their husbands' (Okin 1991: 42). While the state adopted this directly non-neutral relation to personal and domestic life, it also upheld practices within the marketplace which presumed that those engaged in waged-work could rely on the support and care of someone at home (Okin 1989: 134–69). To add to the insult, from the perspective of women, the principle of non-intervention in the private sphere has been used by the state to justify inaction regarding cases of child-abuse, marital rape and domestic violence. In short, liberal states have actually enforced patriarchal power relations within the family, while formally denying their responsibility to intervene in familial disputes on the grounds that it is essential to limit state intervention in civil society and personal relations.

In the light of these three critiques, many feminists have rejected the 'public/private' distinction altogether, believing it to be a central mechanism of the oppression of women within liberal states. Determination to highlight the inequality within the family and to challenge its apolitical status led many feminists to reject the liberal 'respect for so-called private life' (Jaggar 1983: 199) as simply a mystification of patriarchal power. It was argued that the liberal commitment to equality (if applied to women as well as to men) required a rejection of the other liberal commitment to a public/private distinction.

These three different types of critique of the public/private distinction have received varying receptions, even within feminist theory. Some theorists accept one of the critiques while querying the others. For instance, Wendy Brown is sceptical of the second critique, doubting that this historical account of the incorporation of patriarchy into liberalism can help us in our contemplation of gender in contemporary political theory. She acknowledges that Pateman makes a compelling case for the sexual contract as the basis for the social contract, but argues that she 'does not query whether or on what level contemporary liberalism requires a social contract' (Brown 1995: 137). Because Pateman locates women's subordination in contract, she continues to look to contemporary contractual relations as the basis for women's subordination, without considering that liberalism and women's subordination might be sustained without contract.

Brown takes issue with this, arguing that, as women are no longer required to enter a sexual contract for survival or social recognition, 'liberal political orders no longer need refer to an imaginary social contract for their legitimacy' (Brown 1995: 137). While the language of contract may have been needed to justify the establishment of liberal political systems (historically and imperially), it is rarely invoked to justify their continued legitimacy. 'Legitimation is procured, at least provisionally, through the absence of viable alternatives' (Brown 1995: 138). Liberal discourse has become naturalized, no longer requiring the legal fictions of founding moments or social contracts. As social contract becomes less constitutive of liberalism, so too sexual contract becomes less constitutive of women's subordination. In such circumstances Brown argues that 'the legacy of gender subordination Pateman identifies as historically installed in the sexual-social contract is to be found not in contemporary contract relations but in the *terms* of liberal discourse' (Brown 1995: 138). In other words, Brown is deliteralizing and dematerializing contract in order to examine the operation of a discourse premised on sexual contract but no longer dependent on it. As such she hopes to explain, in a way that Pateman cannot, the continued articulation of masculinism within liberal discourse, notwithstanding the erosion of its original mechanism.

Political theory, as we noted previously, need not be viewed as simply reflecting already given social relations; it can also be understood as part of attempts to institute them. On this reading it is the continued use of the terms of debate generated by the social and sexual contracts (notably the formulation of a public/private dichotomy which marginalizes the place of the family) by contemporary liberal theorists that itself perpetuates gender subordination. One of the central tasks of any feminist project must therefore be to reconfigure the terms of political discourse. The existing terms of political discourse legitimate state policies which are fundamentally discriminatory in relation to women, and are able to do so because of women's historical, material and symbolic relation to the domestic.

One of the central ways in which the terms of liberal discourse have been challenged in recent years is through the focus on the question of power. Feminists have found the liberal conception of the political strangely lacking in any analysis of power. The construction of the public/private distinction, and the assertion that those social relations deemed private are non-political, leads liberal theorists to marginalize the political significance of power relations within the private sphere altogether and to recognize only certain forms of power relations within the public sphere. In direct contrast, feminist theorists, aiming to reveal the political significance of women's oppression, have reconceptualized the nature of the political in terms of power relations which cut across state, civil society and familial realms, thereby challenging the power of the liberal discourse itself.

Let us now consider these reconceptualizations of the political and reflect on the ways in which power is redefined such that the power relations in the family become clear. This work on the nature of power has been vital to the task of highlighting women's subordinate role within liberal theory and states. But let us also note that, in focusing on the family as oppressive rather than intimate and fulfilling, the social/personal form of the public/private distinction tends not to figure. Considerations of privacy and intimacy are (temporarily) jettisoned.

## Power

Central to the debate about the nature of politics is the notion of power. The institutionalist conceptions of the political tend not to prioritize power, focusing instead on procedure and norms. This is not to say that the liberal theorists who adopt the institutionalist conception of the political are not concerned with power: they have always been determined above all else to limit the power exercised over the individual, both by the state and by society. For the liberal theorist, Frazer and Lacey point out, 'some power is necessary, and some justified, but all power is undesirable' (Frazer and Lacey 1993: 76). But this normative antipathy to power increasingly seems to have been conflated with reality, leaving liberal theorists without 'the conceptual and methodological tools for the study and analysis of power' (Frazer and Lacey 1993: 76).

Both the narrow instrumentalist and the broader participatory conceptions of politics, on the other hand, rely upon very specific conceptions of power. Those readings of the political which understand politics to be a process rather than an institution define politics as concerned primarily with the allocation and distribution of power. Within this general approach to politics there are substantial differences, generated by radically divergent understandings of the nature of power.

### Conflictual conceptions of power

Political scientists, committed to the use of concepts which work in the project of formulating and testing hypothesis, have developed a standard definition of power: X has power over Y if he can get Y to do something Y would not otherwise do. This formulation allows one to observe Y's behaviour and assess the force X brought to bear. One can observe and quantify empirically verifiable processes. For those intent on understanding the distribution of political power, attention is focused, as Elshtain points out, on the power held by the political institutions of government (national and local) and organizations aiming to influence them (interest groups, unions, NGOs). Power is 'of, by and for elites' (Elshtain 1992a: 112). Power is conceived as a possession, something that is observable and measurable. In other words, empiricist power theorists have confined themselves to one particular locution of power: 'power over'. This corresponds, as Isaac tells us, 'to their belief that a proper social science is a science of behavioural regularities' (Isaac 1987: 21).

Within this general conception of power as 'power over' there are important subdivisions. Steven Lukes helpfully articulates three distinct possible dimensions constituting 'power over'. The narrowest definition adopted by some political scientists is what Lukes characterizes as the one-dimensional view of power. It entails 'a focus on behaviour in the making of decisions on issues over which there is an observable conflict of (subjective) interests, seen as express policy preferences, revealed by political participation' (Lukes 1978: 15). In the words of one of the advocates of this conception of power: 'A has power over B to the extent that he can get B to do something that B would not otherwise do' (Dahl, quoted in Lukes 1978: 11–12).

Those advocating what Lukes calls a two-dimensional conception of power accept that one-dimensional conception of power but argue that: 'Power is also exercised when A devotes his energies to creating or reinforcing social and political values and institutional practices that limit the scope of the political process to public consideration of only those issues which are comparatively innocuous to A' (Bachrach and Baratz, quoted in Lukes 1978: 16). In other words, power may be being exercised even when no observable conflict occurs: the effective use of power entails precluding action and silencing debate.

This second dimension of power is often referred to as the mobilization of bias and requires that one examines not only decision-making but also non-decision-making. Non-decision-making results from the suppression of a latent challenge to the values or interests of the decision-maker. To adopt this second dimension of power is to redefine the boundaries of what is to count as a political issue. Attempts to quantify and map the distribution of political power will, on this conception of power, entail a more extensive field of inquiry. However, similarities between one- and two-dimensional power remain. Both dimensions assume the existence of observable conflict, though in the latter case this conflict is covert rather than overt, and both assume a concept of subjective rather than objective interests – in other words, that interests are consciously articulated and observable.

Lukes finds both conceptions of power wanting in that they focus on the actual behaviour of concrete decisions. This is problematic for two reasons. Firstly, the presumption is that power is about individuals realizing their wills despite the resistance of others. This underplays the significance both of collective action and interests and of systematic effects. Secondly, the presumption that power is only exercised in situations of observable conflict overlooks the importance of power to shape or determine preferences themselves: 'the most effective and insidious use of power is to prevent such conflict from arising in the first place' (Lukes 1978: 23). Conflict may be neither overt nor covert but latent: existing in 'a contradiction between the interests of those exercising power and the *real interests* of those they exclude' (Lukes 1978: 24–5). In other words, the three-dimensional conception of power is much broader than the other two and proposes a distinction between subjective and real interests.

Which of these theories of power one finds most compelling depends in large part on one's general normative frame of reference. Both liberal and Marxist political theorists have tended to conceptualize power as possessional (belonging to either an individual or a group) and conflictual (exercised as a result of conflicting interests). Within this shared conception are significant differences, though. Whereas the liberal conception of power tends to focus upon one- and two-dimensional forms of power, the Marxist one also stresses the centrality of three-dimensional power in the form of ideology. Within liberal theory power is held to be possessed by the state and exercised over its subjects, but it is assumed to be legitimate authority rather than illegitimate domination because it is grounded upon sovereignty and used 'to ensure the peaceable and equitable opportunity of exchange' (Gatens 1992: 123). Within the Marxist perspective, on the other hand, all power is domination, held by one group to dominate and exploit another group that lacks power. The state is viewed as a mechanism for exercising the power of the ruling class. Althusser famously distinguished between repressive state apparatuses (including the police, judiciary and army) and ideological state apparatuses (including schools, religion and the family), which roughly map onto one/two-dimensional and three-dimensional forms of power respectively.

Despite the significant differences between these three conceptions of power, it is important to note that they all share a common core in the notion that A affects B in some significant manner. They could therefore be viewed as three conceptions of a single concept of power, defined by

Lukes as: 'A exercises power over B when A affects B in a manner contrary to B's interests' (Lukes 1978: 27). Others propose quite different concepts of power. Talcott Parsons, for example, argues power to be the use of authoritative decisions to further collective goals. Here power is dissociated from conflicts of interests, coercion and force and associated with the pursuit of collective goals, authority and consensus (Parsons 1967: 297–354). Hannah Arendt offers perhaps the most influential accounts of power as consensual rather than instrumental.

### Capacity conceptions of power

Arendt argues that power:

> corresponds to the human ability not just to act but to act in concert. Power is never the property of an individual; it belongs to a group and remains in existence only so long as the group keeps together. When we say of somebody that he is 'in power' we actually refer to his being empowered by a certain number of people to act in their name. The moment the group, from which the power originated to begin with, disappears 'his power' also vanishes. (Arendt 1969: 44)

From this perspective, then, power is not zero-sum, it springs up whenever people act in concert. Neither is it conflictual, as it arises when people work together rather than when they act against others. It can therefore be distinguished from violence, force and authority.

Critics of this notion of 'power to', which focuses on power as capacity rather than as control, argue that this is a prescriptive rather than a descriptive account. Such definitions of power are held to be persuasive in that they serve to defend and further the authors' distinctive political perspective rather than simply describing what already is. Parsons's definition of power, for example, allows him to 'shift the entire weight of his analysis away from power as expressing a relation between individuals and groups, toward seeing power as a "system property"' (Giddens 1968: 265). Similarly Arendt's definition of power enables her to conceptualize the public sphere as a space in which people behave non-violently and argue rationally free from domination (Lukes 1978: 30). These are 'revisionary persuasive redefinitions', focusing on 'power to' rather than 'power over' in a manner that its critics argue obfuscates or downplays the conflictual aspects of power.

### Practice conceptions of power

There is one further substantial strand to contemporary debates about conceptions of power – that elaborated by Michel Foucault (Foucault

1978: 92–3). In contrast to those who conceptualize power as purely repressive, zero-sum and hierarchical, Foucault offers a concept of power which is much more complex. He is concerned to examine how power relations are created and maintained in more subtle and diffuse ways than have been understood in either conflictual or capacity accounts.

What first distinguishes Foucault's approach to power is the claim of its ubiquity. This leads him to define power even more broadly than the three-dimensional conception. It also means that he perceives power to be present in even the most humane and freely adopted social practices. His claim is that the Enlightenment notion of universal rationality works as a strategy of 'normalization' that is best understood as a form of power. This undermines the liberal distinction between the autonomous and the oppressed. For Foucault, to be a subject is necessarily to be subjected. Power relations are conceived as permeating all levels of social existence. This idea of the ubiquity of power relations, as McNay points out, 'necessitates a radical reconceptualization of the concept of power in general' (McNay 1994: 90).

The first consequence of conceiving power as ubiquitous is the idea that power is not possessional, but relational. 'It is never localised here or there, never in anybody's hands, never appropriated as a commodity or piece of wealth. Power is employed and exercised through a net-like organisation' (Foucault 1980: 98). The second consequence is the idea that power is not uni-directional, but multi-directional. As Foucault says, 'not only do individuals circulate between its threads; they are always in the position of simultaneously undergoing and exercising this power' (Foucault 1980: 98). Power circulates throughout all levels of society and engenders a multiplicity of relations. This gives rise to the third consequence of conceiving power in this Foucauldian manner, which is that, given this multiplicity, it is necessary to conduct an 'ascending analysis' or a microphysics of power. Power cannot be analysed in terms of intentionality, nor should it be assumed to exist only within institutionalized centres of power. No single account (whether deterministic or even reciprocal) can capture the relationship between the microscopic and the macroscopic. The individualist and the structuralist conceptions of power are both rejected.

There is also a fourth consequence generated by this idea of the ubiquity of power relations. This is the idea that power is not only repressive, prohibitive and preventative, but also productive, in that it generates effects. Rather than being the paradigmatic form of power, repression becomes but one form of power relations. The productivity of power is not, though, to be understood as an evaluative concept, signalling a positive, enabling conception of power. For productive power may either constrain or enable, or do both at different points; like preventative power, it can be disciplinary or enabling. The point is simply that it produces effects: it creates (among other things) self-policing subjects.

In his essay entitled 'Governmentality' Foucault distinguishes between the Machiavellian notion of juridical sovereignty and the modern art of government. While the former rests on a monarchical notion of power focused on sovereignty and territory, the latter rests on a pastoral notion of power focused on the efficient management of the population. The pastoral notion of power takes everyday life as its primary object, for governmentality requires the manipulation of the consciousness of individuals. This pastoral conception of power, focusing on the process of subjectification through which individuals are regulated, is then distinguished from violence. An act of violence imposes itself directly on the body and seeks to minimize all resistance. A power relation, on the other hand, occurs only where there is the potential for resistance, that is to say, it arises only between two individuals each of whom has the potential to influence the actions of the other. Whereas violence implies the absence of freedom, power is exercised only over free subjects.

Many have argued that there are acute problems with Foucault's conception of power (Dews 1986, Taylor 1986, Best and Kellner 1991). Fraser, to take one example, maintains that a significant defect of Foucault's work lies in the absence of a clear normative framework. What, she asks, is his implicit condemnation of disciplinary power based upon if not an appeal to Enlightenment values of freedom, justice and liberation (Fraser 1989)? Similarly Jean Grimshaw asks: even if power necessarily generates resistance, 'on what grounds do we (or can we) resist?' (Grimshaw 1993: 54).

Many commentators argue that there is an unresolved tension between conceiving power as both disciplinary and enabling: as both an objectivizing and a subjectivizing force. The positive reading is one in which Foucault successfully presents power as a relation that both 'constrains individuals and constitutes the condition of possibility of their freedom' (McNay 1994: 4). However, two other, more negative readings are commonly articulated: the first finds that he underplays the significance of structures of domination; the second (in direct contrast) feels that he places too great an emphasis on the repressive aspects of power.

From the first of these critical readings it seems to some that, in focusing on the microphysics rather than a macrophysics of power, on the diverse and specific manifestations rather than the centralized institutionalization of power, Foucault comes to conceive power as a primarily enabling phenomenon. The second of these more critical readings entails the claim that Foucault slips unreflectively from an enabling to an essentially dominatory model of power. This tendency, critics argue, is further exacerbated by Foucault's concentration on power from the perspective of those who dominate, rather than those subject to power. This works against his own argument that all power relations are potentially reversible. In short, Foucault is here argued to slip 'too easily from describing disciplinary power as a tendency within modern forms of social control, to positing disciplinary power as a fully installed monolithic force which saturates all social relations' (McNay 1994: 104).

Despite these various contrasting critiques, many have found this Foucauldian conception of power hugely useful. This is particularly so within feminist theory, notwithstanding the fact that Foucault's work on power was notably 'gender-blind' (Ramazanoglu 1993). Foucault summarizes its key elements as: power is a heterogeneous and uneven force, its distribution constantly open to modification (the rule of continual variation); the relationship between the microscopic and the macroscopic cannot be captured in any notion of determination or even reciprocity (the rule of double conditioning); and the discursive formations that transmit and produce power relations are potentially reversible (the rule of tactical polyvalence of discourses); finally, power should be seen as productive and not just repressive (the rule of immanence) (Foucault 1978: 98–101).

If one adopts a definition of politics as relations of power and then conceives power in one of its broader articulations (three-dimensional conflictual power, power as capacity, or power as practice), it becomes immediately evident that the social constitution and cultural manifestations of gender are inherently political issues. For this reason arguments put forward by feminist theorists concerning the need to reconstruct political theory inevitably focus on the issue of power, broadly conceived. Frazer and Lacey, for instance, contend that 'the main substantive component of an adequate political theory . . . is a theory of power' (Frazer and Lacey 1993: 193). Moreover, an adequate theory of power 'must accommodate the ways in which power inheres in practices and discourses such as law, education, psychiatry, which are socially pervasive' (Frazer and Lacey 1993: 193). They argue that the dominant institutional approach to politics (as manifest in liberal theory) has failed to theorize power, and that the other dominant instrumentalist approach to politics (as manifest in positivist political science) has focused exclusively on power as 'sovereignty' or 'property', thereby contributing 'to the myopia of political theory by blinding it to the pervasiveness of powerful discourses in every area of social life' (Frazer and Lacey 1993: 193). Let us turn, then, to consider how power has been conceptualized within feminist theory.

## Feminist Theories of Power

If feminism is indeed politics, it is politics in its broad conception as relations of power. As an 'emancipatory movement which seeks to end a particular kind of power relationship', Yeatman tells us, 'feminism is deeply concerned with issues of how power should be conceived and understood' (Yeatman 1997: 144).

Gender theorists have argued that power is gender-related in several distinct (and not necessarily compatible) ways. Firstly, it is claimed that men and women do not have the same access to resources that are associated with power, and that men have power over women. Secondly, it is held that men and women tend to understand power differently. Thirdly, it is maintained that power relations constitute gender identities themselves. Each of these arguments rests on a distinct theory of power.

Feminists accepting the one- and two-dimensional views of power will tend to be concerned about access to public decision-making – political, economic and social. From the three-dimensional view of power, on the other hand, questions of power tend to be cast in terms of the impact of the ideological constraints placed upon gendered subjects by capitalist society. Gender is here assumed to be 'an ideological effect of the way power "conditions" the mind' (Gatens 1992: 127).

Within this general conflictual and possessional approach to power there have of course been significantly distinct understandings as to the basis for men's power over women. Christine Delphy stresses the economic exploitation of wives by husbands; Shulamith Firestone points to the role of sexual reproduction; Susan Brownmiller focuses on the potential for rape; and Andrea Dworkin explores the nature of sexuality. Despite their differences, these analyses share a notion of patriarchy as a form of 'power over' or domination, where, to the extent to which men hold power, women are powerless.

However, many feminists came to see this adoption of a classic zero-sum, possessional and conflictual model of power (even in its three-dimensional form) as problematic. To represent women as simply powerless, some feminists began to argue, is to work with a narrow conception of power, and to deny the complexity and richness of women's experiences (Elshtain 1992a: 110). Many feminists have followed Arendt in emphasizing the benefits arising from conceptualizing power as empowerment: not as domination but as capacity. This conception of power as 'power to' is claimed to be more inclusive than that of 'power over', comprising both the ability to act and the ability to refrain from action (which is not quantifiable). This distinction is put forward as a means of breaking out of the dualism between being powerless and being powerful, which is thought to be unhelpfully combative and hierarchical.

*Feminist articulations of power as capacity*

Influentially within feminist debates, Hartsock challenges the notion that the exercise of power can best be understood as the ability to compel obedience. There is, she believes, a connection between masculinity itself and the exercise of power over others – 'the repression/ denial of *eros* in a masculinist society underlies the definition of both sexuality and power as domination' (Hartsock 1996: 31). She contrasts this with the theories of power produced by women, which stress those aspects of power related to energy, capacity and potential. While admitting that this constitutes 'only suggestive evidence' that there is a distinct female or feminist conception of power (and despite the fact that Arendt for one would have expressly rejected the idea that her conception of power was in any way an expression of her gendered identity), Hartsock nonetheless wants to argue that, on the basis of the commonality found in these writings, we can speak of 'systematic difference between the theoretical accounts of power produced by women and men' (Hartsock 1996: 32–7).

To assume that demanding more power entails the idea of imposing one's will on others is, Hartsock argues, to work with a masculinist conception of 'power over'. The most effective means of challenging male power is not to enter into competition for power as currently conceived. Rather it is to bring into being the theory and practice of feminist 'power to'. The rejection of the competitive and zero-sum notion of power is important, it is argued, if women want to demand empowerment for themselves, without thereby denying it to others. In recognition of this, feminist theorists have been keen to break the stranglehold of the narrow political science conceptions of power and recuperate the range of everyday uses of the term, which include power not only as a property, but also as the ability to do something. Hartsock does acknowledge the difficulties associated with reconceptualizing power as capacity – notably the refusal to confront the problems attendant on acting on the world, directing attention away from relations of domination that must be confronted and failing to 'address directly the genderedness of power' (Hartsock 1996: 37). But she nonetheless favours it over both the instrumental and the Foucauldian conceptions of power.

This is one significant school of thought within feminism regarding power, characterized by the tendency to consider 'power over' bad and 'power to' good. The former is seen as domination and lack of connection, the latter as enabling and relational. As one commentator puts it, the 'feminist vision of power, as a co-operative non-zero-sum relationship called empowerment, is heralded as better than the masculinist view it opposes. By "better than," feminist theorists mean more humane, less destructive, more fully human' (Deutchman 1996: 8). There are two distinct elements to such a claim: the relation between power and gendered identity, and the relation between the two conceptions of power themselves. Let us look at each in turn.

There is disagreement as to whether this conception of power as capacity can legitimately be claimed as female. There is no historical evidence, critics point out, that the 'power to' conception of power is exclusively or uniformly feminist (Deutchman 1996: 12). Talcott Parsons, for instance, offers an understanding of power as a generalized capacity to secure binding obligation in collectivities, where the obligations are legitimized with reference to bearing on collective goals (Parsons 1967: 308). Hartsock responds to this by stressing that she is claiming not a feminine conception of power, but a feminist one. It is not women's nature that gives rise to a specific way of viewing power, but their particular social role and status (usually caring and private). The systematic and significant differences in life activity experienced by men and women lead to differing world views and distinctive theoretical commitments (Hartsock 1996: 37).

Hartsock's point is that the conception of power as capacity is a part of a 'feminist standpoint', based in historically and materially specific circumstances and realized through a consciousness-raising process. 'Our understanding of power must be rooted in and defined not simply by women's experience but by the systematic pulling together and working out of the liberatory possibilities present in that experience' (Hartsock 1996: 45). The development of a feminist theory of power entails the endorsement not simply of that which women currently understand as power, but rather of that which women might conceptualize once they have worked beyond systematic domination.

Let us now consider the issue of the proposed relation between 'power over' and 'power to'. Although the two are frequently thought to be antagonistic there are also those who claim them to be complementary. Jean Bethke Elshtain, for example, offers a clear argument for viewing these two conceptions of power as complementary. She claims that human societies throughout time have differentiated between maleness and femaleness and 'located complementary forms of power in the two sexes' (Elshtain 1992a: 115). Moreover, she claims, the nature of these sexually differentiated forms of power follows a general pattern: 'One thread that seems to run through the tangle of historic and ethnographic evidence is a picture of *formal* male power being balanced or even underlined by *informal* female power' (Elshtain 1992a: 116). This is an empirical claim from which she derives normative conclusions.

Rather than presuming one form of power to be dominant, Elshtain suggests that we understand such sexually differentiated forms of power (both historically and currently) as genuinely complementary. Where men hold institutionalized, 'political' and juridical power, female power is exercised in informal, communal spheres of life. *Potestas*, the Latin term for political power, control, supremacy and domination, is contrasted with *potentia*, power as ability, potency and efficacy.

The complementarity of these two forms of power is lost, Elshtain suggests, in modern societies where the formal institutions of the state are allotted ever greater significance: 'As the world of female power recedes, the sphere of male power encroaches, absorbing more and more features of social life into the orbit of the juridico-political, and bureaucratized, the "legitimately" powerful: the state' (Elshtain 1992a: 116). In this context women are faced with an unhappy choice: either to 'manipulate their diminished social role as mothers inside increasingly powerless families; or to join forces with the men, assuming masculine roles and identities and competing for power on established, institutionalized terms' (Elshtain 1992a: 116).

### Synthesizing conflict and capacity

In contrast to both these opposing strategies, Elshtain proposes a third route, inviting us to search for new forms of power. Her suggestion is that women are particularly well suited to propose a third way: neither demanding greater 'power over', or *potestas*, nor glorifying *potentia* alone. Women, she implies, are well placed to discern and develop such a conception of power as a result not of their historical link with *potentia* (as Hartsock implies), but in the context of their current role as marginalized from the dominant, but delimiting, norms of *potestas*. 'Perhaps', she suggests, 'women are the "fools" in western political thought and practice whose official powerlessness grants them a paradoxical freedom: freedom from full assimilation into the prevailing public identity whose aims, in our day, are efficiency and control' (Elshtain 1992a: 119). Interestingly, it is Foucault's conception of power that Elshtain invokes as a possible manifestation of this non-dichotomous approach (Elshtain 1992a: 123). Though it is not clear that Foucault's distinction between repressive and productive power actually maps onto her own distinction between *potestas* and *potentia*, what clearly appeals is his recognition of the generative aspects of power.

However, not all feminists have found Foucault's account of power compelling. Hartsock, for example, though sharing the same general objective as Elshtain in relation to theories of power, remains deeply critical of the Foucauldian approach to power. Foucault, she argues, understands power from the perspective of the rulers. His stress on heterogeneity and the specificity of each situation leads him to 'lose track of social structures and instead to focus on how individuals experience and exercise power' (Hartsock 1996: 40). Foucault thereby makes it difficult to locate domination. This is compounded by his use of the image of a net as a way to understand power, for the image carries implications of equality and participation rather than the 'systematic domination of the many by the few' (Hartsock 1996: 40). Moreover, in arguing that analyses of power be conducted starting from the 'infinitesimal mechanisms' rather than from the centre or the top, Foucault seems to suggest that 'those of us at the bottom are in some sense responsible for our situations' (Hartsock 1996: 40). In other words, despite her desire to revalorize the notion of power as capacity, she is concerned that Foucault seems to reduce the significance of power as domination.

This tension arises from the desire both to celebrate power as capacity as important to women's liberation and to invoke a notion of power as the dominance of the state as a significant source of women's oppression. While there has been within feminism a strong desire to retheorize power as capacity, there has also – as Yeatman helpfully points out – been a heavy reliance on the notion of state-centric 'power over' (Yeatman 1997). Yeatman's argument is that within feminism there has been a tendency to collapse power into domination and then to collapse domination into undemocratic force. Yeatman, like Hartsock, wants to distinguish between 'power over' and 'power to', to equate domination only with 'power over'; but she also wants to distinguish between democratic and undemocratic domination.

'Domination', Yeatman argues, 'can be used to control others in order to serve the interests of the powerful, or, domination can work democratically to extend or even constitute the powers of its subjects' (Yeatman 1997: 145). Yet emancipatory movements frequently fail to distinguish between democratic and undemocratic forms of power over, holding democratic institutions (such as the rule of law, freedom of speech and assembly and representative government) as simply a mechanism of domination serving the interests of the powerful (usually capitalist, colonial or patriarchal). The powerful are assumed to manipulate a pseudo-democratic process in pursuit of their own interests, and emancipatory movements have no interest in working with them to further this aim. The result is a negative reaction against all that is currently valued within the political realm as a simple manifestation of domination. Within feminism this perspective takes the form of rejecting all existing political values – including reason, dispassionate judgement and ambition – as patriarchal.

Such an orientation celebrates as virtues 'all those aspects of identity of the oppressed which are associated with strategic self-preservation in a condition of weakness: acuity of perception of the other's feelings; the masking of assertive and direct modes of leadership in those of indirect suggestion and persuasion; the assertion of power through goodness where this works to occlude the subject's interests in power and makes it appear that all they are doing is operating on behalf of the need of others' (Yeatman 1997: 148). In other words, the apparent need to choose between a conception of power as domination and as capacity is itself problematic and neither strategy will be productive. It is the very act of taking too simplistic and cohesive a notion of power as domination that creates the perceived need to define and revalue a directly contrasting conception of power. In other words, the strategy of inclusion here entails adopting a conflictual conception of power. The strategy of reversal entails the positing of a capacity conception of power. The strategy of displacement, here specifically drawing on the work of Foucault, reveals both the conflictual and the capacity conceptions to be mutually constitutive and equally restrictive.

## Democratic forms of power

In order to challenge the celebration of powerlessness entailed in the rejection of all forms of 'power over', Yeatman stresses the importance of the distinction between democratic and undemocratic forms of power over. Centrally, she argues that, while the conception of power as 'power to' stands in an antagonistic relation to undemocratic domination, it may require as a precondition of its realization a democratic form of 'power over' or domination.

Making a distinction between these separable aspects of power entails two significant implications. It allows one to critique undemocratic forms of domination while recognizing and exploring the positive conceptions of power also at play. It also allows one to acknowledge that power is not only manifest as domination, but inheres in all relationships, such that 'any interpretation of reality is itself a manifestation of power, and that those who are relatively powerless still participate in power' (Yeatman 1997: 147).

The political impetus behind Yeatman's conceptual distinction lies in the desire to critique and avoid a 'politics of ressentiment' which she perceives to emanate from the reductive understanding of power as simple domination. What follows from the adoption of this stance is the paradoxical belief both that powerlessness is a moral virtue and that the powerless need someone more powerful than their oppressors to rescue them – neither of which helps to constitute women as autonomous agents. In contrast, Yeatman proposes that empowerment be understood to exist when individuals are 'encouraged to explore their capacities, to discover the contingencies and multiplicity of identity, and to celebrate those moments of transformative practice when their sense of self completely changes' (Yeatman 1997: 148–9). Such empowerment rests on the constraints provided by a democratic form of 'power over'. The statutory constitution of both women and men as rights-bearing subjects 'creates the space for a discourse of what it means to be constituted as a person, how this constitution works, in what ways in what contexts' (Yeatman 1997: 154). In other words, certain forms of democratic domination actually constitute individuals as beings capable of critical self-reflection, exploration and transformation.

By characterizing democratic 'power over' as a requirement for the pursuit of 'power to', Yeatman's discussion of power differs from both those positions which characterize the issue of power as dichotomous: either 'power over' or 'power to'. Rather than feeling compelled to reject the former and celebrate the latter, as many feminists have done, this stance makes an internal distinction within 'power over' and endorses the democratic form as a necessary prerequisite for the pursuit of 'power to'. A similar point is made by Frazer and Lacey, who propose a 'practice conception of power', or a notion of 'power with'. On this conception, they argue, 'power can be thought of as a vital social resource whose creation, allocation and management in the service of the social good is the primary concern of democratic politics' (Frazer and Lacey 1993: 195–6). This approach 'displaces' the apparent dichotomy between the conflictual and capacity conceptions of power.

### Summary

To summarize, one can discern three distinct positions within feminist theories of power. The first concentrates on gaining *potestas* within a perceived zero-sum game, which requires men to relinquish power to women. The second concentrates on revaluing *potentia* in relation to *potestas*, which requires that power be reconceived as its antithesis. The third argues that we should think of power as both *potestas* and *potentia*, and move away from conceiving of these terms as absolute antinomies. These three responses to the perceived exclusion of women from dominant forms of power map out a common frame that we will find recurring throughout this book. The first aspires to inclusion within that which is valued. The second aims at a reversal of these values and the valorization of that which is marginalized. The third views the maintenance of an absolute opposition between these two strategies as itself problematic. These three distinct approaches to the question of power underpin three distinct formulations of gender politics. And, as we shall also find as a recurrent theme, this third strategy of displacement sometimes takes the form of a synthesis of the other two (as with Elshtain) and at other times entails a more genealogical perspective in its own right (as with McNay).

Having gained a sense of the range of ways in which power gets articulated in both contemporary mainstream and feminist discourses, let us now turn to a consideration of how this debate influences the perceived role of politics in relation to public and private spheres of life.

## Reconstructing the Political

Although the claim that the 'personal is political' was central to early feminist strategies for highlighting the oppression of women within the 'private sphere', many feminist political theorists are now revisiting this claim somewhat more critically. Feminist theory offers numerous challenges to traditional conceptions of the public and private spheres. Feminists have explored the ways in which the distinction masks the exercise of power within the private realm and the extent to which the distinction is itself 'a social construction that reflects the exercise of power' (Acklesberg and Shanley 1996: 217). A central element of most of this theorizing has been the argument that it is impossible to distinguish between what is public and what is private because both are constituted by power relations (*potestas*), relations which inscribe and perpetuate the power of men (MacKinnon 1989). For many, this argument seemed to necessitate the jettisoning of the distinction altogether. Yet feminist political theorists are now sceptical that this is a productive way forward and are more concerned to highlight the extent to which 'the meaning and application of these concepts are the locus of severe political struggle' (Acklesberg and Shanley 1996: 220). This is a struggle in which one must continue to engage if one wants to play an active part in defining the terms of political discourse.

Yeatman, for example, argues that we cannot erode the boundaries of the political altogether and proclaim everything to be political. Rather, the feminist project is to redraw the boundary of the political in a manner sensitive to the historical construction of gendered identities, avoiding the reification of these identities in future political structures (Yeatman 1994a: 35–56). This project is articulated in three distinct forms within contemporary gender theory. In other words, the project of redrawing the boundary of the political is being cast in three distinct ways, which correlate with the three distinct approaches to the conception of power outlined above. The first aims at the greater inclusion of women within a public, institutional conception of the political; the second reverses the focus of the instrumental and institutional conceptions of the political and aims to extend the perspective developed by women in the private sphere to the public realm; and the third displaces the boundary between public and private, between conflict and capacity, in order to generate a more heterogeneous and critical conception of the political. These three conceptions of the political, as institutional, ethical and critical respectively, arise from the three strategies of inclusion, reversal and displacement respectively.

## *Institutional*

Okin is perhaps one of the most eloquent feminist political theorists to endorse the fundamental principles of liberalism (Okin 1991: 40) and seeks to realize a truly 'humanist liberalism' by indicating how existing forms of liberalism will need to be modified in order to take gender seriously. She states that, 'if liberalism is to include all of us, women and men, it must address the challenge presented by the claim that "the personal is political"' (Okin 1991: 41). She is conscious that 'adding women in' will require more than simple quantitative change. Some of the central distinctions within liberalism will need to be rethought if this goal is to be achievable. Centrally, the public/private distinction will need to be redrawn.

Although Okin accepts the need for a distinction between public and private, she is concerned that the line has, in practice, been drawn in a manner that has worked to exclude women from the 'crucial political and legal rights defended by liberals' (Okin 1991: 39). She accepts the charge, made so definitively by Pateman (Pateman and Brennan 1979, Pateman 1983, Pateman 1988), that liberalism's past 'is deeply and, for the most part unambiguously, patriarchal' (Okin 1991: 40). But she does not accept the common charge that liberalism is inherently and irretrievably flawed as a result. She views the challenge facing feminist political theorists as the challenge 'of converting a theory that was built on both the separation of public from private and the confinement of women to family life into a theory that can be about all of us as participants in public as well as private life' (Okin 1991: 40).

Okin argues that liberalism can fully include women only if it recognizes the family as a 'fundamental political institution' and 'extends standards of justice to life within it' (Okin 1991: 53). If government is to secure the political conditions that are necessary for the exercise of personal freedom and to remain neutral towards disputed and controversial ideals of the good life, it ought not to continue to support, or even to allow, gendered practices that deny personal freedom to women and children within the family. Because of 'the inextricable connections between the family and its political and legal context', she concludes, 'a liberalism that aspires to be humanist must apply its standards of justice to the most private of our attachments' (Okin 1991: 53).

Yet, while sharing a common feminist critique of the historical delineation of the public/private distinction, Okin nonetheless upholds the central liberal commitment to privacy and the need to respect personal preferences. She agrees with mainstream liberal theorists about the need for a sphere of privacy, maintaining protection of personal and private life from intrusion and control (Okin 1998: 136). What she seeks to challenge is the particular way in which this line between public and private was drawn in classic liberal theory, 'based in the culture and social practices of patriarchy' (Okin 1998: 136). Shklar has argued that 'the important point for liberalism is not so much where the line is drawn, as that it be drawn' (Shklar 1991: 24). Okin's point is that this may be so, but the important thing for a liberalism which embodies gender justice is that the line is drawn in a way that allows women as well as men to enjoy the opportunities of both public participation and privacy.

In making both these claims Okin effectively disaggregates the presumed correspondence between privacy and the family, the personal and domestic. There are, she claims, 'many public policies that could considerably help people to share parenting responsibilities, and in many cases improve the current situation of children, without even raising issues of privacy. The provision of subsidized, first-rate, small-scale day care is one' (Okin 1991: 53). There are also public policies that clearly do raise the issue of privacy. The distinction between them, she suggests, remains as crucial as ever, but can no longer be assumed to be 'anything like as distinct as that which has prevailed in mainstream political theory from the seventeenth century to the present' (Okin 1998: 137).

In short, Okin adopts the institutional, rather than the instrumental or Foucauldian, conception of the political but claims (against the overwhelming consensus within liberal theory) that the family ought to be considered as a political institution. She also accepts the importance of both the state/civil society and the social/personal forms of the public/private distinction, but claims (again contrary to the weight of liberal tradition) that neither corresponds to the public/domestic distinction – which ought to be abandoned.

### Ethical

Okin would use the political power of the state to extend the freedoms of civil society to the domestic sphere. This ambition presumes that the liberal ideals freedom and justice exist in the public (civil society) if not the private (domestic) sphere. Many are cynical about even this presumption.

Echoing the work of Arendt and Habermas, Elshtain argues that the forces of technical rationality have gradually eroded the ideal of a public sphere characterized by justice, leaving only self-interest as a guide to public activity. We are left, she claims, with a polity 'in which the macro-system has been systematically denuded of a set of public moral values' (Elshtain 1974: 471). The public realm is now defined by the operation of a form of politics that is nothing but the pursuit of power. The public morality of justice was overtaken by the forces of power, coercion and violence. Politics has come to be understood as power politics – conflictual rather than consensual. In short, Elshtain argues that, whatever the merits of the institutional conception of politics, it is actually the instrumental that prevails. The proposal that we extend the norms of the public sphere into the private sphere will not therefore extend the norms of justice and fairness to the domestic. It will actually extend the norms of instrumental power relations into a sphere that still manages to operate according to other, more moral, norms.

Elshtain's response is to reassert the integral relation between politics and morals. Politics, she claims, invoking a Rousseauian vision, is to be distinguished from all other activities by moral, not institutional or instrumental, criteria. Politics, for Elshtain, ought to be understood as a dialogue between citizens concerning the community. Such a dialogue will require the re-creation of a shared tradition, a basic consensus of moral values on which we can agree and from which we can communicate ideas in a meaningful way. Elshtain presents us with an enabling conception of politics in contrast to the dominant 'power over' conception. Politics should be an inter-subjective interaction towards communal goals; a mode of activity which cannot be defined by the gender of its actors, the sphere in which it occurs, or the objectives at which it aims (Elshtain 1981: 168). This 'ethical polity' can be created gradually within existing society, starting with 'an inner dialogue' and developing through contemplation and action 'into public speech and principles' (Elshtain 1981: 169).

And women, according to Elshtain, are ideally placed to develop this polity. For it is they who use the language of morality, who have perpetuated and experienced the only real sense of community left in our society – family ties. Although capitalist and liberal forces have increasingly swamped our sense of community, it can be rekindled, and it is the network of family relations which offers the best source of hope for its rejuvenation. This is why it is so important for Elshtain that women develop a political discourse. Because women have been excluded from power politics for so long, they are well placed to develop a communicative politics which will expose the desolation of power politics and 'repoliticize' the polity.

Elshtain's argument here is not simply a rearticulation of the suffragette's claim that women have a responsibility to take the moral purity of the private realm into the public realm and so civilize politics (though it has more in common with this line of argument than many feminists find acceptable). The language of private morality is not the language of an ethical polity. Its form may prefigure this in important ways, but it is only in a community of citizens that it can be realized. While Elshtain rejects the notion of politics as a 'public space', she does stress the importance of 'public imperatives, competing public claims, public morality, public duties, responsibilities, goods' (Elshtain 1981: 347). She wants her politics to be in and of the world, not parasitic on a realm of necessity. Her ethical politics, 'in its public and private aspects, can be sustained only by persons who are committed to the twin values and worth of each' (Elshtain 1981: 166).

Okin emphasizes the oppressive and unequal aspects of domestic life and seeks to extend the norms of public justice to domestic relations. Elshtain emphasizes the ethical and enriching aspects of domestic life and seeks to extend the norms of private morality to political relations. Both emphasize that it is important to recast rather than jettison a public/private distinction, but the recasting takes a very different form in each of their visions. Some theorists see both options as problematically confined by existing conceptual frameworks.

### Critical

Yeatman argues that the 'personal is political' slogan can be drawn out in three distinct directions: de-patriarchalization, ontologization and politicization. De-patriarchalization entails the use of the state and state-sanctioned forces of the social sphere to delegitimize and deprivatize household-based patriarchal power. This is a strategy of appealing to legislative mechanisms and state policing structures to establish and respect individual rights for women in areas in which they were previously defined in a subordinate role with the family and therefore beyond the boundaries of the state. Ontologization, on the other hand, is a strategy of basing politics on identity. Identity politics is elaborated in a manner that derives the social and the political from what is taken to be a given identity. Here the public/private distinction is challenged, but because 'public' political relations and structures are understood to be manifestations of prior 'private' identities.

Finally, politicization is a strategy of 'de-reifying' the patriarchal organization of personal life. In other words, when one claims something to be political which has been viewed as apolitical, one is also asserting that what was perceived to be 'natural' is in fact socially constituted and therefore amenable to change. The private sphere, assumed to include the areas of sexuality, childbearing and childrearing, has invariably been seen as natural or biologically determined, and therefore not political. Yet it is precisely these aspects of life that feminist theorists have argued to be shaped by patriarchal power, as constituting gender identity and sustaining gender inequalities. If the assumption of naturalness is false then the distinction between the public and the private realm 'comes to seem philosophically arbitrary, without reason' (Jaggar 1997b: 53).

These three articulations of the 'personal is political' generate qualitatively different approaches to gender in politics. De-patriarchalization entails the pursuit of a more adequate realization of the liberal as opposed to the patriarchal forms of government. As such it is based on a strategy of inclusion and assumes a conception of the political as institutional. Ontologization entails a desire to express, and have recognized, one's true identity. As such it is based on a strategy of reversal and assumes a conception of the political as ethical. Advocates of politicization stand directly opposed to those of ontologization, but are also sceptical about the viability of using existing forms of state legislation to pursue de-patriarchalization. Politicization is based on a strategy of displacement and proposes a conception of the political as critical practice. Yeatman argues that de-patriarchalization subjects the private lives of households to the forces of normalization, while ontologization delimits the public lives of individuals to the articulation of group identities. These two interpretations of the 'personal is political' therefore 'threaten to displace the political by the social' (Yeatman 1994a: 51).

Pateman also argues that the ontologization strategy 'merely mirrors its adversary', replacing a technocratic, procedural political method with personal morality. This strategy appears to stand in direct opposition to the strategy of inclusion, yet it works within the confines of liberal discourse by simply valuing as political precisely that which liberalism excludes from politics. The personal, Pateman argues, is as much a part of liberal democracy as the fiction of citizenship and the reification of the political. Similarly, Frazer and Lacey maintain that we need to question not only the 'appropriateness and legitimacy of state intervention in the private sphere', but also the endorsement of familial values as the basis of political relations (Frazer and Lacey 1993: 74).

These advocates of a strategy of displacement reject both the attempt to extend the principles of the public sphere more widely such that they encompass women (the strategy of inclusion) and the celebration of women's exclusion from this sphere (the strategy of reversal). They argue that it is more productive to expose the internal tensions and contradictions that lie within any such distinction, which accepts the mythic relations between men and the public sphere and women and the private sphere (Siltanen and Stanworth 1984: 195–207). This is the deconstructive moment in the strategy of displacement.

If there is a reconstructive moment within this strategy, it appears to lie with the rearticulation rather than the rejection of a public/private distinction. Frazer and Lacey, for example, argue that the project of politicization for feminist theorists will entail the 'reinterpretation of some form of public-private distinction along less gender-exploitative lines' (Frazer and Lacey 1993: 74). The distinction between the private and the public is maintained, but does not correspond to discrete separate spheres. Rather, these two entities 'exist in a permanent tension that can never be reconciled' (Mouffe 1993: 72). This requires the explicit recognition that any such distinction will itself be a political intervention. We will always need to scrutinize the configurations of power that have a stake in redefining the political.

Those theorists who adopt a 'practice conception of power' (Yeatman 1997, Frazer and Lacey 1993) now tend to rearticulate the importance of defining and defending both privacy and the limited institutions of democratic governance. The ability to claim privacy for oneself is recognized as an important right of citizenship and a significant measure of political power (Acklesberg and Shanley 1996: 228). The ability to differentiate between abusive and democratically endorsed power is an important function of political studies and a significant control of political power (Frazer and Lacey 1993: 195). The personal may be political but the ability to claim and defend one's privacy is still a central political goal. Power may be pervasive but the ability to distinguish between abusive and legitimate exercises of power is still a vital political task.

## Conclusion

An individualistic liberalism and a competing individualistic instrumentalism have generated the dominant definitions of the political within political theory. Feminists have taken both these conceptions of the political, and their exclusions, to task. They have emphasized the political relevance of social relations characteristic of family and domestic life and drawn attention to the extent to which women's material and symbolic relation to the family and the domestic have limited their access to positions of power within both the state and civil society. They have challenged both the institutional and the narrow instrumental conceptions of the political. The deconstruction of the role of the public/private distinction within liberal theory was central to the rejection of the liberal construction of the political.

Feminist theorists have drawn upon and contributed to the debates about the nature of power in three distinct ways. They have used the conflictual conception of power to argue for the extension of the institutional conception of the political to include the family. They have used the capacity conception of power to argue for recognition of women's distinctive moral voice as the basis for a new ethical polity. And they have developed the practice conception of power to critique both the institutional and the ethical visions of feminist politics and propose a more heterogeneous reconstruction of the political.

# 2

# *Framing Gender*

## Introduction

What is 'gender'? The term 'gender', as used within feminist theory, is a complex and contested concept that can best be understood as a category that was developed to explore what counts as 'woman' and as 'man'.

The ways in which gender might inform and shape the study of political theory are as diverse as the conceptions of gender itself. I shall sketch out the three archetypal approaches to the question of subjectivity which together help map the debate within feminist theory: the determinist, the constructionist and the deconstructionist. In order to understand the difference between these approaches it is helpful to consider the distinction between the terms 'sex', 'gender' and 'corporeality'. Biological determinism works with the category of sex, social constructionism with the sex/gender distinction and deconstructionism with the category of gender, or corporeality.

## Sex and Gender

The distinction between sex, a matter of biology, and gender, a set of culturally defined characteristics, has been central to a significant body of gender theory to date. Here the terms male and female indicate one's sex, a biological status. The terms masculine and feminine indicate one's gender, the complex of socially constructed characteristics, which are held to relate to the two sexes. As Toril Moi notes, 'it has long been

established usage to make "feminine" (and "masculine") represent social constructs (patterns of sexuality and behaviour imposed by cultural
and social norms), and to reserve "female" and "male" for the purely
biological aspects of sexual difference' (Moi 1997: 247). In this sense
the sex/gender distinction maps onto the old nature/nurture distinction.
Gender is distinguished from a biologically determined nature that is
fixed by genetic structure (Gould 1997: xvii).

## Constructionism

This distinction emerges from, and is defining of, the constructionist
approach to gender theory that emerged in the 1960s. The distinction is
made in order to counter the biological determinism from which it is
argued that one's biological sex determines one's social and cultural
characteristics and roles. Equality feminists in particular saw it as vital
to argue that, irrespective of their sex, women were equally capable of
the rational, individualistic and competitive characteristics commonly
deemed to be masculine.

On this constructionist approach sex is still assumed to be an unalterable – and even desirable – biological given. The political project is to
distinguish sex from gender, and to erode the social construction of
gendered identities. The ambition is to accept sexual difference while
realizing gender androgyny. If the link between sex and gender is eroded
in this way, sex becomes politically non-pertinent and men and women
should be expected to participate equally within the public realm.

It was Simone de Beauvoir who developed the theoretical framework
for such an account of the sex/gender distinction. Her claim that 'one is
not born, one becomes a woman' offered a sweeping critique of biological determinism. De Beauvoir stresses the role of tradition and culture
in conditioning women to adopt inferior roles: woman, she argues, is
not natural, she is 'a product elaborated by civilization' (de Beauvoir
1997: 10). She argues for the transcendence of femininity in order that
women too can become human subjects: 'It is not a question of abolishing
in woman the contingencies and miseries of the human condition, but
of giving her the means for transcending them' (de Beauvoir 1997: 11).

This formulation of the sex/gender distinction has been hugely influential, and politically significant. But it has also generated critics among
those concerned at the attempt to deny the significance of the biological
and to assert the universality of existing cultural values. In seeking to
undermine the hold of the connection between sex and gender, some
theorists have tended to assume that 'feminine' characteristics are simply distorted and delimiting features to be jettisoned in favour of the

intrinsically more rewarding and distinctly human characteristics currently perceived to be 'masculine'. Significantly, de Beauvoir accepted the importance of the mind/body split. She viewed the embodied aspects of life, including sexuality and motherhood, as things that feminists ought to try and transcend. The objective is to allow women as well as men to develop and manifest these characteristics, free of cultural stereotyping.

### Structuralist forms of constructionism

When the sex/gender distinction was taken up and developed in the context of a more structuralist framework, attention was placed directly on the power relations that produced and perpetuated gender identities. If gender is not determined by sex, but is a product of socialization, it becomes important – from a structuralist approach – to theorize the nature of the social structures at work. As one commentator argues: 'Gender is never simply an arrangement in which the roles of men and women are decided in a contingent and haphazard way. At any given moment, gender will reflect the material interests of those who have power and those who do not' (Brittan 1997: 113–14).

Gayle Rubin (1975) offered one of the first articulations of such a structuralist account of the sex/gender distinction, and the functioning of the gender system. The central claim of Rubin's arguments was that the gender system which constructs two different sexes is a system that works to concentrate power in the hands of patriarchs (older men who control both younger men and women). The family is the significant site of power and heterosexuality is the central institution that perpetuates the gender system.

This type of analysis generated the idea that women could therefore be viewed as a social class. Where workers were thought to be oppressed by their relation to the mode of production, women were thought to be oppressed by their relation to the mode of reproduction – or reproductive heterosexuality. Liberation required the transformation of these material relations (Delphy 1984).

These were not the only analyses of sex and gender to develop. Numerous theories emerged during the 1980s, each privileging a different aspect of social relations as central to the construction of gendered identities. Reproduction (O'Brien 1983), caring (Gilligan 1982), production (Hartsock 1983) and sexuality (MacKinnon 1989) were all presented as the determining social structure. One of the most influential theses was that developed by Nancy Chodorow (1978).

As Chodorow herself reflects, 'In the early period of the contemporary feminist movement, feminists searched for a grand theory. This single cause, or dominant factor, theory would explain a sexual inequality, hierarchy, and domination that were omnipresent and that defined and circumscribed entirely the experience and organization of gender and sexuality' (Chodorow 1989: 1). In keeping with the times, Chodorow looked for such a grand theory in psychological anthropology and concluded that women's mothering generated a defensive masculine identity in men and a male psychology that sustained male dominance. She drew on a psychoanalytic account of female and male development to argue that mothering was a central constituting element in the social organization and reproduction of gender.

Chodorow's central claim was that girls and boys develop different 'relational capacities and senses of self as a result of growing up in a family in which women mother' (Chodorow 1978: 173). All children identify first with their mother, which means that a girl's gender identification is continuous with her earlier identification in a way that a boy's is not. In addition, in a society where 'father absence' is normal, girls develop a personal identification with their mother based on gradual learning, while boys must develop a masculine gender identification in the absence of a continuous personal relationship with their father. In this context boys develop 'a sense of what it is to be masculine through identification with cultural images of masculinity and men chosen as masculine models' (Chodorow 1978: 176). This is significant in that boys' identification processes are less likely to be embedded in real affective relations. 'Feminine identification processes are relational, whereas masculine identification processes tend to deny relationship' (Chodorow 1978: 176). Women grow up to be more connected with others than do men, who deny dependence and attachment to others. As a result of being parented by a woman, men and women develop different, and often incompatible, relational needs. The less men participate in parenting, the more this will be the case: 'The relational basis for mothering is ... extended in women, and inhibited in men' (Chodorow 1978: 207). Chodorow's political claim was that women's mothering is 'basic to the sexual division of labour and generates a psychology and ideology of male dominance as well as an ideology about women's capacities and nature' (Chodorow 1978: 208). Given this, she advocates new parenting practices, in which children of both sexes might 'develop a sufficiently individuated and strong sense of self, as well as a positively valued and secure gender identity, that does not bog down either in ego-boundary confusion, low self-esteem, and overwhelming relatedness to other, or in compulsive denial of any connection to others or dependence upon them' (Chodorow 1989: 65).

Notwithstanding its originality, this theory shares with those of Hartsock, MacKinnon, O'Brien and others the claim that there is one single social structure that constructs gender identities. The assumption of the singular nature of pertinent social structures created homogeneous concepts of gender. In response to such theories, many feminists have since argued that these articulations of constructionism present too singular an account of power relations and too monolithic an account of gender.

An increasing number of critics now maintain that early articulations of object-relations theory were constrained by a reductive set of assumptions which privileged gender as the only category of difference, marginalizing all other relevant categories in the process. Critics have argued that Chodorow and her followers offered a falsely universalized account of the acquisition of gendered identity, one that actually focused only on the experiences of white, middle-class, Western women. In short, there is concern that object-relation theory offers an account of subjectivity that makes gender the only relevant category of difference. Chodorow's own more recent acknowledgement of the multiplicity of social structures shaping the acquisition of identity adds weight to the contemporary scepticism of such reductionist claims. 'I no longer think', she states, 'that one factor, or even dynamic, can explain male dominance . . . My early writing . . . implied that women's mothering was *the* cause or prime mover of male dominance. I would now argue that these writings document and delineate one extremely important, and previously largely unexamined, aspect of the relations of gender and the psychology of gender' (Chodorow 1989: 5–6).

### From single to multiple social structures

The issue of race was central in propelling the movement from constructionism which proposed singular accounts of social structures (and hence homogeneous conceptions of 'woman') to multiple accounts (and hence differentiated conceptions of 'women'). As Elizabeth Spelman argues: 'Any attempt to talk about all women in terms of something we have in common undermines attempts to talk about the differences among us, and vice versa' (Spelman 1988: 3). Her charge is that the common resolution to this paradox has taken the form of focusing on women 'as women'. Yet to do so has not been to speak of what all women have in common; rather, 'it has been to conflate the condition of one group of women with the condition of all and to treat the differences of white middle-class women from all other women as if there were not differences' (Spelman 1988: 3).

Spelman is aware that many feminists attempt to take differences between women on board, but is sceptical that they actually realize this.

Talking about race and class in addition to gender is not sufficient if one nonetheless continues to insist that we are all the same 'as women', and that the differences among women reside in some non-woman part of us. Adopting this stance allows one to gesture towards difference while continuing only to talk about white middle-class (and, some would add, heterosexual, first-world) women.

An example of what this entails can be seen in Spelman's response to Chodorow's account of the acquisition of gendered identity. Chodorow's account of gender identity falls subject to Spelman's critique because she 'makes it look as if a woman's mothering takes place in a social context that is simply sexist. As if a boy's acquiring a masculine gender identity involves simply the notion that men are superior to women, whoever the men and women are' (Spelman 1988: 171). If this were the case, she argues, 'it becomes impossible to explain why some men are the perpetrators, others the victims, of racism and classism' (Spelman 1988: 171). In other words, in attempting to uncover a single account of gender identity, Chodorow fails to provide a basis for understanding how, for example, some white women come to believe themselves to be superior to some black men. Spelman does not conclude from this that feminism should give up talking about gender, but that 'we do need to keep in mind the full force of the idea that gender is a social construction' (Spelman 1988: 172). In other words, even theorists critical of monocausal accounts of the social construction of gender have themselves used the constructionist approach as the basis for their more pluralized account of gender.

Theories of the social construction of gender have become increasingly multifaceted. But they still, up to this point, take sex as foundational. Accounts of the acquisition of gendered identity are now rarely as monocausal as they were in early articulations of constructionism, but they nonetheless presume a stable category of sex upon which gendered identities are constructed. However, this presumption of the conceptual stability of 'sex' has also become subject to scrutiny. The debates between monocausal and pluralized accounts of gendered identity rest primarily on the social category of gender. The biological category of sex was rarely subject to direct scrutiny. An increasingly large number of gender theorists now view this as a problem. It is argued that, while constructionist accounts of gender emerged to counter the hold of biological determinism, they nonetheless covertly invoked the notion of biological foundations in their reliance on the category of sex (Hawkesworth 1997: 662). The causal connection between sex and gender, however culturally elaborated, is nonetheless presumed. In contrast there are some approaches to the issue of gendered subjectivity that loosen this causal connection altogether.

*From material to discursive constructionism*

It is possible to define the categories of femininity and masculinity not with reference to sex (female and male), but in relation only to one another. This generates a form of relational rather than material constructionism. The question of gender then becomes primarily linguistic or discursive rather than material or social.

In shifting the attention to the discursive, relational constructionists recuperate an element of de Beauvoir's original discussion of 'woman' that was not prioritized in earlier constructionist accounts. Humanity, argued de Beauvoir, is male 'and man defines woman not in herself but as relative to him . . . He is the Subject, he is the Absolute – she is the Other' (de Beauvoir 1997: 5). Otherness, she argues, is a fundamental category of human thought: 'no group ever sets itself up as the One without at once setting up the Other over against itself' (de Beauvoir 1997: 6). Woman is defined not by biology, or even by material structures based on this biology, but by her otherness to men.

In this context 'gender' becomes a fundamentally political category. Without a material referent, its meaning is generated within linguistic structures. To understand the nature of gender upon this approach, one need not explore the relation between femininity and the biological female, or masculinity and the biological male. Instead one needs to explore the ways in which femininity is articulated as the other of masculinity. This necessitates a 'linguistic turn' within gender theorizing, shifting attention from material to discursive structures. On this approach the meaning of femininity has no ontological foundation. It is relational and contextual.

While advocates of pluralized accounts of constructionism have moved from talking about 'woman' to 'women', discursive accounts of gender reject the idea that even 'women' exist in any stable form. One of the key theorists of this perspective has been Denise Riley. She argues that:

> 'women' is historically, discursively constructed, and always relatively to other categories which themselves change; 'women' is a volatile collectivity in which female persons can be very differently positioned, so that the apparent continuity of the subject of 'women' isn't to be relied on; 'women' is both synchronically and diachronically erratic as a collectivity, while for the individual, 'being a woman' is also inconstant, and can't provide an ontological foundation. (Riley 1988: 1–2)

Riley's 'historical constructionism' differs from the previous renderings of constructionism in that it offers no static or structural account of the material causes of the construction of gender.

The concern about the category 'women' here is not the same as that voiced by those who argued its formulation to be too racially or culturally homogeneous. Debates about differences within women still presume the category of 'women' (Riley 1997: 245). Yet it is unclear whether it is possible or desirable to try to fix the meaning of femininity at all. Feminist theory, which created the category of gender in order to answer the question 'what is a woman?' in a non-deterministic manner, now finds itself unable to speak of 'woman', or even 'women', without major discomfort. The project is not to discover some essential ontological nature for women, but to insist that the category of 'woman' is historically contingent.

Given an entirely relational conception of gender, the category of 'women' will be highly volatile. For example, Julia Kristeva refuses to give any substantive content to femininity. She argues that femininity is simply 'that which is marginalised by the patriarchal symbolic order' (Kristeva 1997: 248). On this definition 'femininity' has a stable relationship only to dominant patriarchal power. Interestingly it has no necessary relationship to the biological category of the female, and can be located in the biological male. This is the logical conclusion of the sex/gender distinction. If there is no causal relation between sex and gender there is no reason why the construction of masculinity will accrue exclusively to the bodies of males or femininity to the bodies of females. Moreover, there is no reason to assume that there will only ever be two genders.

Judith Butler has pointed out that the 'presumption of a binary gender system implicitly retains the belief in a mimetic relation of gender to sex, whereby gender mirrors sex or is otherwise restricted by it' (Butler 1990: 6). The more critical one is of the singular, deterministic accounts that present tightly causal theories of the relation between sex and gender, and the more one theorizes gender as 'radically independent of sex', the less rationale there seems to be for assuming that the gender system will be binary. The categories of masculinity and femininity no longer have any stable referent in biology and would therefore appear to be lacking in definitional logic.

### Summary

So far the debate about gender can be seen as a debate within social construction. It is accepted that sex is biologically determined, and gender is socially constructed. There are three main sources of conflict within constructionism. Firstly, there is the question of whether one considers gender as a manifestation of contingent stereotyping or of structural power relations. Secondly, there is the question of whether one considers these structures to be singular or multiple. Thirdly, there is the question of whether one considers these structures to be material or linguistic. The debate is not about whether gender is constructed or not, but rather the extent to which the structures of social construction are open to modification, and are multiple. Degrees of mutability range from the universal and atemporal to the historically and socially contingent and infinitely mutable. Degrees of multiplicity range from the singular to the many. As Susan Moller Okin puts it: 'At one end of the spectrum are those whose explanations of the subordination of women focus primarily on biological difference as causal in the construction of gender, and at the other end are those who argue that biological difference may not even lie at the core of the social construction that is gender' (Okin 1989: 6).

## Beyond Sex and Gender

The constructionist account of sex and gender takes the focus off biological sex to a large extent, first by introducing a notion of gender as socially constructed, and then by defining the feminine as relational to the masculine, without any substantive content in its own right. But this still leaves the category of the female and male in place: the category of gender becomes highly sophisticated, but sex is untheorized. However, the category of sex has itself come under scrutiny of late and the sex/gender distinction looks increasingly untenable. As Donna Haraway has noted: 'There is nothing about being "female" that naturally binds women. There is not even such a status as "being" female, itself a highly complex category constructed in contested sexual scientific discourses and other social practices' (Haraway 1990: 197). The sex/gender distinction, comments Lynne Segal, 'is now seen by many as a misleading distinction' (Segal 1994: 226).

The idea of biological sex difference, left unchallenged in constructionist theories, is now challenged. This development appears counterintuitive to many readers. 'In our culture', argues Bob Connell, who has done much to promote the denaturalization of sex, 'the reproductive dichotomy is assumed to be the absolute basis of gender and sexuality in everyday life . . . For many people the notion of natural sex difference forms a limit beyond which thought cannot go' (Connell 1987: 66). Yet, he asserts, doctrines of natural difference (and there are feminist as well as sexist versions of these) are fundamentally mistaken (Connell 1987: 67). In contrast to both biologically determinist accounts (where society 'registers what nature decrees') and material constructionist accounts (where society culturally elaborates the distinction between the sexes), Connell contends that social practices themselves construct sexual difference by 'converting an average difference into a categorical difference' (Connell 1987: 80).

The body itself is transformed in social practice. As Connell says in relation to masculinity: 'My male body does not confer masculinity on me, it receives masculinity' (Connell 1987: 83). In other words, not only is biological determinism rejected, the constructionist tendency to accept sex as presocial is also condemned. The physical sense of maleness or femaleness is a consequence, not simply of chromosomes or the possession/absence of a penis, but of a personal history of habits of posture and movement, of particular physical skills, the image of one's own body and so on. 'The social definition of men as holders of power is translated not only into mental body-images and fantasies, but into muscle and tensions, posture, the feel and texture of the body' (Connell 1987: 85). Nature may be opposed to culture and the body to history symbolically, but in practice the body is never outside history and history never free of bodily presence.

The neat distinction between the physiological and the socially constituted becomes increasingly strained. In the context of recent studies of technology and nature, it is now commonly argued that the attempt to identify a clear presocial sense of biology is a doomed project. It follows from this that the conceptual distinction between sex and gender that earlier feminists painstakingly established also looks shaky. As Jaggar argues, 'if we acknowledge human biology, including human sex differences, as created partly by society, and if we acknowledge human society as responsive to human biology, then we lose the clarity of the distinction between sex and gender' (Jaggar 1997b: 52–3).

## Corporeality

The claim that biology itself is a result of systems of social organization has been recognized by a wide spectrum of theorists. Mary Daly famously noted that the effects of prohibition of women's bodies prevented women from developing their capacities in various ways – from Chinese footbinding to contemporary American gynaecology (Daly 1987). Andrea Dworkin has maintained that the sex distinction itself may be in part a social product – 'inter-sex' individuals being less likely to be chosen as marriage partners (Dworkin 1974). Dorothy Dinnerstein has asserted that 'Man-made and physiological structures have ... come to interpenetrate so thoroughly that to call a human project contrary to human biology is naive' (quoted in Jaggar 1997a: 51). Monique Wittig has argued forcefully against the idea that there is natural division between men and women. Her belief is that nature itself has been used to oppress women and deform their bodies (Wittig 1992). The erosion of a clear presocial sense of biology is not new, and not confined to postmodern political theorists. Yet this insight has come to appear particularly significant in the light of recent challenges to structuralist accounts of sex and gender.

The sex/gender distinction was formulated much as Marxists conceived the material/ideological distinction: with femininity and masculinity standing in opposition to an identity which counts as truth (and which can be discovered through consciousness-raising) and in a secondary position relative to their material determinants – the body. The constructionist perspective aims to explore how men and women become masculine and feminine subjects. While arguing for a clear relation between sex and gender, these theoretical perspectives nonetheless presume analytical separability and focus upon gender as a conditioning of the mind.

In contrast, deconstructionists tend to invoke the Foucauldian notion of discourse, in which the discursive and the material are intertwined. Discourse 'is to be understood as an amalgam of material practices and forms of knowledge linked together in a non-contingent relation' (McNay 1994: 108). Both the material and the non-material are mutually determining. Gender is therefore both a material effect of the way in which power takes hold of the body and an ideological effect of the way power 'conditions' the mind. This erodes the clarity of the sex/gender distinction. From this perspective it makes no sense to conceive of the body as simply an anatomical fact and the mind as socially conditioned. The biological and the social are themselves 'bound together' (Foucault 1978: 152).

The deconstructive approach to subjectivity draws heavily upon Foucault's claim that notions of subjectivity are merely the result of the operations of power upon the body. Particular technologies of power give rise to a corpus of knowledge, which naturalize a specific notion of subjectivity, reinforcing the effects of this power. As Foucault states: 'I ... believe that there is no sovereign, founding subject, a universal form of subject to be found everywhere ... I believe, on the contrary, that the subject is constituted through practices of subjection, or, in a more autonomous way, through practices of liberation, of liberty' (Foucault 1988: 50). The constraints of power are regarded as simultaneously the precondition of, and a threat to, individual subjectivity.

One of the most important advocates of this position has been Judith Butler. Her claim is that gender ought not to be conceived merely as the cultural inscription of meaning on a pregiven sex; gender must also designate the very apparatus of production whereby the sexes themselves are established. As a result, gender is not to culture as sex is to nature; gender is also the discursive/cultural means by which 'sexed nature' or 'a natural sex' is produced and established as 'prediscursive', 'prior to culture' . . . (Butler 1990: 1–25)

Butler's work has been enormously influential. Many feminists now endorse her insistence that the distinction between the material and the intangible, body and mind, be eroded.

Moira Gatens, for example, argues that the 'anatomical body is itself a theoretical object for the discourse of anatomy which is produced by human beings in culture' (Gatens 1992: 131). In other words, it is a particular culture that chooses to represent bodies anatomically. This means that 'the sexed body can no longer be conceived as the unproblematic biological and factual base upon which gender is inscribed, but must itself be recognised as constructed by discourses and practices that take the body both as their target and as their vehicle of expression' (Gatens 1992: 132). In this context theorists are now beginning to argue that the sex/gender distinction needs to be replaced by 'an understanding of a single, but variegated . . . porous, permeable, notion of corporeal subjectivity' (Prokhovnik 1999: 113).

## Essentialism and Autonomy

The wide range of perspectives possible within the basic social constructionist distinction between sex and gender means that constructionism can be used to endorse an equally wide variety of advocacy projects. One could use the distinction to argue that, because gendered identity is socially constructed, individuals are able to reflect rationally and determine autonomously their own identities. One could equally argue that, because gendered identity is socially constructed, it will inevitably be severely constrained and can never be autonomously chosen. The constructionist account of gender can therefore be used to argue both for and against the possibility of autonomy.

This means that, while constructionism was originally conceived as a means of refuting biological determinism, it can entail either a form of cultural determinism or a form of individual autonomy. If 'construction' is used to imply that certain laws (material or linguistic) generate gender difference along universal axes, then constructionism implies a form of determinism. If the culture or society that constructs gender operates according to immutable laws, gender is as determined as it was under the biological determinist account. If, on the other hand, 'construction' were used to imply a form of choice informed by individual reflection, gender would appear to be a matter of free will. Constructionism can then encompass either determinism or free will, depending on its particular rendering.

Within feminist debates about subjectivity, the conventional philosophical dichotomy between determinism and free will has more commonly been articulated as a debate between the poles of essentialism and autonomy. Let us look at each in turn.

### Essentialism

I have avoided using the term essentialism so far because it is much overused and very confused within feminist theory. But it is worth indicating how the notion of essentialism relates to the determinism/constructionism distinction. Diana Fuss, in her classic attempt to undermine the hold and pertinence of the assumed clear-cut distinction between essentialism and constructionism, defines essentialism as 'a belief in true essence – that which is most irreducible, unchanging, and therefore constitutive of a given person or thing' (Fuss 1989: 2). In feminist theory, she notes, essentialism is cast in the form of 'appeals to a pure or original femininity, a female essence, outside the boundaries of the social and thereby untainted (though perhaps repressed) by a patriarchal order' (Fuss 1989: 2). Constructionism, on the other hand, stands in direct opposition to essentialism, insisting that what appear to be essences are actually historical constructions. Whereas the essentialist would assume the natural to be determining of social and political practices, the constructionist would argue the natural itself to be a construction of the social and/or political.

Yet, although the essentialist and anti-essentialist perspectives appear to be both analytically distinct and politically antagonistic, in practice it is rather difficult to disentangle the two. While constructionism stands in opposition to biological determinism, it nonetheless contains essentialist aspects. Essences can be materially and symbolically, as well as biologically, given. As Moi notes, it is no less essentialist 'to hold that there is a historically or socially given female essence' than it is to propose a biologically given one (Moi 1997: 247). Once this is acknowledged, it becomes evident that constructionist accounts of the sex/gender distinction may themselves entail essentialist claims. Indeed Fuss argues that 'there is no sure way to bracket off and to contain essentialist manoeuvres in anti-essentialist arguments' (Fuss 1989: 4). It is possible, however, to categorize forms of essentialism and to evaluate their relative desirability.

Ferguson helpfully unpacks the term essentialism, showing that it commonly entails at least three different positions: these she labels 'essentialism per se', 'universalization', and 'coherent categorization'. Essentialism per se is defined as that which 'attributes women's psychological and social experiences to fixed and unchanging traits resident in women's physiology or in some larger order of things' (Ferguson 1993: 81). The biological determinism that we have been considering would therefore fall within this category, but so too would some of the more rigid and 'grand' culturally determinist theories. Universalization is defined as that which 'takes the patterns visible in one's own time and place to be accurate for all' (Ferguson 1993: 82). Most of the early, singular forms of constructionism (including the theses of Chodorow and Hartsock) have been charged with this tendency. The final form of essentialism distinguished by Ferguson entails 'any constitution of a unified set of categories around the terms *woman* and *man*' (Ferguson 1993: 82). Given that any analysis requires some set of categories about which generalizations can be made, it is unlikely that even the most trenchant critic of 'essentialism per se' or of 'universalization' will avoid this form of essentialism.

Despite the constructionist rejection of biological determinism, many constructionist accounts have been labelled essentialist. Here the charge of essentialism is usually a form of universalization. And, despite the deconstructionist rejection of both biological determinism and universalization, many deconstructionists are deeply ambivalent about the jettisoning of the category of 'women' and therefore open themselves up to charges of essentialism that accompany an invocation of a coherent gender category.

Theorists such as Braidotti, Fuss, Ferguson and Quinby are trying to move feminism beyond the essentialism/anti-essentialism impasse that has beleaguered it over the years. As Quinby notes: 'even this many years after Diana Fuss's illuminating demonstrations of how the "bar between essentialism and constructionism is by no means as solid and unassailable as advocates of both sides assume it to be", essentialism remains a term still uttered in a tone of contempt' (Quinby 1997: 150–1). Both Fuss and Quinby argue that the language of essence is not necessarily reactionary. Ferguson shows how it is, in some form, necessarily present within any feminist discourse, however self-consciously anti-essentialist.

### Autonomy

There is a presumption within most contemporary political theory that autonomy is just what women want (Di Stefano 1996: 95). Autonomy does indeed appear to be a central feminist objective: control of one's body, labour, resources and life decisions have all been key feminist demands. Yet autonomy has also been seen as an ideal that represents an abstract, disembodied and profoundly masculine conception of the self.

This ambivalence about the concept of autonomy was first signalled, as Di Stefano notes, by de Beauvoir, in that she insists both that women should claim the role and benefits of male subjects, and that 'the feminized Other functions as a prop for the virile, autonomous self' (Di Stefano 1996: 96). The ideal of autonomy may require the notion of 'feminized alterity' for its definitional identity. If feminized heteronomy and masculine autonomy are two halves of a dichotomous whole, it is simply not possible to jettison the former without destabilizing the latter. In other words, gender theorists who aim to achieve autonomy for women as well as for men are pursuing an impossible goal. The very concept of autonomy has been defined in a masculine manner and cannot be simply appropriated by all people without severe definitional disruption.

Di Stefano argues that this conundrum continues to inflect Western feminist thinking about autonomy (Di Stefano 1996: 96). While many women have campaigned for women's legal and political right to autonomy, Jean Baker Miller, for instance, argues that the notion of autonomy 'derived from men's development, not women's' (Miller 1976: 95). The emphasis upon the ability to give up affiliations in order to become a separate and self-directed individual is one that emerges from a male developmental trajectory and is a 'dangerous' ideal for women to pursue. Elizabeth Grosz, on the other hand, argues that the notion of autonomous self-determination is gender-neutral. For her autonomy is about the 'right to political, social, economic and intellectual self-determination' and implies the right to self-definition. As such it does not require that women fit into male-defined norms (Grosz 1987: 193).

What we usually find, then, is a split with regard to the concept of autonomy. On the one hand we find gender theorists arguing that 'autonomy is an emancipatory concept from which many women and some men have been unfairly excluded and to which they do and should aspire' (Di Stefano 1996: 98). On the other hand we find more sceptical gender theorists arguing that autonomy is part of the oppressive political discourse which privileges men's behaviour and norms. These two positions are manifestations of the strategies of inclusion and reversal respectively. In the former, the valued concept of autonomy is assumed to be gender-neutral in conception, and is claimed for women as well as for men in practice. In the latter, autonomy is deemed to be an inherently patriarchal concept and so rejected in favour of a more relational ideal. The strategy of displacement here entails going beyond autonomy/ heteronomy (authenticity) and proposing a modification of the presumed opposition. Within this, there are deconstructive and reconstructive moments. In a deconstructive move Butler proposes that we view autonomy as an illusionary effect (Butler 1992: 12). In a more reconstructive move Jean Grimshaw proposes that we salvage a modified autonomy which 'neither assumes the original unitary self . . . nor ignores the needs of women' (Grimshaw 1988: 105).

If we now consider this debate about autonomy in the light of the previous one about essentialism, it is clear that both concepts have a highly charged and deeply ambivalent role within feminist theories of subjectivity. They are, in many respects, antithetical. One would expect theorists unambiguously to embrace one or the other as central to their project. Yet, in reality, most theorists are concerned about the potential dangers of both essentialism and autonomy. The idea that women's experiences can be attributed to fixed and unchanging traits resident in their physiology and the idea that women's experiences can be entirely attributed to self-determination and abstract reflection are both viewed sceptically. Nonetheless, the majority of theorists have adopted some form of essentialism in order to reflect upon 'women' as a category and have endorsed some form of autonomy in order to campaign for women's legal and political rights.

## Mobile Subjectivities

Intriguingly, despite the heated debates between advocates of determinism, constructionism and deconstructionism, many theorists are now adopting an eclectic position in which they attempt either a theoretical synthesis or a pragmatic compromise between the three approaches.

Many feminists who are theoretically committed to the deconstructionist approach to the question of subjectivity nonetheless invoke some form of essentialism in the context of political strategy. Despite the theoretical deconstruction of the category of 'woman' it is common to find theorists advocating a politics of 'as if women existed', since the world behaves as if they unambiguously did. This has sometimes resulted in a confusing vacillation between essentialist and anti-essentialist moments. For instance, Kristeva states that: 'believing oneself "a woman" is almost as absurd and obscurantist as believing oneself "a man". I say almost because there are still things to be got for women: freedom of abortion and contraception, childcare facilities, recognition of work etc. Therefore, "we are women" should still be kept as a slogan, for demands and publicity' (quoted in de Lauretis 1984: 95). This attempt to negotiate the tension between theoretical vision and pragmatic policy is viewed by many as simply incoherent. Fraser, for instance, argues that Kristeva has a tendency to manifest 'alternating essentialist gynocentric moments with anti-essentialist nominalistic moments, moments that consolidate an ahistorical, undifferentiated, maternal feminine gender identity with moments that repudiate women's identities altogether' (Fraser 1997a: 166). Nonetheless, it is common to find deconstructionist theorists advocating a form of 'strategic essentialism' (Spivak 1987).

Against these deconstructionist endorsements of strategic essentialism Butler counters: 'Strategic essentialism won't do: for strategies always have meanings that exceed the purposes for which they are intended' (Butler 1990: 5). She does allow that provisional unities 'might emerge in the context of concrete actions that have purposes other than the articulation of identity. An open coalition, then, will affirm identities that are alternately instituted and relinquished according to the purposes at hand; it will be an open assemblage that permits of multiple convergences and divergences, without obedience to a normative telos of definitional closure' (Butler 1990: 16). But, as Ferguson points out, Butler uses passive constructions and indirect grammar ('whatever aims are in view') to avoid saying 'what we have in view'. She does so to hide the fact that, contrary to her own explicit assertion, she presumes some group who have enough in common to use first-person plural pronouns (Ferguson 1993: 181). In other words, she implicitly adopts the third form of essentialism delineated by Ferguson.

If Butler is deeply resistant to the idea of invoking an essentialist notion of femininity (however minimal), others are far more enthusiastic. The simultaneous adoption of a deconstructionist account of subjectivity with a political affirmation of 'the feminine' is given a particular theoretical coherence by the post-Freudian linguistic theories of Lacanian feminists. These theorists adopt a particularly structuralist account of language to account for the constitution of gendered identity. Notably, Irigaray offers a universalist account of linguistic identity formation, coupled with an essentialist notion of the authentic feminine to be found in the pre-linguistic realm. On this perspective femininity loses its material referent, but remains a coherent and politically significant category. From a related theoretical perspective Drucilla Cornell insists 'on the affirmation of the feminine' (Cornell 1993: 100). Hers is not a biological or even a material feminine, it is a metaphorical one. The metaphorical feminine adopted here is not a form of biological determinism. In Cornell's words: 'the remetaphorisation of the feminine within sexual difference does not try to capture the truth of femininity. We are not to accommodate to what we have been forced "to be" under the gender hierarchy. The opposite is the case' (Cornell 1993: 142).

Although Irigaray and Cornell affirm the feminine, their theoretical stance is quite distinct from the earlier constructionist perspectives that generated apparently similar affirmations. Cornell perceives Gilligan's notion of the different female voice to be 'part of our artificial mythology. As we tell a story, however, we are beginning to create the reality in which the very economy of desire perpetuated by phallogocentrism is undermined' (Cornell 1993: 110). For Cornell, then, it is not that her 'feminine' is symbolic and Gilligan's structural, but rather that both are symbolic and that Gilligan's metaphor of the feminine reinforces gender hierarchies whereas hers undermines it.

However, others fear that this 'remetaphorization of the feminine' may actually underline rather than undermine gender hierarchy. Those theorists who adopt a form of discursive constructionism, but who embrace a less structuralist account of linguistic structures, are far more sceptical about the affirmation of the feminine. For example, Brown argues that gender identities are diverse, fluid, and 'ultimately impossible to generalize' (Brown 1995: 166). However, gender *power* may nonetheless 'be named and traced with some precision at the relatively general level' (Brown 1995: 166–7). Brown argues that these modes of power are far more circumscribable than their particular agents, vehicles and objects. Rather than leading to the endorsement of the symbolic feminine, this articulation of discursive constructionism generates a commitment to destabilizing the notion of stable binary gender identities altogether.

Others still attempt another resolution of the tension between theoretical sophistication and political effectivity. Riley, for example, claims that essentialism overfeminizes women by defining us maternally while deconstructionism underfeminizes us by insisting that 'women' don't exist:

> There are alternatives to those schools of thought which in saying that 'woman' is fictional are silent about 'women', and those which, from an opposite perspective, proclaim that the reality of women is yet to come, but that this time, it's we, women, who will define her. Instead of veering between deconstruction and transcendence, we could try another train of speculations: that 'women' is indeed an unstable category, that this instability has a historical foundation, and that feminism is the site of the systematic fighting-out of that instability – which need not worry us. (Riley 1997: 244)

Similarly Fraser argues that: 'Complex, shifting, discursively constructed social identities, provide an alternative to reified, essentialist conceptions of gender identity, on the one hand, and to simple negations and dispersals of identity, on the other' (Fraser 1997a: 166). In other words, the attempt to position oneself within the debate about sex, gender and corporeality in a way that that is both theoretically cogent and politically effective increasingly leads to an endorsement of 'mobile subjectivities'.

## The Politics of Subjectivity

The debates about the nature of 'women', about sex, gender and corporeality, are of intense political significance. They underpin differing conceptions of the nature of politics and the appropriateness of various political strategies and objectives.

For example, if one accepts the deconstructionist arguments put forward about the construction of sex as well as gender, this means that one cannot rule out the biological as a political concern. As Gould argues: 'If nothing is natural, then the area of human social life that political theory has taken traditionally as its domain can now be seen to be too narrow' (Gould 1997: 53). This has particular significance for those theorists who adopted the sex/gender distinction as a way of transcending the constraints of female biology. These theorists would make women equal to men by uncoupling the link between sex and gender, eroding the distinction between gendered identities within the public sphere in favour of a universal humanism, and confining the significance of sexual difference to the private sphere. But this goal, it now appears, will always be self-contradictory because it fails to address the social construction of biology itself. The underlying dichotomy between male and female sexual difference remains unchallenged. The fact that female biology appears so disruptive in the public sphere (creating demands for maternity leave, sick leave for premenstrual tension and claims of sexual harassment) needs to be understood in the light of social constructions of female and male sexual difference. As Pateman has highlighted, it was social contract theory itself that helped to define women by their reproductive heterosexuality and so constitute the political significance of sexual difference (Pateman 1988).

But it is not only the parameters of mainstream political theory that are challenged by the developments within debates about subjectivity. The premises of feminist politics are also challenged. As Butler argues, if 'a stable notion of gender no longer proves to be the foundational premise of feminist politics, perhaps a new sort of feminist politics is now desirable to contest the very reifications of gender and identity, one that will take the variable construction of identity as both a methodological and normative prerequisite, if not a political goal' (Butler 1990: 5).

Contrary to the impression given by many of her detractors, Butler does not actually argue that contesting the processes of reification is *the* political goal. She does suggest that contesting the very reifications of gender might be *a* political goal. The problem, which is not specific to Butler, is that it is not clear what other forms of politics might be compatible with this metatheoretical position. Elsewhere she acknowledges that 'the political task is not to refuse representational politics – as if we could' (Butler 1990: 5). But the vital question regarding what difference the recognition that gendered identities are reified might make to how we negotiate representational politics is left unexplored.

This silence has led some to presume that such a politics will inevitably involve relinquishing any presumption of solidarity and jettisoning the unity of the category of woman. This is a worrying prospect for many. Kate Soper, for example, argues that 'feminism, like any other politics, has always implied a banding together, a movement based on solidarity and sisterhood of women, who are linked by perhaps very little else than their sameness and "common cause" as women' (Soper 1990: 235). As Naomi Scheman argues, there is problem of when and how to say 'we' (Scheman 1993: 190). Women became suspicious of the 'we' invoked by hegemonic male discourse, only to invoke a new 'we', the different voice that women spoke, 'committing precisely the epistemological and political sin we had been attacking in masculinist thought' (Scheman 1993: 190).

This problem remains unresolved. As Scheman articulates it: 'the case against saying we seems overwhelming: politically as a piece of imperialist presumption, and epistemologically as a fiction that equates autonomy with universality.' Yet, and is a politically crucial yet: 'the epistemological and political need to say we remains' (Scheman 1993: 190). Assertions of sameness, which the invocation of 'we' presumes, need not rest on claims to essential sameness. Of central importance is the question of self-definition. A 'historically specific *we* of political identity and alliance' is liberatory in a way in which a group identity imposed by oppressive power relations is not. Distinguishing between the two, and creating space for the former, is the vital role of gender in political theory. It keeps us continually aware of the contingency of claims to group sameness and mindful of the power relations which produced the conditions of identity.

The debate about subjectivity is ultimately a political debate. The vast literature that has emerged in response to the question 'what is gender?' is politically focused and driven. Underpinning the reflections on subjectivity are political considerations about oppression and liberation. The way in which the question 'what is gender?' gets asked makes it clear that this has primarily been a question framed by feminist politics. The gender in question has been the female one. Gender has all too often been taken as a synonym for woman (Carver 1995). The 'we' in question is always a collectivity of women (however conceived).

## Masculinities

The debate concerning subjectivity has emerged largely within femininist theory and has focused, sometimes exclusively, on the question of female ontology and feminine identity. However, each stage in the debate surveyed above entails a more or less overt theory of male ontology and masculine identity. Also, as the debate has progressed, a more inclusive approach to all aspects of gender – masculine as well as feminine – has emerged. In other words, debates about sex and gender have been inspired and shaped largely by feminist politics. The focus has therefore been overwhelmingly on women rather than on men. But as the literature has shifted from theorizing sex, to the sex/gender distinction (in all its forms) and finally to corporeality, so the logic of considering only one gender has dissipated.

Throughout the discussion about subjectivity in this chapter it may have appeared as though theorizing female subjectivity is essentially different to, and therefore analytically distinct from, theorizing male subjectivity. This reflects the way in which the debate has developed within feminist theory, the major site of reflection of gendered subjectivity to date. Nonetheless, this presumption needs to be questioned. There is an increasingly prevalent perception within feminist debates that gendered identities are more complex and less binary than previously assumed. In addition to this, there has also emerged a discrete literature about masculinity itself. The tendency (among both advocates and critics) to assume that gender is a synonym for women and that to explore the politics of gender is to engage with feminist political theory stands in need of revision.

Given the relational nature of the masculine and the feminine, one inevitably needs to explore each in relation to the other. And, if one accepts the notion that there is no single feminine identity, it makes sense to assume that there is similarly no single masculine identity but rather many. It is, notes Spelman, always easier to see how privilege works in others than in ourselves, 'but the insights so gained may be entirely lost if we can't imagine that we are anything like those others' (Spelman 1988: 5). Spelman uses this insight to critique the tendency of feminists to conflate one form of womanhood with all. But it can also be used to critique the tendency to conflate one form of masculinity with all – something which many feminists, attuned to the importance of differentiating between women, continue to do in regard to men. Spelman herself makes the important acknowledgement that it is not a threat to the coherence of feminism to recognize the existence of many genders, but continues to equate this with 'many kinds of women' (Spelman 1988: 176). Recognition of the existence of 'many kinds of men' is there in Spelman's work, but only fleetingly mentioned (Spelman 1988: 186), not explicitly theorized.

There is still reluctance within much feminist theory to engage fully with the literature on masculinity. Yet its insights and developments are essential and profoundly helpful to a full understanding of gender theory. Arguments for the recognition of many genders as articulated within feminist theory resonate with similar claims from within recent literature on masculinity. Arthur Brittan, for example, challenges the notion that masculinity is timeless and universal. 'My position', he states, 'is that we cannot talk of masculinity, only masculinities' (Brittan 1997: 113). Like Spelman, he argues that this position does not lead to the abandonment of gender studies altogether: masculinity does not become so variable that we cannot identify it as a topic, but it does require that it must be theorized in a historically and culturally specific manner. The claim that gendered identities (both feminine and masculine) are continuously subject to a process of reinterpretation and are never static does not mean that they should be viewed as ephemeral or irrelevant. Given the extensive theorization of masculinities now in existence, the notion that gender might be synonymous with women, while masculinity remains untheorized, has now been overturned. De Beauvoir may have been right to argue that 'A man would never set out to write a book on the peculiar situation of the human male.' But, as John MacInnes notes, 'half a century later it seems that every man and his dog is writing a book on masculinity' (MacInnes 1998: 1).

In recent years – as Jeff Hearn tells us – we have seen the 'naming of men as men' (Hearn 1999: 1). Men and masculinities can now be subject to explicit scrutiny. This state of affairs was brought about by numerous factors. One of the most influential has been the impact of feminism on men, but others include the gay movement, queer politics and the proliferation of sexual politics generally. Also significant has been the recent transformation of employment practices: during the last two decades of the twentieth century in Britain the number of men in employment shrank relative to the number of women in employment. Within this, numbers working in manufacturing fell while numbers working within retail, catering and leisure, and within finance, estate agency and business services, rose (Hearn 1999: 4). These employment changes have transformed the relation of many men to their work, to their families and to themselves. The rights and responsibilities that accompany fatherhood have been the subject of complex, and ambivalent, policy-making and public debate: state intervention to impose the responsibilities of fatherhood has increased, but so too have the rights of fathers. There has been a greater and more diverse interest in men in advertising and popular culture. And a plethora of academic discourses has emerged studying men: from ethnographic descriptions of particular men's activities to structural interrogations of different masculinities (Brod 1987, Brod and Kaufman 1994, Connell 1995, Hearn and Morgan 1990, Seidler 1989).

It is interesting to note that debates paralleling those within feminist theory have developed within the literature on men and masculinity. Connell argues that 'masculinity' ('to the extent the term can be briefly defined at all') is: 'simultaneously a place in gender relations, the practice through which men and women engage that place in gender, and the effects of these practices in bodily experience, personality and culture . . . terms such as hegemonic masculinity and marginalized masculinities name not fixed character types but configurations of practice generated in particular situations in a changing structure of relationships' (Connell 1995: 71, 81). The desire to reject any form of biological determinism leads Connell and the numerous theorists of 'masculinities' to deny any connection between 'being male' and 'doing masculinities' (Morgan 1992: 47). But there is a paradox here, which arises from the unresolved question of the relation between the biological and the social.

Echoing the question posed by Butler in relation to feminist debates about gender, MacInnes asks: 'what is *male* about *masculinity*?' (MacInnes 1998: 61). What is the relation, he asks, between men's social behaviour and 'their sexual organs'? If it has none, 'then they are not "doing masculinities"; they are doing "humanities". If it has, then they are being male' (MacInnes 1998: 63). In other words, if the concept of gender (masculinity) becomes so radically independent of sex (male) and so pluralized and relational, can we really justify continued use of the concept of masculinities? Is it a coherent enough entity to categorize? The parallels with the debates concerning women should be evident.

Nonetheless, the dynamics within gender theory as applied to males and masculinity are inevitably distinct from gender theory as applied to females and femininity, given the power imbalances between the two. The primary motivation behind most gender theorizing in relation to women has been a feminist one, where feminism is a political position aiming to alter the power balance between men and women in favour of women, complicated by the perception that there are power imbalances between women and that the category of women may itself be a product of patriarchal relations. This political motivation inevitably shapes the terms of debate. The various accounts of subjectivity outlined above are informed by, and manifest themselves within, distinct strategies towards this single political end.

The concern in most manifestations of men's studies, on the other hand, is to delineate (and possibly to alter) the power imbalances between men. This leads to a focus on differences within the category of masculinity and to the development of the notion of multiple masculinities. In other words, in relation to the sex/gender distinction, most gender theory that is concerned with men has focused on the internal dynamics within gender such that the relation of gender to sex is largely unarticulated. This has not been the case within gender theory concerned with women because, although increasingly concerned about the power imbalances between women, such theorizing never relinquishes a prior, and some argue more defining, concern with the power imbalances between women and men.

## Conclusion

There are three archetypal approaches to the question of subjectivity within feminist theory: determinist, constructionist and deconstructionist. Determinism has largely been rejected. Constructionism has been extremely influential, generating the distinction between sex and gender. There have been many different versions of constructionist accounts of the acquisition of gendered identity. These accounts have tended to become less singular and more pluralized, shifting attention from the category of 'woman' to that of 'women'. Nonetheless, despite the increasing sophistication of constructionist accounts of gender, the basic sex/gender distinction upon which all such theories rest has come under fire. An increasing number of theorists now argue that the dichotomy is not sustainable, given that sex is itself socially constructed. This provides the grounds for a deconstructive perspective that shifts attention away from 'women' to 'subjectivities' and takes us beyond the sex/gender distinction towards a concern with corporeality conceived in a non-dualistic manner.

These debates about sex, gender and corporeality influence the manner in which political theory is conceived and pursued. The adoption of a biological determinist stance, which draws no distinction between sex and gender and views the sexes to be binary and contrasting, results in the explicit need to theorize political theory from either a male or a female perspective. There are two different ways of engaging in and conceptualizing the political arising inevitably from two different sexed identities. The adoption of a social constructionist stance, which draws a distinction between sex and gender and views gender to be socially constructed, results in a determination to denaturalize the presumptions of sexual difference that underpin deterministic approaches to politics. This process of denaturalization could take the form of eroding the link between sex and gender such that sex becomes politically non-pertinent and men and women are expected to participate equally within the public realm. This is the strategy of inclusion. It could also take the form of elaborating the extent to which one's engagement in, and perception of, the political will be socially constituted, and highlighting the extent to which gender has influenced the form of this engagement in significant ways. This could in turn lead to the endorsement of the notion that the form of women's engagement in the political should be recognized and revalorized. This is the strategy of reversal.

The adoption of a deconstructionist stance, which destabilizes the sex/gender distinction upon which the constructionist accounts worked and therefore challenges the idea that gender need be thought of as cultural elaborations of two distinct sexes, results in a commitment to deconstruct rather than to interpret gender practices. This is the strategy of displacement. Rather than challenging the dominance of men by reclaiming and articulating a voice and set of experiences distinctive to women, this approach would destabilize and reject the dualism of 'male' and 'female' itself. This leads to an exploration of the ways in which dominant discourses (one of them being political theory itself) have constituted the category of gender. Many feminists are concerned that the deconstructionist position regarding subjectivity is not compatible with solidarity or collective action. Its project undermines the assertion of solidarity in that it alerts us to the fact that any commonalities declared may themselves be the effects of power, and that recognition of commonalities may itself become an instrument of regulation and subordination.

The strategy of inclusion aims at equality between the sexes and assumes that, if achieved, gender would no longer be a significant category. The strategy of reversal aims not to transcend gendered characteristics, but to revalue the feminine in relation to the masculine. In other words, whereas the project of the former is to unpick the relation between sex and gender, the project of the latter focuses on the relations within gender and seeks to revalue the feminine *vis-à-vis* the masculine. The strategy of displacement – like the strategy of inclusion – works to challenge the pertinence of the sex/gender distinction, but in the opposite direction. The displacement theorist views the category of 'sex' as itself a product of an existing gender order, which needs to be challenged. While advocates of the strategies of inclusion, reversal and displacement all see the specific features currently deemed feminine to be in some way oppressive, they formulate this perception in distinct ways. The strategist of inclusion views the *substance* of the characteristics to be negative. The strategist of reversal views their *evaluation* to be negative. Finally, the strategist of displacement views their *positioning* as negative.

# 3

# *Framing Theory*

## Introduction

What form should theory take? Having considered the debates concerning the nature of politics and of gender within feminist theory, let us now turn to reflect on the third central issue vital to any consideration of gender in political theory, that of theory.

Rather than engaging in the substantive debates of political theory, this approach takes a step back and asks, what is the project of political theory? Theoretical debates are framed by 'metatheories' which both enable us to ask certain sorts of questions and render other sorts of question invisible. These frames order our thinking, making understanding possible. They also delimit the form of understanding deemed appropriate to the project of theorizing the political.

For example, Raymond Plant asks: 'Is the project of political theory to provide some universal values as a foundation for practical reasoning in politics, or is it to bring to a fuller consciousness the values which are implicit in the communities of which we are a part?' (Plant 1998: 80). These two distinctive ways of understanding the project of political theory generate two distinct notions of the subject matter and methodology appropriate to theorizing the political. As Plant argues: 'The answers given to these questions clearly determine the scope of political theory and the vocation of the political philosopher' (Plant 1998: 80). If we are to understand how gender relates to and inflects political theory, we will need to have a sense of the terrain of political theory with which it engages.

I shall argue that there are three archetypal understandings of the nature of political theory: the objective, the interpretative and the genealogical. From the objectivity frame the project of political theory is the elaboration of abstract universal values. As Plant indicates, within this frame the vocation of the political philosopher is to 'provide some universal values as a foundation for practical reasoning in politics' (Plant 1998: 80). From the interpretative frame the project is to uncover and interpret the values which already exist within concrete communities. As Plant says, the aim is to 'bring to a fuller consciousness the values which are implicit in the communities of which we are a part' (Plant 1998: 80). Within this general project some variants of interpretivism place greater emphasis on the power imbalances within communities. The project of interpretation is then 'to interpret appearances properly in order to uncover an underlying meaning, a reality distorted but not destroyed by the power of those able to construct the appearances in the first place' (Ferguson 1993: 6). From the genealogical frame the task of political theory is to unsettle existing values by questioning their claims to self-evident status. Or, in the words of Ferguson: 'to deconstruct meaning claims in order to look for the modes of power they carry and to force open a space for the emergence of counter-meanings' (Ferguson 1993: 6).

The metatheoretical frames of objectivity and interpretation represent the strategies of inclusion and reversal in relation to discussion about the nature of political theory itself. The genealogical frame which has emerged as a third methodological perspective within debates about political theory represents the strategy of displacement, characterized by its determination to destabilize the dichotomy between inclusion and reversal.

The methodological debates to be addressed in this chapter, coupled with the debates about subjectivity addressed in Chapter 2, together comprise the essential background to the perspectives on politics articulated in Chapter 1. As Frazer and Lacey tell us, political theories presuppose ontological and epistemological positions which are not necessarily articulated by the political theory itself, but which have 'some influence in shaping political arguments, albeit not decisive influence' (Frazer and Lacey 1993: 187). These 'second-order' assumptions provide a framework within which 'first-order' political views are developed.

The three frames of objectivity, interpretation and genealogy are common to both mainstream and gender political theory, but they take a somewhat different form in each. Specifically the interpretative perspective varies most between its mainstream and its gender articulations. The ways in which it does so will become clear in the course of the chapter. I shall outline the core characteristics of each of the three frames proposed and consider how and when each gets employed in relation to both mainstream political theory and gender theory. Finally, I shall consider how the three inter-relate in the context of gender in political theory.

## Objectivity

Inquiry undertaken from within this frame entails the basic conviction that there is some permanent, ahistorical framework to which we can ultimately appeal in determining the nature of truth. This framework provides constraints that are secure and stable, enabling the pursuit of objective knowledge. These constraints commonly take two forms: the empirical and the rational. The empirical guarantee of objectivity is located in a world that is independent of our perception of it; the rational guarantee is located in an 'a priori' universal and necessary structure to human knowledge. In other words, knowledge claims appeal to standards of either material reality or transcendental principle, but not to those of social convention.

The form of objectivism that focuses on the empirical guarantee of objectivity is often labelled empiricism. It asserts that there is a world of objective reality that exists independently of us and that it has a determinate nature that we can know (Bernstein 1983: 9). Reality (the 'object') is assumed to be independent of us (the 'subject'). The recognition and affirmation of subject/object split is vital to the generation of objective knowledge claims. The form of objectivism that focuses on the rational guarantee of objectivity is often labelled rationalism. It asserts that there is an 'Archimedean point', a detached perspective transcending prejudices, tradition and opinions which is revealed through reason. Reason (objective) is presumed to be detached from identity (subjective).

Objectivism entails two distinct forms of reasoning, inductive and deductive. Empiricism adopts an inductive form of reasoning, which proceeds from the particular to the general. One starts with observation of material things and works towards the formulation of an abstract hypothesis. Rationalism adopts a deductive form of reasoning, which proceeds from the general to the particular. One starts with the perception of an abstract principle and works through its logical application to specific circumstances. These generate two distinct forms of truth claims: correspondence and coherence respectively. Correspondence truth claims are made inductively via appeal to observation of an independent world. Coherence truth claims are made deductively via appeal to universal structures of reason. Although quite distinct in form, both coherence and correspondence truth claims are a manifestation of cognitive objectivism: truth claims are objective to the extent to which they either correspond to a material reality or derive coherently from an a priori given.

How, then, does this relate to objectivity within political theory? Here we are concerned primarily with *moral* objectivism. The objective frame is committed to defending the existence of some universal values as a foundation for practical reasoning in politics. These can be conceived either empirically or transcendentally, but are in either case universal and independent of social convention. Although critical of some forms of cognitive empiricism and rationalism, Kant is a central exponent of moral objectivism: 'he does not', Bernstein notes, 'question the need for an ahistorical permanent matrix or categorical scheme for grounding knowledge' (Bernstein 1983: 10). Kant sought to explain and establish the objective foundation of morality. He rejected all attempts to ground morality on experience, insisting on a rigorous distinction between Is and Ought. His aim was to establish the existence of a basic, universal, objective moral law for all rational beings: this was his 'categorical imperative'. This is a rationalist rather than an empiricist form of objectivism, applied specifically to questions of morality. The claim is that there is an objective moral law that can be grounded by an appeal to pure reason.

## Interpretation

The interpretative frame offers a very different account of the project of political theory. As Ferguson argues, 'within this project the task of theory is to interpret appearances properly in order to uncover an underlying meaning, a reality distorted but not destroyed by the power of those able to construct the appearances in the first place' (Ferguson 1993: 6). The claim that political theory can provide some universal values as a foundation for practical reasoning in politics is the object of the interpretative theorist's scorn. In claiming to articulate such universal values the political theorist working from this perspective appears to demand recognition of the objectivity frame as itself objective and neutral. This, its interpretative critics argue, is simply not the case. Rather, it represents a particular consensus about the project of political theory which itself requires justification.

From the interpretative frame the relationship between reality and our perception of it is not one of simple representation. It is always a matter of interpretation. All knowledge is mediated through language. Language, it is argued, is itself socially constituted, historically and culturally specific, and an outcome of pre-existing configurations of power. Both empirical and rational claims to truth are made within communities which themselves construct the criteria according to which such claims appear true. The clear-cut division between fact and value, or description and evaluation, proposed by empiricists is undermined. Similarly, the clear-cut division between reason and evaluation, or truth and belief, proposed by rationalists is undermined. Instead the concepts of interpretation and judgement are proposed. Political theory is understood not as the pursuit of universal truths, but rather as the practice of deliberative judgement in particular situations.

Standards of rationality are themselves judged to be meaningful only within particular contexts. For example, in his influential articulation of an interpretative perspective, Peter Winch argues that, although witchcraft is irrational in our society, it can nonetheless be judged rational when viewed from the perspective of the participants of the Zanda way of life in which it is practised (Winch 1970). The implications of such a claim are significant, for this approach would seem to repudiate the idea of universal criteria of rationality and so undermine the objectivist project (see Hollis 1970, Lukes 1970, and MacIntyre 1970 for useful discussions of Winch's claim).

Given this, the theorist committed to interpretation is suspicious of all claims to rationalism and the idea that there is a single universal form of rationality. Interpretivists view those who make such a claim with scepticism, or open hostility. As Connolly says of rationalism: 'In the name of reason, it construes the unfamiliar to be unreason; in the name of criticism, it closes off avenues to self-criticism; in the name of the universal it celebrates the provincial' (Connolly 1981: 33). In short, claims to objectivity are actually as partial as the contextualized interpretative perspectives they would seek to distinguish themselves from.

Reason is not a faculty that can free itself from its historical context. It is always situated. Understanding, interpretation and application are internally related. The primary task is not, as with objectivity, to distinguish knowledge from experience, reason from belief, but to assert a different set of experiences and beliefs in order to produce a different and/or better way of thinking. The aim is not to break the link between knowledge and experience, but to enable a different set of experiences to provide the basis for new knowledge claims. Whether these knowledge claims are better, more objective, or simply different, and incommensurable, is a source of intense debate.

The adoption of an interpretation frame is widely held to generate a commitment to cultural relativism. If cultures can only be understood and judged from within there would appear be no rational way to adjudicate between different standards of rationality. Some advocates of an interpretative frame, however, refute this. Significantly Winch himself points out that there are minimal standards of coherence that may be universal: rationality he says, 'is limited by certain formal requirements centring around the demand for consistency' (Winch 1970: 100). This indicates that, while interpretation may entail relativism, it is not necessarily synonymous with it.

There are those who think interpretation necessarily entails a commitment to relativity and those who maintain that its project is to move beyond the objectivity/relativity dichotomy. The relativist claims that 'there can be no higher appeal than to a given conceptual scheme, language game, set of social practices, or historical epoch. There is a non-reducible plurality of such schemes, paradigms, and practices; there is no substantive overarching framework in which radically different and alternative schemes are commensurable – no universal standards that somehow stand outside of and above these competing alternatives' (Bernstein 1983: 11–12). There are four central elements to an unambiguous relativism: the rejection of the idea that there are laws governing social reality; the rejection of the idea that knowledge might be value-free; the assertion that we inhabit different paradigms or social worlds which validate knowledge claims internally; and the assertion that there is no transcendent or foundational authority to mediate between these paradigms. All world views become equally valid. Given that theory is simply a way of understanding everyday life in terms which people themselves understand it, this conclusion naturally follows.

However, if one accepts that knowledge is also a means by which one group of people may dominate another, one problematizes the relativist form of interpretation. Accordingly, some Marxists invoke a distinction between interests and beliefs, which allows them to theorize false consciousness and to reintroduce the notion of objectivity. The idea that one can assess the beliefs operative within a world view against the criteria of interests invokes a notion of objectivity, but one rather different from the empiricist or rationalist forms outlined above. Here it is a concept of 'interests' rather than 'reality' or 'reason' that is being appealed to. The extent to which the concept of interests propels one into either objectivity or relativity has been a matter of debate. Significantly, the idea that one must locate oneself clearly one or other side of an objectivity/relativity divide itself springs from the objectivity frame. As an increasing number of theorists now argue, this mutually exclusive and exhaustive formulation of an objectivity/relativity debate makes sense only if one accepts some version of Cartesianism. Notably, Catharine MacKinnon argues that: 'Unlike the scientific strain in Marxism or the Kantian imperative in liberalism, which in this context share most salient features, feminism neither claims universality nor, failing that, reduces to relativity' (MacKinnon 1987: 137). Such articulations of interpretation would reject objectivity without endorsing relativity.

While objectivism structures inquiry around the pursuit of objectivity, this rendering of the interpretation frame structures it around the uncovering of ideologies. Whereas objectivism seeks to draw a clear divide between objectivity and ideologies, the interpretivist views this move as itself an ideological position. As with objectivism, the aim of interpretation is to discover truth, but in contrast with objectivism its strategy is to critique the misleading appearances that disguise underlying realities (Ferguson 1993: 5).

Explanations as to why objectivist political theorists claim universality for their particular conception of rationality also vary. One articulation of this critique asserts that objectivist political theory is a simple reflection of interests. This has most frequently been argued with respect to socioeconomic interests (in the case of Marxist critiques of liberal theory) but is also debated with respect to male interests (in the case of feminist critiques of patriarchal theory). This approach can, in its most extreme form, appear deterministic in that it assumes that the principles of political theory are the epiphenomena of deeper causal forces and are themselves without effect (Skinner 1988: 107). It also generates the question of how individual theorists are able to articulate the interests of their class or gender so exactly. Within feminist theory this question is usually answered with an appeal to psychology, with the argument that political theories articulated by men will reflect the interests of men because they are psychologically predisposed to adopt a particular masculine perspective. Here theory reflects the underlying reality of the nature of men. If political theory as articulated by men is rational, abstract and universalist, then this must be because that is what men are like.

An alternative approach sees objectivist political theory as a means of mystification or legitimation of deeper causal forces. Here the theory has a much more active role to play. Rather than reflecting that which already exists, theory plays a part in bringing what does not exist into being and perpetuating a state of affairs which is complex and ambiguous by claiming it to be singular and just. Here, if political theory is rational, abstract and universalist it is probably because some (men) have something to gain from the assumption that this is how we should be. But the often-noted problems with this approach are that it assumes interpretation theorists to have some access to the 'truth' which other people lack. There become different levels of truth, with only the privileged having access to the reality behind the ideology. The potential elitism and tensions produced by such a claim have led many to accept a paradigm shift away from a theory of ideology to one of discourse. This approach has the benefit of allowing for multiple discourses which are both disciplining and enabling but also moves one closer to a genealogical than to an interpretation frame.

## Genealogy

The distinctive challenge of genealogical theory is that it adopts a self-consciously critical relationship to established philosophical and political traditions. As the interpretative frame encompasses substantially distinct theoretical schools (including hermeneutics, historicism, idealism and so on), so the genealogical frame is here assumed to encompass schools of thought that are importantly distinct in many respects. The Derridean textual practices of literary deconstruction and the Foucauldian project of denaturalizing claims of power are, for the purposes of mapping three archetypal methodological frames, here grouped together.

From the genealogical frame meaning is not the simple representation of ideas or things: the meaning of words does not correspond in transparent fashion to something external; it is acquired through specific, mutable social processes. The rejection of a straightforward correspondence theory of meaning is not, however, replaced by a consensus theory of meaning (as with the interpretative frame). Meaning is not stable or static; it is conflictual and mobile. Language, Joan Scott argues, is 'any system – strictly verbal or other – through which meaning is constructed and cultural practices organised and by which, accordingly, people represent and understand their world, including who they are and how they relate to others' (Scott 1997: 759). Language is therefore taken to be more than words or sets of grammatical rules; it is that which constitutes meaning.

While all meaning is a contextual construction, some meanings gain the status of objective truths. 'The power of these "truths" comes from the ways they function as givens or first premises for both sides in an argument, so that conflicts within discursive fields are framed to follow from rather than question them' (Scott 1997: 760). For example, the theorist located within the genealogical frame would argue that the meanings of 'male' and 'female' are located neither within some biological given, nor within a universal transcendental essence, but rather are negotiated through dynamic power relations. Because their meanings seem to be beyond dispute these terms usually act as premises to work from rather than questions to be explored. The genealogical approach to language demands that one subjects such premises to particularly close scrutiny: for it is precisely where terms appear to be beyond dispute that it is most important to explore the construction of the apparent objectivity. Premises must be scrutinized. As Ferguson argues, from the genealogical frame 'gender' becomes the first question, not the first premise, to one's theorizing (Ferguson 1993: 89).

Developing an understanding how it is that particular meanings emerge while others are eclipsed entails exploring the power dynamics embedded within specific claims to knowledge. As Ferguson argues, the project of theorizing from the genealogical frame is to make the familiar strange. This entails questioning why accepted notions are accepted; giving a history to that which seems atemporal; and breaking apart unified categories by allowing internal tensions to emerge (Ferguson 1993: 122–3). The genealogical gender theorist is therefore interested not in what is said by or about women, but how 'woman' gets said (Ferguson 1993: 124).

The commitment to recasting, as opposed to sustaining or rejecting, derives much of its theoretical legitimacy from deconstructionism. This is a particular approach to the way meanings work. There are two central claims to deconstructionism that have proved enormously influential to political and gender theory. The first is that 'meaning is made through implicit or explicit contrast, that a positive definition rests on the negation or repression of something represented as antithetical to it' (Scott 1997: 760). The second is that fixed oppositions conceal the extent to which things presented as oppositional are, in fact, interdependent. Oppositions that appear natural are constructed. The construction of oppositions entails making what is complex and heterogeneous appear binary and hierarchical.

The meaning of a concept is established by placing it in opposition to another term. Its meaning is therefore relational rather than absolute. Moreover, the relation between concepts has, in the Western philosophical tradition, been constructed in a binary and hierarchical fashion. Dominant concepts (accredited with positive normative connotations) derive their meaning from their relation of opposition and dominance to a second, derivative concept. The project of deconstructionism is to highlight the existence of such binary oppositions, to reveal the oppositions to be constructed rather than natural, and to show the extent to which the difference *between* the binary terms is created by repressing other differences *within* the terms. As Barbara Johnson writes: 'The "deconstruction" of a binary opposition is thus not an annihilation of all values or differences; it is an attempt to follow the subtle, powerful effects of differences already at work within the illusion of a binary opposition' (quoted in Scott 1997: 761).

Theorists working within the frame of objectivity accept some form of the correspondence or coherence theory of truth. Those working within the interpretation frame reject such theories but subscribe to a consensus theory of truth. Their aim is to discover shared understandings. Those working within a genealogical frame reject the aspiration to all three forms of truth and instead emphasize the extent to which discourses constitute that which they claim to have discovered. Where the objectivity theorist views language as a neutral medium of communication, interpretivists perceive language to be primarily expressive and genealogists point out its semiotic dimensions.

## Three Frames of Political Theory

Each of the frames outlined above has had a distinct and significant impact upon the study of political theory. Let us briefly consider in turn what the project of political theory appears to be from the perspective of the objectivity, interpretation and genealogical frames.

### *Objectivism and political theory*

Objectivism has had two distinct and contradictory effects on the status and nature of political theory in recent decades. The arguments in favour of *cognitive* objectivism (both empiricist and rationalist), as proposed by positivists, challenged the very legitimacy of the discipline itself. Neo-Kantian articulations of *moral* rationalism have, on the other hand, provided it with a clear identity and status that rejuvenated the discipline in the wake of positivism.

When considering objectivity in relation to political theory it is moral objectivism that is being contemplated. Specifically, following the writings of John Rawls and his articulation of a Kantian rather than a utilitarian defence of liberalism, the project of political theory has commonly been cast in the light of a moral rationalism. It is worth elaborating on this point here in order to clarify the debates that are to follow about gender in relation to this conception of political theory.

There is an extensive literature that has emerged within gender studies that would challenge the dominance of both empiricism and rationalism. The empiricist form of cognitive objectivism is clearly a dominant frame through which many engage in scientific inquiry. The rationalist form of cognitive objectivism is a dominant frame in analytic philosophy. Gender theorists have been deeply critical of both. For instance, Sandra Harding and Helen Longino offer critical considerations of empiricism in relation to science (Harding 1987, Longino 1993), and Genevieve Lloyd and Karen Green develop critiques of rationalism in relation to philosophy (Lloyd 1984, Green 1995). In order to understand how these relate to the debate under consideration about gender in *political theory* it is worth briefly surveying how political theory is situated *vis-à-vis* scientific and philosophical discourses. It is, I am arguing, a rationalist form of moral objectivism that represents one of the central approaches to contemporary political theory.

*Empiricism and rationalism*

The cognitive and moral forms of objectivism have had significantly divergent receptions in recent times. Notably, during most of this century cognitive objectivism found success and support at the expense of moral objectivism. As Bernstein notes, 'a combination of cognitive objectivism and moral relativism has been taken to be the most attractive and supportable option' (Bernstein 1983: 13). This combination usually takes the form of a clear distinction between descriptive statements (empirically objective), formal statements (rationally objective) and normative statements (morally relative).

This formulation was underpinned by the prevalence of positivism. The positivists' assertion was that all knowledge claims must be either empirically testable or formally derivable. And, while positivism states that objectivity requires both observation and reasoning, it is argued that within the natural sciences the function of formal deductive reason is primarily a secondary one in that it allows for the analysis of the empirical inductive knowledge claims. The impact of positivism not only further legitimated the primacy accorded to the natural sciences as the location of objectivity. It also heightened the aspiration among social scientists to ape either natural science methods or analytic philosophy methods in pursuit of the prestige that accompanies claims to objectivity (both empirical and rational).

Given the positivist claim that this frame was pertinent to not only the natural sciences but also the social sciences, many political theorists felt compelled to adopt the norms of cognitive objectivism and aspire towards either empirical veracity or analytical clarity (Stanley and Wise 1993). From the positivist perspective the discipline of politics could be bifurcated into political science and political philosophy. The role of the political scientist was to carry out empirical research of the kind undertaken by natural scientists, the role of the political philosopher to 'expose and elucidate linguistic muddles' (Weldon 1962: 23). In the 1950s, when the effects of positivism could most clearly be seen in the field of politics, political theorists – hovering in something of a normative quagmire between political science and political philosophy – were frequently uncertain 'as to the nature of the truths which were to be discovered' (Weldon 1962: 25).

Concerned that political theory could not survive as a legitimate project in the face of the empiricist and rationalist demands, some announced its 'death' (Laslett 1956: ix). Others argued, in opposition to positivism, in defence of a distinctly normative discipline. Political theory, the early critics of positivism argued, differs from political science, or any other empirical inquiry, in being concerned with questions which cannot avoid human evaluation (Berlin 1962: 6). This led many to reject the pursuit of objectivity altogether and endorse the interpretation frame, claiming the social sciences to be distinct from the natural sciences by virtue of the object of their study. Accordingly, it was argued, political theorists need to adopt a methodology which understands the political 'from the inside' through its own concepts (Winch 1958: 123). This allowed for a simultaneous endorsement of two frames: cognitive objectivism in relation to the natural sciences and interpretation in relation to the social sciences. However, it is worth noting that there have been two strong counters to this resolution: the upsurge of interpretation within the natural sciences, and the reassertion of (moral) objectivism within the social sciences. Let us look at each in turn.

### The interpretivist challenge to empiricism

The empiricist defence of objectivity has come to look increasingly vulnerable in the light of debates concerning the actual operation of the natural sciences. Karl Popper's defence of objectivism was formulated with an awareness of the growing tendency to question the actual objectivity of the natural sciences. The positivist concern to isolate all ideological elements from synthetic and analytic knowledge is echoed in Popper's concern to destroy the hold of the Hegelian/Marxist metatheoretical frame. 'If scientific objectivity were founded', Popper comments, 'as the sociologistic theory of knowledge naively assumes, upon the individual scientist's impartiality or objectivity, then we should have to say goodbye to it' (Popper 1977: 217). However, Popper is adamant that objectivity is a product of the social character of scientific method. Science, he claims, advances by conjectures and refutations: via the assertion of hypotheses and subsequent attempts to falsify them. Drawing a clear division between science and ideology, Popper argues that in ideology the origins of the 'ideologist' and the interests in putting the hypothesis forward are important. In science, on the other hand, it does not matter who puts forward a hypothesis or for what motives. As long as the scientific community is 'open' and everybody is free to criticize and falsify, objectivity is assured.

This rearticulation of the positivist concern to isolate correspondence and coherence theories of truth from consensus theories of truth is achieved only by allowing that objectivity is a product of particular social relations. This is not positivism per se, but a modified form which ties positivism closely to questions of social context.

A further modification to the positivist assertions of cognitive objectivism occurred with the acknowledgement that the cognitive practices of science – observation and reasoning – are themselves both social. Objectivity, comprising both inductive and deductive thought, cannot avoid reference to social norms. Despite the positivists' aspirations to keep correspondence and coherence forms of truth analytically distinct, it might be argued that both these forms of cognition actually presume a third, 'consensus theory', of truth, which is inherently social. For example, consider the argument that, although a correspondence notion of truth takes the form of observation, descriptions of observations must be inter-subjectively verifiable, ordered and organized, all of which rest on a consensus as to the centrality of categories of perception and organization. Data is therefore an outcome of both experience and social interaction. A coherence theory of truth on the other hand takes the form of reasoning. Reasoning, like observation, is also social: 'assigning evidential relevance to a set of data, and evaluating a hypothesis or theory on the basis of such assignment' (Longino 1993: 264). In other words, just as not any old observations will do, so not any old assumptions or reasons will do. Both require legitimization with reference to 'background assumptions'. Assumptions about evidential relevance are learned within a community of researchers. It is, as Longino argues, not the individual's observation and reasoning that matter even in scientific inquiry, it is the community's (Longino 1993: 265). The distance between this modified version of cognitive objectivism and interpretation is interestingly not too great. Indeed, taken only one stage further, as in the work of Thomas Kuhn, discussion about those social values that apply in the pursuit of objectivity ceases to be a modified defence of objectivism and becomes a form of critique.

The work of Kuhn played a significant role in undermining the force of cognitive objectivism within the social sciences. The scientific community, he claimed, is not one with an impartial interest in the quest for truth; it is a political community in which authority is imposed and novelty and deviance are suppressed. The normal condition of science involves the acceptance by scientists of a 'paradigm', a network of assumptions, which the individual scientist learns from the scientific community via the examples of 'good research'. It is because paradigms rest not only on reason but also on conventionally based assumptions that they become so deeply entrenched. Only when the scientific community can no longer evade the growing body of anomalies is the paradigm rejected for one that offers a better fit between observation and expectation. The truths that the scientific process throws up are inter-subjectively agreed truths. The attempt to distinguish clearly between science and ideology, or between correspondence and coherence truths on the one hand and consensus truths on the other, looks perilously close to failure. The objectivist claims about the nature of inquiry must defend themselves against the charge that this project is itself a product of a socially specific consensus rather than a permanent ahistorical empirical and rational framework.

### The rationalist defence of political theory

Political theory engages with primarily normative considerations. It entails inquiries into the nature of justice, the best form of government, the sources of government legitimacy and so on. Engagement in such considerations inevitably involves making some appeal to a conception of 'the good'. It is simply not obvious how ideas as to what constitutes 'the good' are supported by or derived from empirical or rational foundations. The desire to avoid chaos and relativism is therefore particularly fraught within political theorizing. Yet there is a clear desire nonetheless to be able to distinguish between the legitimate and the illegitimate, and to do so on some basis with greater force than subjective preference alone appears to provide. Without external standards of right and wrong, how is one to evaluate and judge political decisions and structures? It would appear that we need a rational foundation for political theory.

In this context Rawls's strongly foundationalist articulation of political theory offered a way of dispelling the positivists' charge of meaninglessness, articulating a rationalist defence of the objectivity of political theory. The foundation proposed by Rawls was neither empirical nor transcendental, but 'a form of thought and feeling that rational persons can adopt within the world' (Rawls 1971: 587). There is, he proposes, a particular form of reasoning which everyone is equally able of adopting which will 'bring together in one scheme all individual perspectives and arrive together at regulative principles that can be affirmed by everyone as he lives by them, each from his own point of view' (Rawls 1971: 587). In other words, it is proposed that there is an 'Archimedean point' from which a detached observer can come to a 'true' understanding of the good. The aim is to move beyond one's own individual beliefs and communal values and to engage in that form of abstract reflection that is both universal and foundational. The fear of moral nihilism and fragmentation propels the pursuit of 'rationally compelling rules which could underpin practical political reasoning in a world in which first order moral agreement has become fragmented' (Plant 1991: 323). This is a form of moral rationalism or objectivism in that it proposes that there is something (in this case a form of reasoning) whose existence is independent of our beliefs, and which generates objective truths.

### The genealogical challenge

From the genealogical perspective, this Rawlsian rearticulation of Kantian liberalism represents a reassertion of objectivity that requires the creation of an opposing, subordinate 'other' against which it distinguishes itself. The growth of a communitarian antithesis to this neo-Kantian liberalism is therefore essential to the identity of the latter. The establishment of a dichotomous debate between liberals and communitarians arises, on a genealogical reading, from the nature of the moral objectivism that underpins contemporary neo-Kantian articulations of liberalism.

Objectivism defines reasoning as very specific forms of thinking. It then places inordinate value on these forms of thinking and asserts the importance of protecting such reasoning from all external distortions. In the process of drawing the boundaries to its metatheoretical frame, objectivism relies on the exclusion of all that it deems irrational. It creates a constitutive outside regarded as a threat. As Bernstein and Bordo have both noted (Bernstein 1983, Bordo 1987), Descartes' writings have a symbolic role within contemporary theoretical debates. They instil in us a sense that 'either there is some support for our being, a fixed foundation for our knowledge, or we cannot escape the forces of darkness that envelop us with madness, within intellectual and moral chaos' (Bernstein 1983: 18).

It is this 'Cartesian anxiety' in the face of the threat of madness and chaos that propels us to endorse fixed, permanent constraints to which we can appeal as safeguards of the soul. The effect of this anxiety is to generate either/or oppositions. Kant argues that unless we control our passions we cannot speak in the voice of impartial reason. His ambition to demonstrate that there is a universal, objective moral law is underpinned by a presumption that if this cannot be done the concept of morality is itself vacuous. Similarly contemporary advocates of liberalism have repeatedly argued that without universal standards of morality we will have no resources with which to evaluate competing conceptions of the good.

This need to establish a non-negotiable boundary between objectivity and 'its other' is central to the construction of the other two frames delineated. The interpretation and the genealogical frames are two distinct responses to the objectivist claim to metatheoretical superiority. The interpretative response is one of reversal, the genealogical response one of displacement. The former seeks to valorize and defend that which objectivism excludes and denigrates; the latter seeks to undermine the credibility of the either/or boundary itself. The interpretation frame can therefore be understood as a reaction to the objectivist frame, which engages within a terrain, mapped out by objectivism itself. The genealogical frame can be understood as a critique of the contours of debate themselves.

## Three Frames of Gender Theory

The three frames outlined are articulated rather differently within political and gender literatures. Objectivist forms of political and gender theory are largely interchangeable (as they simply focus on different barriers to achievement of the same ideal). Interpretivist political and gender theories are more distinct. This is because the interpretivist gender theory frame argues that the objectivist frame is not only mistaken, but also patriarchal. It is a manifestation of masculinity and has been used to exclude a distinctly feminine frame. The objectivity/interpretation debate is recast along gendered lines.

Whereas many mainstream advocates of interpretation have viewed objectivity as a manifestation of a particularly capitalist or Western set of interests, the gender interpretivists argue it to be a manifestation of male interests (the fact that many men have articulated the interpretivist and genealogical positions being frequently overlooked). There are some attempts to consider how the interpretivist forms of political and gender theory might inter-relate (see Frazer and Lacey 1993) but by and large these two projects are quite distinct. They frequently involve opposing political ambitions with regard to community and family values.

Gender theorists and political theorists occupy the genealogical frame in almost identical manner because the perspective is understood as a means of deconstructing gender dualisms rather than as an articulation of them. Indeed, many interpretivist gender theorists have argued that the genealogical position cannot be a specifically gender theory at all because it deconstructs the feminine and masculine subject. (See Coole 1998, Flax 1997, Fraser and Nicholson 1990, Waugh 1997, and Wright 1989 for a discussion of the relation between feminism and postmodernism.)

When categorizing feminist theory it has been common to distinguish between liberal, radical and postmodern feminisms. These three perspectives might be broadly located within the objectivity, interpretation and genealogy frames respectively, but this tight mapping is not inevitable. It is possible for similar political perspectives to be grounded in different metatheoretical frames. It is also common within feminist theory to find mention of the epistemological typology proposed by Sandra Harding. She distinguishes between feminist empiricism, standpoint and postmodernism (Harding 1987: 3–5). Empiricism (or the 'adding women in approach') leaves existing presumptions unchallenged and seeks to rectify 'bad social science', which is responsible for bias. Standpoint theory emphasizes the extent to which knowledge is grounded in material experiences. Postmodernism (in which Harding includes the disparate theoretical schools of semiotics, deconstruction and psychoanalysis) is sceptical of universalizing claims to reason and insists that there are always subjugated knowledges (Harding 1987: 6–10). I have modified this schema by shifting attention from empiricist cognitive objectivism (pertinent in the natural sciences) to rationalist moral objectivism (more pertinent to our consideration of political theory), and by adopting Ferguson's categories of interpretation and genealogy rather than Harding's categories of standpoint and postmodernism. This is because interpretation is broader than standpoint (incorporating all arguments for a women's perspective) and genealogy less burdened by political connotations and conceptual confusions than postmodernism.

## Objectivist gender theory

Harding characterizes feminist empiricism as an objection to social bias that distorts the research process. Social bias is conceived as 'prejudices that are based on false beliefs (due to superstition, custom, ignorance or mis-education) and hostile attitudes' (Harding 1987: 182). Such bias, she argues, enters the research process at both the observation and reasoning stages in both the collection and interpretation of data. What is demanded by the feminist empiricist is 'stricter adherence to the existing methodological norms of scientific inquiry' (Harding 1987: 182). Only in the assertion of the importance of the social bias against women and its contingent effects on the results of empiricist inquiry does a feminist articulation of objectivity differ from objectivism per se.

Feminist articulations of rationalism are also largely indistinct from rationalism per se. A commitment to objectivity in its rationalist form entails endorsing human reason as the absolute authority in questions of morality. This reason is held to be generic to the human species, though frequently distorted by the workings of passion, prejudice or ignorance. The project of the rationalist gender theorist is to assert, and demand recognition of, women's equal capacity for reason, and to confront and eradicate the distortions of prejudice, which work against this recognition. The bias is not thought to be inherent to the rationalist frame itself and can therefore be distinguished and removed from it. The reason for jettisoning social bias is to bring us closer to the realization of the impartial observer and the detached thinker.

## Interpretative gender theory

From this frame reason is not neutral. The 'woman problem' is not simply that prejudice and ignorance have worked against women's full development and utilization of their equal capacity for rationality; it is more profound than this. Rationality itself is here held to be masculine. It excludes 'the feminine' in principle and not just in practice.

The basic assumptions underpinning the variety of perspectives within this frame is that knowledge is not objective and the commitment to rationalism is itself a partial perspective in need of justification. The social identity and interests of the inquirer always delimit knowledge claims. In a patriarchal context, where knowledge has been generated primarily by men, what is perceived as objective will actually prove to be an articulation of men's experiences and men's perspectives. Interpretivist feminist critics of objectivism view rationality as a mistaken ideal reflecting masculinist preoccupations. Given that knowledge is based in experience, any knowledge claims based exclusively in the experiences of men will be partial, silencing the experiences of ways of knowing of women.

The feminist form of interpretation comprises two elements: the ambition first to reveal the patriarchal gender priorities within dominant knowledge claims and then to reverse them. As Ferguson argues: 'The creation of a women's voice, or a feminist standpoint, or a gynocentric theory, entails immersion in a world divided between male and female experiences in order to critique the power of the former and valorise the alternative residing in the latter' (Ferguson 1993: 3). The primary task is not, as with objectivism, to distinguish knowledge or theory from identities and interests, but to assert a different set of identities and interests in order to produce a different and/or better way of thinking. The aim is not to break the link between experience and knowledge, but to enable a different set of experiences to provide the basis for new knowledge claims.

Unlike proponents of mainstream articulations of interpretation, feminist interpretivists have frequently made appeal to psychoanalytic theory in order to explain why it is that men are more likely than women to adopt objectivist rather than interpretivist ways of thinking. This is where the interpretation frame takes a distinctive character, quite marginal to mainstream renderings of this frame. The focus of debate is not only why the objectivist account won't do, or even why the objectivist account is complicit with modernity, or capitalism, or the West, but also why and to what effect the objectivist commitment to rationality is masculinist.

Object-relations theory, a particular form of sociological psychoanalysis, has proved a central tool of analysis in the formation of this interpretative frame. As outlined in Chapter 2, this account suggests that, because it is women who adopt the primary parenting role, male and female children will have differing relations to their primary carer and as a result will develop distinct gendered personalities. The masculine and feminine ways of knowing and behaving manifest in contemporary society are not biologically determined, but are shaped by boys' and girls' differing identification with their mother. Objectivity and impartiality are masculine because these are the forms of thinking which arise in the context of a specifically male psychological development, where that development takes place in relation to a female primary carer.

Chodorow's articulation of object-relations theory has been highly influential in providing an account of the hold of objectivism in patriarchy. Object-relations theory offers a basis for claiming distinct epistemological frameworks – the separateness of the male psyche tending them towards the separation of experience and reason in a manner that does not resonate with the connectedness of the female psyche. Evelyn Fox Keller, for instance, argues that science – and the concept of reason that it invokes – is gender biased (Keller 1984). She claims that the character traits required by a good scientist (and a good researcher), such as detachment and objectivity, are those that mother-centred forms of childrearing encourage in boys but not in girls. Susan Bordo also uses Chodorow's theory to argue that Descartes' writing is a prime example of the detachment sought as a denial of the feminine within. She characterizes the conception of reason developed by Descartes as one 'which regards all sense-experience as illusory and insists that the object can only be truly known by the perceiver who is willing to purge the mind of all obscurity, all irrelevancy, all free imaginative associations, and all passionate attachments' (Bordo 1987: 26).

Objectivity, on this account, is equated with detachment from context: 'the confusion and obscurity of its bodily swamp' (Bordo 1987: 92). In other words, as Atherton points out, what Chodorow finds in the male personality structure as a result of male upbringing, Bordo finds in Descartes' intellectual writings as a result of his cultural upbringing (Atherton 1993: 21). Where Chodorow focuses on the individual boy's anxiety at separation from his mother, Bordo focuses on 'Cartesian anxiety': the defensive assertion of autonomy in the face of separation from nature. Cartesian rationalism is, accordingly, characterized by Bordo as the drive to separate from and control nature (and, by extension, women). In short, the gendered patterns of identity formation structure the dominant concept of reason.

This sort of argument draws tight links between subjectivity and knowledge. Reason is not generic to humans, but particular to specific groups of people in specific contexts. The conception of knowledge that underpins both modern science and liberal politics (empiricism and rationalism) is argued to be but one form of reasoning, and a form that requires the exclusion and subordination of its antithesis: relativism and subjectivism. Gender theorists have been quick to point out the extent to which women have been cast as the 'other' of reason. Not only is this narrow conception of reason one which has excluded women socially, it also entails the repression of the feminine psychologically.

Where masculinity comes to be identified with reason, femininity is associated with the inferior: that which is to be excluded. This gendered interpretivist critique of objectivism presents the Enlightenment in its totality as a repression of the feminine. Descartes and Kant are held up as the twin foundations of a rationality that is based upon a disembodied and disembedded conception of personhood. Whether this commitment to rationalist objectivity is inherently male or a historical construct has been the source of many debates, with essentialist notions of natural difference largely losing out to social constructionist notions of historical experience. Not all theorists accept that reason is itself inevitably or essentially male, or that its antithesis is paradigmatically female. But the interpretivist gender theorist does hold that the project of gender theory is to counter the dominance of male reason with an assertion of the value of female forms of thinking.

The two central characteristics of this proposed female form of thinking are experience and emotion. In direct opposition to the objectivist rejection of the distorting influences of social context and bodily passions, interpretivist gender theorists celebrate the subjective and emotional aspects of thought. They take what is devalued and reaffirm its significance.

Experience as a criterion of meaning 'is a fundamental epistemological tenet' of both African-American and feminist thought, according to Patricia Hill Collins (Collins 1991). One's experiences determine not only what one thinks, but also how one thinks. Working squarely within an interpretivist frame, Collins argues that women as a group are more likely to use concrete knowledge and dialogue than are men (Collins 1991: 201–19). They are less likely to adopt the abstract form of reasoning advocated by Kant and less convinced by the attempt to reduce ethical thinking to an abstract and universal form of reason. As with most advocates of this position, she rejects the straightforward essentialist grounding for this argument and proposes a social constructivist one, which draws on object-relations theory.

Similarly, Sara Ruddick, in her writing on 'maternal thinking' (Ruddick 1997: 299–305), emphasizes the practical origins of reason. Ruddick argues against the notion that thought might transcend its social origins: there is, she maintains, 'no truth to be apprehended from a transcendental perspective' (Ruddick 1997: 300). All truth is relative to the practices in which it is made. Given this, 'maternal practice' generates its own truths. There are three central commitments within maternal work: the preservation, growth and social acceptability of one's children.

These demands are both practical and epistemological. To protect, nurture and train, mothers must think, and think in specific ways. It is not possible to evaluate maternal thinking, Ruddick claims, echoing Winch's earlier argument, without practising maternal work.

Yet maternal thinking has not been valorized: 'Mothers have been a powerless group whose thinking, when it has been acknowledged at all, has most often been recognised by people interested in interpreting and controlling rather than listening' (Ruddick 1997: 304). It is important that they should now have time to think for themselves. It is also desirable that maternal thinking should develop its own critical practice. For although such criticism would be grounded in its originating practice, and therefore only ever one discipline among others, its particular perspective may offer distinctive critical advantages that could aid social change.

Ruddick's thesis of 'maternal thinking' is archetypally interpretative. She explicitly draws on the work of Wittgenstein, Winch and Habermas to develop her account of reason as contextual. She gives a specifically gendered focus to this frame by drawing attention to mothering as a social practice worthy of epistemological consideration. But the interpretivist frame takes a further distinctive turn in its gendered forms. Unlike Ruddick, who is happy to endorse relativism, many interpretivist gender theorists want to maintain that the particular form of thinking originating in the experiences particular to women is not just different to, but better than, the abstract form of reasoning manifest by men. These are the advocates of a feminist 'standpoint' perspective.

The 'feminist standpoint' methodology was developed by Nancy Hartsock and drew explicitly on a Marxist methodological framework. It shares with relativist forms of interpretation the perception that knowledge originates in practice, but introduces the notion that in 'systems of domination the vision available to the rulers will be both partial and perverse.' The vision available to the oppressed group, on the other hand, 'exposes the real relations among human beings . . . and carries a historically liberatory role' (Hartsock 1997: 153).

The standpoint of the oppressed is a contextual knowledge, but it is not just one among others: it comprehends both the 'surface appearance' generated by the standpoint of the dominant group and the deeper reality perceived by the oppressed group. It is not just different; it is less partial. As Alison Jaggar, another advocate of a standpoint form of interpretation, argues:

> the perspective on reality that is available from the standpoint of the subordinated, which in part at least is the standpoint of women, is a perspective that offers a less partial and distorted and therefore more

reliable view. Subordinated people have a kind of epistemological privilege in so far as they have easier access to this standpoint and therefore a better chance of ascertaining the possible beginnings of a society in which all could thrive. (Jaggar 1997a: 192)

On the basis of this standpoint argument, Jaggar offers an account of interpretation that is a significant modification of Ruddick's relativist statement. Jaggar shares with Ruddick the idea that reason originates in practice and that women's experiences have been different enough to generate distinctive ways of thinking. But she goes further than Ruddick in claiming the merits of this female form of thinking in relation to dominant male forms. Ruddick proposes maternal thinking as one form among others. Jaggar suggests that the 'emotional acumen' gained by women through their work in emotional nurturance 'can now be recognised as a skill in political analysis and validated as giving women a special advantage both in understanding the mechanisms of domination and in envisioning freer ways to live' (Jaggar 1997a: 193).

These, then, represent the two distinct versions of interpretation discussed above, here articulated within gender theory. Both insist that knowledge is contextual and that different practices generate different forms of knowledge. Both also insist that women's experiences (particularly, but not exclusively, mothering) shape a distinctive female knowledge which is relational rather than autonomous, concrete rather than abstract, empathetic and imaginative rather than abstract and instrumental. Both call for this form of knowledge to be recognized and its potential contribution valued. One central difference between relativist and standpoint versions of interpretation lies in the differing responses to the fact that not all women think in the same way or share the same standpoint. As MacKinnon critically points out, the relativist form embraces any version of women's experiences that a biological female claims as her own whereas the standpoint version regards some women's views as 'false consciousness' (MacKinnon 1987: 181, fn 5). Both have come to be seen as problematic.

In relation to the first strategy, Kathleen Jones speaks of the 'political and epistemological quagmires produced by the strategy of invoking experience as the source of knowledge that can best serve feminist purposes' (Jones 1993a: 193). She challenges the idea that the language of experience is transparent: it relies on an unexamined truth of the subjective and simply substitutes one sovereign regime of truth for another (see Grimshaw 1986: 90–103 and Grant 1993 for similar critiques of the invocation of experience as a grounding for truth). In short, this rendering has the tendency to sink into radical subjectivism.

In relation to the second strategy, numerous theorists have argued that, having accepted that different standpoints generate different epistemologies, one is obliged to address the political issue of what constitutes a group unified enough to share a single standpoint. This issue has led to severe criticism of the notion that there might be a single women's perspective. In her defence, Hartsock does distinguish a feminist from a feminine standpoint, though 'she does not elaborate upon a set of political values that are separable from Woman' (Grant 1993: 124). Many gender theorists, sensitive to the charge that they have failed to acknowledge difference, have, like Chodorow, shifted their position away from 'feminist grand theory' to a more pluralistic notion of feminist theories, accepting that the complexity of gender is best captured by decentred theories.

## Genealogical gender theory

Rather than seeking to revalorize 'female ways of knowing', genealogical gender theorists aim to reveal the extent to which the gendering of reason is a historical and contingent process. Or, as Scott argues: 'We need theory that will enable us to articulate alternative ways of thinking about (and thus acting upon) gender without either simply reversing the old hierarchies or confirming them' (Scott 1997: 758).

Adopting the genealogical perspective, Scott argues that these 'old hierarchies', entrenched within a long tradition of Western philosophy, 'have systematically and repeatedly construed the world hierarchically in terms of masculine universals and feminine specificities' (Scott 1997: 758). Given this, the pursuit of universals works to confirm the dominant perspective, while the pursuit of woman-specific unities works to confirm its subordinate other.

Where it has worked within this schema, gender theory has served to shore up a dichotomous form of thought that is itself a product of patriarchy. To propose that we destabilize the inclusion/reversal dichotomy is to challenge a central tenet of patriarchal thought itself. This means that, while both objective and interpretative forms of gender theory have consciously aspired towards the rejection of patriarchy, they have both – in different respects – unconsciously perpetuated its underlying logic. Rather than presuming that gender is irrelevant to one's capacity to reason, or that reasoning is a manifestation (whether essential or social) of gendered identity, genealogical gender thorists aim to show how reason has become gendered.

Consider, for example, the accounts of the gendering of reason developed by Naomi Scheman and Genevieve Lloyd. Scheman argues that

Cartesian method 'is a form of discipline requiring acts of will to patrol a perimeter around our minds, allowing in only what can be determined to be trustworthy, and controlling the influence of the vicissitudes of our bodies and of other people' (Scheman 1997: 349). If perception of truth comes from within us, we must be free from external constraint. And, on a conception of the person where mind and body are distinct, the body is itself an external force. In other words, to be rational one needs to discipline the distracting influences of the body, the passions and the external world.

The democratic ethos of the Cartesian-Kantian subject was revolutionary: 'epistemic authority', or the legitimate power of reason, was held to lie within the person and to be universally present. The irony is that, despite this initial democratic ethos of universalism, it took hold within a society that was itself far from equal. As Scheman argues: 'Those who succeeded in embodying the ideals of subjecthood oppressed those whose places in the world (from which, for various reasons, they could not move) were (often) to perform the labour on which the existence and well-being of the enfranchised depended and (always) to represent the aspects of embodied humanness that the more privileged denied in themselves' (Scheman 1997: 351). In other words, those with power both repressed the 'irrational' within themselves via acts of internalized discipline, and represented the less powerful as lacking in self-discipline and therefore in need of external discipline. This process, Scheman argues, had a particularly oppressive effect upon women who were so closely defined by their bodies, and therefore so easily represented as irrational and in need of discipline.

Genevieve Lloyd also argues that a particular way of thinking derived from Descartes' theory of reason has been associated with masculinity and has as a result worked to suggest that women are not fully rational. Where she differs from Bordo is that she assumes both Descartes' concept of reason and his motivation in adopting it to be gender-neutral. The problem arises because Descartes' concept of reason was so narrow that it became possible to think of it as only one way of thinking, rather than as a more general account of thinking itself. This made it possible to develop a contrasting model of thinking and emphasize the differences between them. Lloyd argues that this bifurcation of concepts of reason was used to construct the conceptions of masculinity and femininity employed today. As Atherton comments, 'Lloyd's claim is that it is the concept of masculinity that has been shaped by the concept of reason, not that reason has had masculine characteristics incorporated into it' (Atherton 1993: 24).

From this perspective it is simply wrong-headed to respond by asserting an alternative 'feminine kind of reason'. The genealogical gender

theorists' concern, as articulated by Lloyd, is that the feminist appropriation of maternal thinking or a standpoint epistemology risk perpetuating that contingent alignment which actually constituted the
oppressive gender identities that such theorists are trying to work against.
Might not deconstructive strategies be better employed to expose that
contingent link: 'trying to understand its operations in order to break its
grip?' (Lloyd 1993: 76).

As a result of the impact of feminist interpretation, the assertion of
the intrinsic relation between masculinity and rationalism has become
commonplace. This is a link that genealogical theorists are keen to
refute. As Diana Coole notes, 'The irony, and danger, of this equation is
that it appears to assert the very association which patriarchy always
insisted on anyway, when it claimed that men are *naturally* more adept
at abstract thinking while women are *naturally* more practical and
emotional' (Coole 1998: 111). If this claim is to be critical politically,
it must avoid appeals to essentialism. But even if it does not entail
essentialist appeals, invocations of 'the feminine' are still treated with
scepticism from the genealogical frame.

Most interpretation theorists do themselves repudiate essentialism 'per
se' (as with Hartsock and Jaggar), offering structural accounts of the
femininity of women's thinking. But it is worth noting that the schema
that I am drawing is complicated by the existence of a strand of theorizing within the genealogical frame that also affirms 'the feminine'. Here
the feminine is neither essential nor material, but symbolic. In the structural account it is men and women who reason differently (adopting a
structural view of gender as materially constructed). In the symbolic
account it is the masculine and the feminine that represent different
forms of reasoning (adopting a metaphorical view of gender as symbolically constructed). Both are keen to distinguish themselves from those
who might offer a biological account of sex rather than a material or
symbolic account of gender. Both deny charges of essentialism: their
projects are not designed to reveal an essential feminine. But where the
structural account falls within the interpretation frame, the symbolic
account falls within the genealogy frame.

Notably Irigaray proposes a metaphorical link between multiplicity
and the feminine and Kristeva equates the semiotic (that which is repressed in phallocentric culture) with the feminine. Kristeva works within
a genealogical frame in that she is committed to transgressing the boundaries between conscious and unconscious, symbolic and semiotic, rational and irrational, masculine and feminine. She clearly distinguishes her
project from the classic interpretative one with the introduction of the
notion of desire. Drawing on Freudian theory, Kristeva emphasizes the
limitations of assuming that meaning exists 'through the connection of

two terms from a stable place and theory' and foregrounds the 'unpredictable signifying effects which must be called *an imaginary'* (Kristeva 1997: 231). She suggests that 'the wise interpreter give way to delirium so that, out of his desire, the imaginary may join interpretive closure' (Kristeva 1997: 231). She celebrates that which subverts the binary oppositions that order the symbolic, and all that undercuts the dualistic oppositions of gender. But she nonetheless calls for that form of thinking and writing that disrupts phallocentric culture, the feminine.

But Lloyd argues that the repudiation of essentialism can give a false security, masking perhaps a more elusive perpetuation of damaging sexual stereotypes. She is wary of celebrating a feminine, even if metaphorical: 'We can gain the crucial insights into the maleness of reason without appropriating the residue of "excess" as female' (Lloyd 1993: 76). 'I remain', she concludes, 'sceptical about the generalized affirmation of the feminine that has characterized some contemporary feminist critiques of reason' (Lloyd 1993: 82). I shall take this scepticism as more clearly characteristic of the genealogical perspective than the endorsement of a symbolic feminine.

The issue, from this genealogical frame, is not whether one wants to endorse rationality, or its other, but how this particular form of reason came to acquire normative dominance. Where objectivism sees rationality as a human ideal, and interpretation sees it as an oppressive form of masculinity, genealogy explores the particular forces at play in the historical constitution of rationality itself.

## Relating Objectivity, Interpretation and Genealogy

Richard Bernstein has argued that 'An adequate social and political theory must be empirical, interpretive and critical' (Bernstein 1976: 235). One might read this as a proposal that one invokes all three methodological frames outlined. Let us then briefly consider the relation between these frames within gender theory and explore whether, and in what ways, one might negotiate a perspective within and between the three.

Should one, Harding asks, 'have to choose between feminist empiricism and the feminist standpoint as justificatory strategies?' (Harding 1987: 186). Her answer is that we should not. Both are useful when appealing to different audiences: they are transitional epistemologies, 'and there are good reasons to see that as a virtue' (Harding 1987: 186). Both share a central concern to ground accounts of the social which are less partial and distorted than the prevailing ones. Harding is, however, reluctant to embrace postmodernism, as it would seem to require that feminists 'give up the political benefits which accrue from believing that we are producing a new, less biased, more accurate, social science' (Harding 1987: 188). For Harding, then, far from metatheoretical approaches dictating political perspectives, political objectives shape epistemological allegiances.

Others have proposed the integration of objectivity and interpretation, not as a form of methodological pragmatism, but in the form of a more synthetic metatheoretical frame. Here the work of critical theorists has proved significant. Notably, Seyla Benhabib argues:

> The retreat from utopia within feminist theory in the last decade has taken the form of debunking as essentialist any attempt to formulate a feminist ethic, a feminist politics, a feminist concept of autonomy, and even a feminist aesthetic. . . . Postmodernism can teach us the theoretical and political traps of why utopia and foundational thinking can go wrong, but it should not lead to a retreat from utopia altogether. (Benhabib et al. 1995: 30)

The appeal to 'foundational thinking' here is significant. Benhabib's rendering of critical theory represents a very particular negotiation of the objectivity and interpretation frames (see Benhabib 1992: 69–70).

In her attempt to assimilate Gilligan's insights concerning an ethic of care into a Habermasian model of discourse ethics, Benhabib offers a sophisticated attempt to negotiate afresh the relation between objectivity and interpretation within political theory. Her aim is to develop a 'universalist moral theory', but one which avoids projecting the narrow vision of the moral domain present in the work of other objectivists (including Rawls and Habermas). Hers is a procedural notion of universalism, but one – she claims – which is not as exclusive as the other versions that she criticizes (Benhabib 1992: 86). Given this, it can incorporate and valorize forms of thinking – commonly associated with women – which have been excluded and devalorized by other renderings of moral objectivity. The detail of this approach will be considered in Chapter 5. The relevant point here is simply to note that there is a move within gender and political theory to negotiate a position between objectivity and interpretation.

It has also been common within recent gender theory to attempt to negotiate a position that draws on both interpretation and genealogy. Speaking from a genealogical perspective, Scott states that: 'Until we understand how the concepts work to constrain and construct specific meanings, we cannot make them work for us' (Scott 1997: 762). The implication is that deconstruction is an invaluable tool in the process of understanding how concepts work to constrain and construct meanings.

But what is the theoretical frame needed to makes concepts 'work for us'? Here substantial disagreement exists. Some argue that a genealogical feminism does all the work, others that it needs to be adopted alongside an interpretation frame. Some view any attempt at reconstruction as suspicious; others view deconstructionism as a moment in a broader project of reconstruction.

Viewed from the genealogical frame the feminist project entails critique, questioning, destabilizing, creating uncertainty and challenging accepted meanings. Even if one accepts these techniques and commitments – and by no means all feminists do – there remains disagreement as to whether this frame equips one with a sufficient range of tools to engage with the entirety of 'political theory'. As Hirschmann and Di Stefano comment, one of the central features of political theory has been the 'creation of new pictures and visions of politics' (Hirschmann and Di Stefano 1996: 2). Given this, they ask whether the visionary dimension of political theory is something that feminists must in the end avoid. 'Is the very term "feminist political theory" an oxymoron, and is "political theory" *per se* something feminists should avoid except from the perspective of tearing it apart? Or has this enterprise of critical deconstructive techniques, having been extremely powerful for feminist critique, occluded other feminist endeavours *vis-à-vis* political theory?' (Hirschmann and Di Stefano 1996: 3).

Perhaps ironically, certain of the genealogical gender theorists – committed as they are to deconstructing binary oppositions – are firmly wedded to maintaining the opposition between deconstruction and reconstruction, critique and utopia. For example, Kristeva argues that 'If women have a role to play . . . it is only in assuming a negative function: reject everything finite, definitive, structural, loaded with meaning, in the existing state of society' (Kristeva 1980: 166). A feminist practice does not have a positive function; it should not aim at reconstruction, for it can only be at odds with what is. Similarly Judith Butler argues that 'The pursuit of the "new" is the preoccupation of high modernism; if anything, postmodernism casts doubt upon the possibility of a "new" that is not in some way already implicated in the "old"' (Butler 1992: 6).

Others, attentive to the failings of simple strategies of reversal, and conscious of the effectiveness of deconstructive techniques, are nonetheless keen to promote a more synthetic approach. For the refusal to engage in reconstructive enterprises has a concrete impact on women's daily lives. Political concepts, Hirschmann and Di Stefano argue, 'are not simply the private domain of intellectuals who are paid to engage in esoteric debates over abstruse intellectual notions; they play a vital role in the structuring of social relations' (Hirschmann and Di Stefano 1996: 4). The charge here is that, while remaining solely within the genealogical frame, refusing to engage in a reconstructive task at all, is to stay metatheoretically pure, it is also to remain politically ineffective.

Given this, there are feminists who propose that both the interpretative and genealogical frames be adopted in the pursuit of a rounded engagement with gender in political theory. But even within this grouping there is another subdivision to be made. For there are two strategies of co-existence proposed: one based upon an interpretative pursuit of synthesis, the other upon a genealogical celebration of irony. Genealogical gender theorists open to the gains possible from inhabiting the interpretation frame are happy to live with the irony of this contradiction. Interpretative gender theorists open to the virtues of viewing problems through a genealogical frame are usually more concerned to resolve the tension, drawing on the best points of each while moving beyond the limitations of both.

For example, Frazer and Lacey argue that there is a danger in over-reliance on deconstruction, in that it may re-erect binary oppositions where critical analysis has already unsettled them. Therefore they recommend the use of deconstruction as just one useful critical tool of analysis (Frazer and Lacey 1993: 171). Similarly Nancy Fraser argues against those who present different frames of feminist thinking as incompatible: 'instead, we might reconstruct each approach so as to reconcile it with the other' (Fraser 1995a: 60). Her overall aim 'is to preserve the best elements of each paradigm, thereby helping to prepare the ground for their fruitful integration in feminist theorizing' (Fraser 1995a: 60). Fraser sees the clash of theoretical paradigms as 'a false antithesis' capable of resolution and synthesis.

Adopting a less synthetic stance, Christine Sylvester, usually perceived to be a thoroughgoing postmodern feminist within international relations theory, actually argues for 'cacophonous feminisms' which will draw on the various epistemological strategies discussed. The virtue of empiricist epistemology is that it acts as a reminder that we need the workaday efforts of feminist scientists to uncover all the stories (if not all the truth) about men and women. Meanwhile standpoint epistemology grows increasingly sophisticated as the recognition of multiple realities blurs the distinction between standpoint and postmodernist thinking. Finally postmodern epistemology ensures that we retain a humility concerning theory itself and a longing for what cannot fully be had (Sylvester 1994: 66). In adopting this pluralist approach to metatheoretical frames Sylvester is representative of many genealogical gender theorists who, far from rejecting other epistemologies, rejoice in the contradictions and tensions of adopting and exploring all. It is this tendency to accept the value of other (possibly incommensurable) frames that leads to confusion as to whether postmodern theorists are adopting a distinctive genealogical frame, or whether they are simply recommending a playful acceptance of all existing frames. Many appear to advocate both these stances. Sylvester, for example, argues that, 'as the feminisms of yesterday and today commingle, it is important to bear in mind that each makes a contribution to knowledge in a postmodern era' (Sylvester 1994: 66).

This celebration of contradiction has received an ambivalent reception, even among those who share a commitment to negotiating a perspective between the frames. Scheman, for instance, contends that epistemologies need to be politically usable and grounded in a particular set of political practices. 'Subversive playfulness is not enough, nor is noncritical pluralism' (Scheman 1993: 189). The playful eclecticism of some genealogical appropriations of objectivity and interpretation is too frivolous for many more firmly grounded within these frames. Benhabib is compelling here when she asserts that it may well be that there is no either/or. Each method and approach should learn from and benefit from the other, she tells us, but we should clarify 'what the conceptual constraints' of each approach are before 'we can issue a Pollyanna call to all parties of the debate' (Benhabib et al. 1995: 114).

The theorist who most clearly articulates what a positive engagement between the frames might entail is Kathy Ferguson. 'It is possible', she states, 'to be enframed within interpretation (feminist or otherwise) or within genealogy, seeing only the battles each practice names as worthy and missing the ways in which contending interpretations or rival deconstructions co-operate on a metatheoretical level to articulate some possibilities and silence others' (Ferguson 1993: 7). Arguing against the merits of being wholly 'enframed', she suggests that these be seen as 'contrasting pairs within a complex field rather than exclusively binary couples' (Ferguson 1993: 10). It is, she says, the 'rootedness in one position or the other that I am attempting to problematize' (Ferguson 1993: x).

Adopting something akin to a deconstructive method itself, Ferguson argues that genealogy and interpretation should not be projected as binary oppositions. They rely upon one another: interpretation can be used to push aside hegemonic claims to dominant truths; genealogy tells us that reconstructed concepts and theories 'must themselves be scrutinized for their tendency to echo that which they oppose' (Ferguson 1993: 28). In short, Ferguson maintains: 'Genealogy keeps interpretation honest, and interpretation gives genealogy direction' (Ferguson 1993: 30). Each tempers the possible excesses of the other. The danger of subduing dissonances inconvenient to its unities present within interpretation is checked by genealogical critique. The danger of political inactivism with genealogy, lacking as it does any criteria for distinguishing between differences that should be cultivated and those that should be eradicated, is checked by interpretative vision.

It may perhaps be possible, despite the theoretical tensions, to endorse both the genealogical and the interpretative frames. One could use the genealogical frame in order to trace the heterogeneous and changing discursive regimes that constitute any particular subject position, thereby enabling one effectively to transgress their operation. One could use the interpretative frame in order to perceive structural discrepancies in power accruing to distinct identifications, to discern shared experiences across subject positions, and to map affinities as the basis for collective action. Whether these two distinctive frames could also engage with a modified form of objectivity has, to date, received less attention. This is perhaps the central methodological question that feminist political theorists now need to address.

## Conclusion

Focusing on metatheoretical differences within gender theory can help one to understand and evaluate the various confrontations that continue to rage within it. However, it is important also to recognize that most theorists invoke, both knowingly and unwittingly, multiple metatheoretical frames. The unwitting conflation of frames has tended to generate confusion. The knowing invocation on the other hand has become an important political strategy. Because of the politically charged nature of much gender theory its advocates have perhaps been more willing than many mainstream political theorists explicitly to recognize metatheories as 'justificatory strategies' and make pragmatic appeal to whichever promises the greatest political benefits (Harding 1987: 186; see also Lloyd 1993: 83, Frazer and Lacey 1993: 171, Sylvester 1994: 66). The relative merit of the frames is 'at least as much political as it is epistemological' given that each frame allows one to ask particular questions – questions which may be more or less appropriate to the political task in hand (Ferguson 1993: 22).

In short, debates about the project of political theory can usefully be understood as debates about whether one's frame should be objective, interpretative or genealogical – or, indeed, a complex negotiation or pragmatic conflation of some combination of these. The nature of political theory is differently conceived from each of the objectivity, interpretation and genealogy frames. So too is the relation between gender and political theory. From the objective frame gender is deemed nonpertinent, and the project of 'gender in political theory' is simply to render it so in practice. From the interpretative frame gender shapes political theory, and the project of 'gender in political theory' is to reveal the ways in which political theory is currently gendered in patriarchal ways and could be rearticulated in alternative feminist ways. From the genealogical frame political theory is one of the discourses that constitutes gender, and the project of 'gender in political theory' is to destabilize the hold of particular gendered discourses and create space for the emergence of alternative corporeal subjectivities.

# PART II
# Reconstructing the Political

# 4

# *Equality*

## Introduction

The debate that has most clearly and decisively shaped feminist theorizing during the 1980s and 1990s has been the 'equality/difference' debate. Equality and difference, both rich, complex and contested terms in their own right, have come to represent distinct and competing perspectives within feminist theory, in which they stand for two fundamentally antagonistic accounts of the nature of gender and of the feminist project. Those interested in delineating ideological positions have mapped the pursuit of 'equality' onto liberal or socialist forms of feminism and the pursuit of 'difference' onto radical or cultural feminism. Those more interested in geographical diversity have mapped equality and difference perspectives onto Anglo-American and French or Italian feminisms respectively.

If one augments the ideological and the geographical frames of analysis with a chronological perspective, one might reasonably depict the trajectory of feminist theory in relation to equality/difference as starting with equality, shifting to difference, and then moving on to resolution of the dichotomy. Some commentators have chosen to label these stages of feminism as waves, first-wave feminism being characterized by the commitment to equality, second-wave by the commitment to difference, and the present third wave by a commitment to diversity. Others see the move from equality to difference as internal to second-wave feminism: Nancy Fraser, for example, argues that the shift occurs within the US women's movement in the late 1970s (Fraser 1997a: 100). While each of these chronological narratives undeniably captures something of the feeling within feminist debates, each is perhaps overly schematic and itself embedded within a particular normative frame. It is equally possible to characterize the dynamic nature of the equality/difference debate not as a progression from hypothesis, via antithesis to a stable synthesis, but rather as an ever-present and unresolved oscillation between binary opposites, the deconstruction of which is central. The hope of resolution and reconstruction is viewed from this perspective with scepticism.

I shall attempt to map the equality and difference debates from the perspective of current attempts to move 'beyond' equality and difference. It is the 'going beyond' that most clearly characterizes the present moment of gender theorizing. In order to evaluate this project, one will need to understand not only the nature of the dichotomy between the 'equality' and 'difference' perspectives as commonly defined (along with their respective critiques of one another), but also the various strategies adopted for moving beyond dichotomous thinking. The strategies of inclusion, reversal and displacement take the form, in the context of this debate, of endorsements of equality, difference and diversity respectively.

The status of the third diversity perspective is complex. It is not intended to encompass all the various attempts made to 'go beyond' or to synthesize the equality and difference perspectives. These are best understood as complex negotiations of existing archetypes rather than articulations of a new one. However, the particular attempt to 'go beyond' equality and difference that is inspired by a desire to explore the workings of paradox, without the illusion of resolution, can, I think, be seen as a third distinctive archetype.

## Equality and Difference

'Throughout its history', argue Bock and James, 'women's liberation has been seen sometimes as the right to be equal, sometimes as the right to be different' (Bock and James 1992: 4). The central tension between these two positions arises from a dispute as to whether a commitment to gender-neutrality can ever be achieved by pursuing a strategy of equality. Some feel that, in the context of a patriarchal society, the pursuit of equality might inevitably result in requiring everyone to assimilate to the dominant gender norm of masculinity. Those who believe the former to be possible fall within the 'equality' perspective; those who are sceptical adopt a 'difference' perspective. Put bluntly, women appear to be faced by a clear choice: in a society where the male is the norm, one can – as a woman – seek either assimilation or differentiation. One can aim to transcend one's gendered particularity, or to affirm it: pursue 'gender-neutrality' or seek 'gender-visibility'.

## Equality

Those who approach gender and political theory from an equality perspective firmly believe that gender ought to be politically irrelevant, or
non-pertinent. The fact that men and women are commonly understood
to be different is insufficient reason to treat them differently within the
political sphere. The project of any polity truly committed to liberal
principles of equality should be to transcend sexist presumptions about
gender difference which have worked to discriminate against women, to
grant women equal rights with men and to enable women to participate
equally with men in the public sphere. Gender difference is viewed as a
manifestation of sexism, as a patriarchal creation used to rationalize the
inequality between the sexes. The widespread presumption that women
were not fully rational was repeatedly used as a justification for continuing to exclude them from full citizenship. The equality theorist's
argument that there is a manifest need to counter such myths is upheld
in the face of all evidence which might appear to indicate that there
actually are gender differences (such as differing educational aptitudes
or vocational ambition). These, they maintain, are simply the result of
generations of sexual inequality. If different gender characteristics exist,
they are socially constructed in a sexist society to the benefit of men and
the disadvantage of women.

Given that the equality theorist believes gender differences to be created and perpetuated in the interests of men, their project is to advocate
the transcendence of gender differences. The idea that women 'are different' has been used to exclude women from valued and fulfilling social
engagement. The notion that women might not be capable of the rational, abstract, universalizing form of reasoning needed to engage in public arenas of work and politics needs to be countered with an assertion
of women's similarity to men. As Fraser notes, 'From the equality perspective, then, gender difference appeared to be inextricable from
sexism. The political task was thus clear: the goal of feminism was to
throw off the shackles of "difference" and establish equality, bringing
men and women under a common measure' (Fraser 1997a: 100). From
the equality perspective gender difference is synonymous with inferiority and is to be rejected in the name of a more genuinely inclusive just
social order.

## Difference

In contrast, difference theorists accept and even celebrate gender differences. Men and women are different, they argue, but difference should

not be read as inferiority. Equality theorists argue that 'gender difference' is either a straightforward myth or a contingent result of social conditioning, but in either case needs to be transcended. Difference theorists, on the other hand, argue that 'gender difference' is either a biological given or a result of social conditioning (see Chapter 2), but in either case needs to be recognized and valued.

Whereas the equality theorist argues for women's integration into the existing social order, the difference perspective seeks to reverse the order of things: to place at the centre that which is currently marginalized, to value that which is currently devalued, to privilege that which is currently subordinated. The nurturing, peace-loving, intuitive and emotional qualities of women are celebrated rather than subordinated. The individualistic, competitive, rational qualities of patriarchal society are viewed with suspicion and hostility rather than admiration and longing. The aim is to lessen the power, not to join the ranks, of the male order. In the specific context of political theory this involves replacing male-ordered thinking with a discourse that privileges women's experiences and women's perspectives. The political task here is the reversal of that proposed by the equality theorist. The goal of feminism is to make clear the fundamental difference between men and women and to enable women to gain a positive sense of their common identity as women. Once this is gained, women can then demand that their distinctive voice is heard and perspective valued.

Ferguson succinctly summarizes this approach. 'The creation of women's voice, or a feminist standpoint, or a gynocentric theory, entails immersion in a world divided between male and female experience in order to critique the power of the former and valorise the alternative residing in the latter. It is a theoretical project that opposes the identities and coherencies contained in patriarchal theory in the name of a different set of identities and coherencies, a different and better way of thinking and living' (Ferguson 1993: 3–4). From the difference perspective the denial of gender difference represses women's authentic nature. A genuinely inclusive just social order will necessarily recognize women's specificity and embody female as well as (or perhaps instead of) male values.

*Between equality and difference*

The fundamental disagreement between equality and difference theorists centres on the question of neutrality. Equality theorists accept the basic claim underpinning most liberal political theory and its practical political institutions, that the liberal ideal of equality is itself neutral *vis-à-vis* gender. If women are in practice not equal with men, this is as a result of contingent distortions of the ideal of neutrality. The appropriate response to the inequality between the sexes is for women to pursue the ideal of neutrality more rigorously: to hold liberalism accountable to its own professed ideals. Difference theorists on the other hand see the ideal of neutrality as itself partial. Rather than perceiving the liberal commitment to gender-neutrality and equality as an inspiring, if sadly unfulfilled, ideal, difference theorists argue that what appears neutral is actually androcentric or male-defined. Appeals to gender-neutrality are therefore complicit with the structures that denigrate the feminine. If there is no genuinely neutral position to adopt with regard to gender, one is forced to choose between assimilation to the dominant male norm or celebration and revaluation of the subordinate female other: inclusion or reversal.

A practical example here should help to indicate the nature of the dispute. When considering how employment legislation ought to be drafted in order to deal with the fact that women may require pregnancy leave and benefits, two distinct strategies both aiming at gender justice have repeatedly emerged. The first approach proposes that pregnancy should be included within general gender-neutral leave and benefit policies. Such policies would be relevant to any physical condition that renders anyone, male or female, unable to work. One formulation of this equality perspective would be simply to apply leave and benefit laws developed for a male workforce to both men and women. Many feminists have been quick to point out that this does not actually constitute the pursuit of gender-neutrality, as it takes male lives as the norm and so disadvantages women (Williams 1983). More genuinely gender-neutral policies would require the adoption of a concept of equality that recognizes and accommodates the specific needs of everyone, not just those of the dominant group. The pursuit of such a gender-neutral advocacy project might entail large-scale reform of existing legislation and a significant restructuring of most workplace policy (Taub and Williams 1986). The equality project might then aim at integration, but in practice this frequently entails quite fundamental transformation of existing practices.

The difference theorist, however, remains unhappy with even this 'radical' rendering of the equality approach. For, as Young argues, 'it implies that women do not have any right to leave and job security when having babies, or assimilates such guarantees under the supposedly gender-neutral category of "disability". Such assimilation is unacceptable because pregnancy and childbirth are usually normal conditions for normal women, because pregnancy and childbirth themselves count as socially necessary work, and because they have unique and variable characteristics and needs' (Young 1990a: 175). The problem is not only that policies claiming to be neutral are actually partial, it is also that the distinctiveness of women's contribution is not positively recognized. In contrast, the difference theorist proposes a gender-differentiated approach that might positively recognize, and give public confirmation of, the social contribution of childbearing.

In response to such a move, critics have argued that, while the importance of pregnancy benefits should not be overlooked, neither should they be overemphasized. Deborah Rhode, for instance, attempts to shift the focus from difference to disadvantage. She argues that: 'Pregnancy-related policies affect most women workers for relatively brief intervals. The absence of broader disability, health, child-rearing and caretaking assistance remains a chronic problem for the vast majority of employees, male and female, throughout their working lives' (Rhode 1992: 154). In other words, to focus exclusively on the differences between men and women may be to misrepresent the complex realities of both women's and men's lives.

The gender-neutrality perspective entails an affirmation of the belief that women are individuals possessed of reason, and that this potentiality entitles them to full human rights. The emphasis is not upon equality of outcome, but on equality of opportunity. Given that women have an equal capacity for reason, they are worthy of equal respect and entitled to equality of opportunity. The argument is not that everyone should be required to be the same in some substantive sense. This is not an end-state approach to the question of equality. It is a procedural approach whereby the concern is that all people – irrespective of gender – are subject to the same procedural rules and formal evaluations in order that they may equally choose to pursue their own ends in their own way. It is not that 'differences' are denied or frowned upon. Indeed the central premise of this approach is that individual autonomy and ability to choose one's 'different' projects and beliefs is vital to a just society.

The difference perspective, on the other hand, would emphasize and seek recognition for that which the equality perspective would transcend. The claim is that what appears to be neutrality within the equality perspective is actually partiality: treating people as equals only in respect to those capacities and needs commonly associated with men. Rather than demanding 'gender-neutrality', this concern about the falsity of a claim to neutrality leads to a call that women's *specificity* be recognized.

In relation to citizenship debates, for example, this has meant that calls to extend the ideal of citizenship to encompass women have been tempered by the insistence that women's citizenship be differentiated from that of men. As Ruth Lister comments in her exploration of feminist perspectives on citizenship:

the most fundamental either/or choice that has faced feminist theorists and activists pressing women's claims as citizens is whether our aim is a genuinely gender-neutral conception of citizenship or a gender-differentiated conception. The former would accord women equal citizenship rights with men and enable them to participate as their equals in the public sphere; the latter would recognise women's particular concerns and contribution and value their responsibilities in the private sphere. (Lister 1997: 92–3)

This second gender-differentiated approach frequently draws on the symbol of motherhood to emphasize the distinctiveness of women's possible contribution to citizenship. The practice of motherhood cultivates, it is claimed, a form of maternal thinking centred around 'attentive love' (Ruddick 1983: 227). The central issue regarding gender and citizenship should not be viewed, difference theorists argue, as a question of how to help women to leave this role and to transcend this form of thinking in order to play a more active role as citizens. Rather, the issue is how to develop a conception of citizenship that might incorporate maternal thinking. Gender-neutral theorists, by contrast, are concerned both that this project reinforces existing stereotypes of women and that it aims to introduce into the public arena values and relationships that are not properly political (Dietz 1998: 390–4) (see Chapter 6 for a fuller discussion of this debate).

This, then, is the character of the equality/difference debate. Its central features are neatly captured by Fraser, who argues that:

The proponents of equality saw gender difference as the handmaiden of male domination. For them, the central injustices of sexism were women's marginalization and the maldistribution of social gods. And the key meaning of gender equity was equal participation and redistribution. Difference feminists, in contrast, saw gender difference as the cornerstone of women's identity. For them, accordingly, androcentrism was sexism's chief harm. And the centrepiece of gender equity was the revaluation of femininity. (Fraser 1997a: 100)

The existence of these two distinct strategies within feminism is not new, nor is the ambivalence about their relative merits. Indeed, the ambivalence regarding equality and difference perspectives recurs throughout the history of feminist writings. Pateman labels the simultaneous demand for both gender-neutral and gender-differentiated citizenship 'Wollstonecraft's dilemma' (Pateman 1989: 196–7). The source of the dilemma emanates from the mutual incompatibility of the two options given the dominant tendency to view a patriarchal model of citizenship as a neutral model. Pateman's argument is that the existence of this patriarchal conception of citizenship permits only two incompatible and partial feminist options. 'The debate therefore continues', she says, 'to oscillate between "difference" (maternal thinking should be valued and brought into the political arena) and "equality" (citizenship not mother-hood is vital for feminists) and so remains caught in Wollstonecraft's dilemma' (Pateman 1992: 21).

Scott makes a very similar point. 'When equality and difference are paired dichotomously', she argues, 'they structure an impossible choice. If one opts for equality, one is forced to accept the notion that differ-ence is antithetical to it. If one opts for difference, one admits that equality is unattainable' (Scott 1997: 765). Recognition of the negative effects of this dilemma upon feminist theory and practice has motivated many to attempt to negotiate a path beyond the dichotomy. Indeed, it is rare to find anyone actually espousing either an equality or a difference perspective in a totally unqualified manner.

## Beyond Dichotomy

Recognition of the partiality and limitations of the gender-neutral model of equality has repeatedly propelled feminists to the endorsement of its opposite, adopting a strategy of reversal. In place of abstraction, ration-ality, universality and equality, 'difference' feminists have asserted the value of the embedded and the emotional, of particularity and differ-ence. However, the problem with simply affirming all that gender-neutrality excludes has become apparent to many feminists themselves. For, as Anne Phillips argues: 'in challenging a narrow version from one side, feminists risk simply situating themselves on an opposite of a false divide . . . in sharpening up what is distinctive in the new position, it is easy to reproduce an over-simple dichotomy' (Phillips 1993: 67).

Although both 'equality' and 'difference' have been promoted with great vigour within feminism, there has been a long-standing and in-creasingly prevalent perception that neither of these two stances offers an unambiguously positive way forward. As Martha Minow states, 'Both focusing on and ignoring the difference risk recreating it. This is the dilemma of difference' (quoted in Scott 1997: 762). To seek to transcend difference is to perpetuate the conflation of masculine partial-ity with neutrality. To focus on difference is to reaffirm the relation between feminine partiality and deviance. The 'problem' of gender in political theory might not be resolved by simply pursuing a strategy of reversal, revaluing that which is devalued and claiming recognition for that which is excluded. For although this strategy aims to challenge the core tenets of liberal impartiality, it might inadvertently reinforce their hold by working with the terms of debate they have created. As Scott argues: 'it makes no sense for the feminist movement to let its arguments be forced into pre-existing categories and its political disputes to be characterized by a dichotomy we did not invent' (Scott 1997: 765). In this vein Phillips also states: 'I argue ... against a polar opposition between what is abstract, impartial, gender-neutral, and what is specific, relational, engendered; and I suggest that the best in contemporary feminism is already steering a more middle route' (Phillips 1993: 58). This 'middle route' can take many forms. Some opt for a pragmatic endorsement of whichever policy appears best to further women's interests in each particular circumstance; others pursue a more theoretically integrated approach.

This third way, or strategy of displacement, argues against remaining within the terms of existing political discourse and seeks to show why neither an equality nor a difference approach will ever be a satisfactory one given that both work within parameters of debate constructed according to patriarchal norms. Assuming that the displacement project is currently prevalent, gender theorizing has increasingly distanced itself from both the strategy of inclusion, which would 'add women in', and the strategy of reversal, which would refuse existing norms, and has embraced the deconstruction of binary oppositions as a central theoretical, and political, task.

In the context of justice, for instance, there has been a clear trajectory. The attempt to realize gender justice according to existing norms of justice as impartiality, provoked a counter-literature arguing 'justice' to be a masculinist way of thinking about morality, and developing an alternative, feminine, ethic of care. In response to this rejection of justice as impartiality, writers as diverse as Seyla Benhabib, Susan Moller Okin and Iris Marion Young have all claimed that the distinction between an ethic of justice and one of care has been overdrawn (Benhabib 1992, Okin 1989, Young 1996a). These theorists argue, in various ways, that moral reasoning ought properly to draw upon both these approaches (see Chapter 5 for a fuller discussion). In relation to citizenship debates also, one finds that current theorists most frequently argue that one ought to draw on the strengths of both individualist and relational approaches. With regard to the gender-neutral/gender-differentiated dichotomy Ruth Lister argues that: 'a feminist reinterpretation of citizenship can best be approached by treating each of these oppositions as potentially complementary rather than as mutually exclusive alternatives' (Lister 1997: 92). In short, the current mood in gender theory is to a large extent characterized by an attempt to find a resolution of the equality/difference dichotomy. Equality and difference are increasingly seen as ideal types rather than as workable or sufficient models for political action in their own right. But, before we consider attempts to negotiate a settlement between these two perspectives, let us focus on the third perspective that has emerged within gender theory, the strategy of displacement.

The precise manner in which theorists attempt to resolve or 'go beyond' the apparent dichotomy between equality and difference perspectives requires some attention. For there are significant differences within the strategies adopted. Some propose synthesis as the best way forward. This resolution is rarely presented as a distinctive perspective in its own right, and is more frequently seen as a historical account of cumulative change. As such it can appear lacking in theoretical clarity and innovative contribution. Phillips makes this point: 'If feminists take up the high ground of empathy and emotion *versus* abstract and impartial reason, they are I believe wrong. If they situate themselves more firmly in the middle ground – as increasingly it seems that they do – they may be right but not so strikingly original' (Phillips 1993: 67). In contrast to this synthetic resolution, there is a strategy for 'going beyond' equality and difference perspectives which does offer a distinctive and theoretically innovative perspective in its own right.

## Diversity

The diversity perspective is not located on either side of the equality/ difference divide, but rather gains its definition from its commitment to deconstructing the division itself. Grosz articulates the contrast between difference and diversity perspectives. Whereas the difference theorist is concerned to reverse the privileged terms in oppositional pairs, the issue for diversity theorists 'is not to privilege one term at the expense of the other, but to explore the cost of their maintenance' (Grosz 1994a: 32). If a difference approach aims to 'put women in the centre', this diversity approach in contrast aims to 'deconstruct centres'. Both are transformative projects: both seek to problematize the very foundations of political theory in the light of taking gender seriously. Both recognize – in a way that an equality approach does not – that dominant modes of political theorizing have been founded upon patriarchal gender priorities. As such both are analytically distinct from an equality approach which merely seeks to 'add women' in to the existing schema: they are transformative rather than integrative. And, in this respect, it is their shared rejection of equality politics that unites them.

However, as the terms of debate concerning gender and political theory have gradually shifted from the integrative to the transformative, it is the dissimilarity between the difference and diversity forms of gender politics that has increasingly preoccupied gender theorists. The distinction between these two approaches manifests itself in the contrast between the sort of transformation envisaged. 'In the first stance', Ferguson states, 'men – male power, male identities, masculinity as a set of practices – are problematized; in the second, the gendered world itself becomes a problem' (Ferguson 1993: 3). This is a distinction between those who would reverse patriarchal gender priorities and those who would displace them. Rather than *re-centring* political theory around a female- as opposed to a male-gendered perspective, the diversity approach seeks to *de-centre* political theory with respect to gender altogether.

One of the most significant political consequences of this approach is that the apparently clear-cut distinctions between oppression and resistance become blurred. Diversity theorists are keen to point out that the 'reinscription of conventional power strategies can occur even in places where one might most confidently expect liberation' (Ferguson 1993: 123). In other words, while both equality and difference feminisms overtly aim to challenge the dominant patriarchal order, each might actually work further to entrench its underlying premises, perpetuate its logic and thereby prolong its dominance. Until the logic of binary dualisms is itself challenged, the political project of feminism will always be bound by Wollstonecraft's dilemma.

Scott makes one of the clearest statements of the need to 'go beyond' the equality/difference debate in this deconstructive manner. The entire equality versus difference debate is, she maintains, premised upon a false choice. Difference does not entail inequality, nor does equality presuppose sameness. In place of a dichotomy between sameness and difference Scott introduces the category of diversity. In other words, she destabilizes the duality between inclusion and reversal and proposes a third, heterogeneous, option. There is, she argues, a need to unmask the power relationship constructed by positing equality as the antithesis of difference, and to refuse the consequent dichotomous construction of political choices. The determination to 'go beyond' the equality/difference debate does not therefore signal a simple desire for agreement and synthesis. It represents the emergence of a new perspective that takes the deconstruction of binary oppositions to be its central task.

There are several important ways in which the equality/difference dichotomy can be displaced. The first strategy focuses on de-coupling the apparent opposition. The 'oppositional pairing', argues Scott, 'misrepresents the relationship of both terms' (Scott 1997: 765). The dilemma with regard to equality and difference emerges from the common acceptance of several distinct, and dubious, assumptions. Notably, it is commonly assumed that equality is synonymous with sameness and that difference is synonymous with dichotomous sexual difference. It is also commonly assumed that one must either be different from or the same as a particular ideal type and, given that the male is the norm and female its subordinate other, this ideal type is assumed to be male. Given all these assumptions, to be 'equal' is to be the same as a male norm, to be different is to deviate from it. For women to demand equality is simultaneously to deny their sexual difference and to claim sameness with a dominant norm of maleness. Two distinct aspects of this form of reasoning are worth considering. The first is the equation of difference with dichotomous sexual difference, the second the equation of equality with sameness.

### Difference and dichotomy

The strategy of displacement, involving an exploration and critique of binary oppositions, has come to be a central aspect of gender theory. Not only the equality/difference dichotomy, but dichotomous thinking itself has been subject to extensive critique (see Flax 1992, Lloyd 1984, Grosz 1994a, Green 1995, Prokhovnik 1999). The proposal that we move beyond the dichotomies that have structured debates within feminism is underpinned by a new theoretical commitment to the project of challenging binary thinking in all its manifestations. The deconstruction of dichotomies, revealing the ways in which each side of a binary division implies and reflects the other, is one of the central methodological devices of an increasingly prevalent theoretical approach, frequently labelled post-structuralism. This approach is now highly influential within feminist theory. Surveys of recent trends within feminist theory indicate that 'the critique of dichotomies, of dualisms, of falsely either/or alternatives, has become a major theme in feminist writing' (Barrett and Phillips 1992: 8). Given this, the amount of energy spent by feminist theorists in constructing and debating an equality/difference opposition is particularly bemusing to those feminists who view dichotomous thinking itself as the problem. In the context of the claim that dichotomous thinking is oppressive, it is intriguing that feminists have so often worked to constitute the significance and hold of the dichotomy between equality and difference.

Before surveying the nature of the critiques levelled at dichotomous thinking, let us briefly consider the central features to dichotomous thinking. Prokhovnik helpfully lists these as: an opposition between two identities; a hierarchical ordering of the pair; the idea that between them this pair sum up and define a whole; and the notion of transcendence (Prokhovnik 1999: 23–31). Opposition entails not simply an opposition between two things held in tension which are equally valued, but an opposition between two things held in tension, only one of which can be right. Hierarchy entails the ranking of two polarized terms such that one becomes the privileged term, the other its subordinate counterpart. One side of the pairing is defined by its not being the other. The dominant term is dependent upon its exclusion of the subordinate term, such that the secondary status of the subordinate term is a condition for the possibility of the dominant one. Moreover the two are not only mutually exclusive; they are also mutually exhaustive. They are held to constitute a whole, not simply parts of an open-ended plurality. Together they comprise all the possible options.

Numerous feminist critics of dichotomous thinking have argued that dichotomies are, in effect, a particular form of metaphor in thinking and language. Dichotomy, as Prokhovnik contends, is one of the many possible metaphors that can be used to explain the world, but one that has been particularly potent and instrumental in setting out the condition of thinking in the modern period. Ironically, one of the effects of the dominance of this particular metaphor in thinking is the devaluation of the significance of metaphor itself. Rather than presenting itself as only one metaphorical mode among others, dichotomous thinking adopts an adversarial, zero-sum stance whereby any form of reasoning not dichotomous in form is both other than and subordinate to dichotomous thinking. In further insisting upon the dichotomous distinction between form and content, dichotomous thinking underplays the extent to which its own form structures the content of thinking and debate. (See Chapter 3 for a consideration of the extent to which dichotomous thinking could be said to be male or masculine.)

Critiques of dichotomous thinking are not specific to gender theorists. However, gender theory has become particularly preoccupied with the hold of dichotomies because of the perceived centrality of 'maleness' as the privileged term, which not only posits 'femaleness' as its 'suppressed, subordinated, negative counterpart' but also sets up a range of other equally hierarchical dichotomies. In short, the political significance of dichotomous thinking is that it maintains inequalities of power.

### Equality and sameness

Within the equality/difference debate, 'difference' theorists criticize equality as assimilatory, as requiring 'sameness', specifically gender sameness. The problem, implicitly assumed though rarely explicitly conceived, is not therefore 'equality' but 'equality as sameness'. This is important, because it means that critics of this stance could, and some argue should, reject sameness without rejecting equality. Diversity theorists tend to share the difference theorists' scepticism about existing formulations of equality as sameness, but, rather than rejecting equality, they highlight the problems of sameness.

One such theorist is Wendy Brown. Brown argues that the definition of equality as a condition of sameness, 'a condition in which humans share the same nature, the same rights, and the same terms of regard by state institutions', is intrinsic to liberalism (Brown 1995). Within liberalism, she maintains, individuals are guaranteed equality, in the sense of the right to be treated the same as everyone else, because we are regarded as having a civil, and hence political, sameness. Her point is to endorse the feminist claim that, as long as equality is understood as sameness, gender consistently emerges as a problem of difference: human equality contrasts with gender difference. Because equality is conceived as sameness, its conceptual opposite is not, she claims, inequality, but difference. 'Equality as sameness is a gendered formulation of equality, because it secures gender privilege through naming women as difference and men as the neutral standard of the same' (Brown 1995: 153).

But in what ways does this generic liberalism under consideration assume equality to be sameness? The equality theorist would argue that the point of the liberal distinction between the civil and the political was precisely to allow for the existence of political equality despite civil differences of religious belief and cultural identity. Brown's point, though, is that 'an ontology of masculine sameness' requires its differentiation from women. Her claim is not of course that all men *are* the same, but that differences among men are named 'woman' and thereby displaced from men onto women. Women's status as difference becomes intrinsic. Difference is not primarily a descriptive term but a symbolic one. The liberal conception of equality 'allegorizes' gender. The discourse of liberalism requires, produces and then disavows the feminine as symbolic difference in order to secure the masculinist liberal norm.

It is not only equality theorists who have made this mistake. The conflation of equality with sameness is clearly manifest by many of the advocates of a difference perspective. Take, for example, Irigaray's claim that: 'Women merely "equal" to men would be "like them", therefore not women. Once more, the difference between the sexes would be in that way cancelled out, ignored, papered over' (quoted in Sellers 1991: 71). This statement only works, and the arguments for asserting the importance of difference are only compelling, if one assumes equality to be synonymous here with gender-sameness. To make this assumption is, as critics of the equality/difference dichotomy claim, to confuse a contingent convention for a definitional truth. Moreover, the assumption that equality is gender-sameness rests on a specifically patriarchal set of contingencies.

To ask if women should seek justice in terms of (masculinist liberal) sameness or in terms of (feminist) difference is to remain constrained by the form of dichotomous thinking adopted by 'liberal masculinism'. Neither strategy offers the possibility of 'subversive resolution' (Brown 1995: 165). Both equality and difference perspectives work to reaffirm the masculinist norm in different ways. The equality perspective does so by emancipating certain women to participate in the terms of masculinist justice and by extending an unreconstructed discourse of rights and autonomy to the domains of childrearing, health and sexuality. The difference perspective does so by proposing a norm of female caring as the basis for a counter-discourse of responsibility and inter-dependency. Both work within the confines of dichotomous thinking, accepting the claim that there can only be two oppositional, mutually exclusive options.

From the diversity perspective, equality feminism is perceived to accept the substantive content and normative value of the dominant pairings of dichotomous thinking. It simply seeks to distance these terms from the male/female binary. Difference feminism, on the other hand, accepts both the substantive content of the binary terms and their correlation with the male/female binary, but seeks to reverse their dominant/subordinate status. From the diversity perspective the equality approach is internally contradictory and inevitably self-defeating. In seeking to extend the scope of the dominant category of the pairing, equality feminism is inattentive to both the defining role of the subordinate and the constructed nature of the binary. The difference approach on the other hand is potentially self-defeating in that it may work to sustain that which it seeks to erode. The attempt to reject masculinist thought by affirming its opposite actually works to reaffirm binary logic, which is central to the operation of masculine thought. Such a celebration of the feminine might then 'discursively entrench' the masculine ideal that it seeks to denounce (Brown 1995: 21). To celebrate the 'feminine' as currently conceived is, from the diversity perspective, to celebrate a feminine contingently constituted through masculinist discourses. As such there is a danger that this approach might operate 'inadvertently to resubordinate by renaturalizing that which it was intended to emancipate by articulating' (Brown 1995: 99).

Equality is not to be confused with sameness. The whole conceptual force of 'equality' rests on the assumption of differences, which should in some respect be valued equally. To advocate equality is not necessarily to assume or to demand sameness in some material concrete sense; it is to propose that concrete differences be treated equally. What might constitute equal treatment is the subject of intense debate (equality of opportunity versus equality of outcome being a classic debate within political theory) but it is only one particularly regressive conception of equality that is being critiqued by the advocates of 'difference theory'.

To claim that two discrete entities are 'the same' is to invoke some standard of evaluation: they are the same with respect to some specified criteria. Given that all entities have more than one property, they will probably be different with respect to other criteria. Two pencils may be the same colour but different lengths. Two people may be the same age but different heights. All this tells us is that things can be both the same and different with respect to each other simultaneously. To determine whether they are also equal is to engage in a different form of inquiry: here we must evaluate both entities with respect to an agreed upon norm. To be equal to another is to be regarded as equivalent to another. Whether one is regarded as equivalent is a matter of social agreement not objective fact. Such agreement will necessarily be made in specific contexts for specific purposes. In effect it is an agreement to regard diverse persons as equivalent despite manifest differences deemed non-pertinent to the context of evaluation. The central issue is not whether people aré the same or different, but what criteria of evaluation are employed and who has the power to specify these. This is significant because, as Scott notes in the context of democratic citizenship, 'the measure of equivalence has been, at different times, independence or ownership of property or race or sex' (Scott 1997: 765). In other words, the criteria of evaluation have shifted over time and are subject to future contestation.

To recognize that equality does not necessarily imply sameness is not, however, to jettison the concerns of difference theorists. The criteria of evaluation adopted to assess equivalence may be relational and flexible, rather than objective and immutable, but they have nonetheless in practice worked fairly consistently against women. Significantly, women have rarely been in a position to specify these criteria. Even where the criteria have been other than sex, it has almost uniformly been one deemed characteristic of men – or more precisely of hegemonic masculinity. This has worked to define women as deviant. While the feminist 'equality theorists' aspire to ensure that women are deemed equivalent to men with respect to the specified criteria of evaluation, feminist 'difference theorists' point out that the criteria of evaluation were not only defined by men but, more importantly, embody ideals of masculinity. This means that women are not only excluded in practice but also subordinated in principle.

Feminist 'diversity theorists' on the other hand point to the weaknesses in both these approaches. The 'equality' perspective fails to recognize the socially constructed and patriarchal nature of the criterion of evaluation deemed pertinent to social inclusion. The 'difference' per-

spective (in focusing on sexual difference as the only criterion of evaluation) fails to theorize the extent to which 'maleness' and 'femaleness'
are themselves socially constructed and also underplays the significance
and plurality of other forms of difference. As Scott usefully summarizes:
'In effect, the duality this opposition creates draws one line of difference, invests it with biological explanations, and then treats each side of
the opposition as a unitary phenomenon. Everything in each category
(male/female) is assumed to be the same; hence, differences within either
category are suppressed' (Scott 1997: 766). A crucial issue, then, is
whether the norms of equivalence are in fact neutral, male or masculine.
Equality theorists argue that they are in practice, or could in principle
be, neutral. Identity theorists argue that the norms of equivalence are
not, and can never be, neutral with regard to gender, because a central
norm is that of maleness itself. Diversity theorists argue that the norms
of equivalence are more plural and contingent than appeals to maleness
alone allow. The existing norms are neither neutral with respect to
gender nor an expression of it. Rather they are a part of the very
discursive practices that constitute gender itself.

Arguing for this third approach, Scott states: 'It is not sameness or
identity between women and men that we want to claim but a more
complicated historically variable diversity than is permitted by the opposition male/female, a diversity that is also differently expressed for
different purposes in different contexts' (Scott 1997: 766). The diversity
perspective focuses not only on differences between the sexes, but also
on the differences within gender groups. The binary opposition between
equality and difference is displaced. So too is the binary opposition
between the sexes.

Diversity theorists are, then, highly critical of equality theorists, but
they tend to be even more vehemently opposed to difference theorists.
They do not view this as a three-stage progression towards an ideal
synthetic position. Young, for example, notes that: 'It may be true that
the assimilationist ideal that treats everyone the same and applies the
same standards to all perpetuates disadvantage because real group differences remain that make it unfair to compare the unequals. But this is
far preferable to a re-establishment of separate and unequal spheres for
different groups justified on the basis of group difference' (Young 1990a:
169). The risk of the difference approach is that one will re-create the
stigma that difference carried before the formal attempt to transcend it
by asserting equality. This is a risk avoided, according to Young, only if
one rejects the 'oppressive meaning of group difference' as 'absolute
otherness, mutual exclusion, categorical opposition' (Young 1990a: 169).

Drawing heavily on the diversity perspective, Young is concerned to
reveal the extent to which both the equality and difference perspectives

arise from a single attempt to 'measure all against some universal standard' which actually 'generates a logic of difference as hierarchical dichotomy' (Young 1990a: 170). The real risk in working within this logic, even if with a view to reversing it, is that difference is here absolute. The failure to see difference as relational has two negative results: groups marked as different appear to have nothing in common with those considered as the norm; and differences within these groups are repressed. 'In this way', Young tells us, 'the definition of difference as exclusion and opposition actually denies difference' (Young 1990a: 170). In other words, to claim one's identity as 'woman' serves not only to perpetuate the idea that women are totally different from men, but also to repress the significant differences between women.

This insight is pursued by Bonnie Honig, who characterizes difference as 'that which resists or exceeds the closure of identity' (Honig 1996: 257–8). For Honig difference is a perpetual and unruly presence within any assertion of identity. She views the attempts of difference theorists to locate difference solely between stable identity groups as mistaken. Her project is to affirm the 'inescapability of conflict and the ineradicability of resistance' within, and not simply between, identity claims (Honig 1996: 258). This move would appear to distance her from even Young's modified reading of difference. Notably, she argues that her understanding of difference 'renders problematic . . . certain identity- and interest-based conceptions of pluralism' (Honig 1996: 271). On this perspective the real political potential arises not from stable subjectivities (however conceived), but from decentred subjects 'who are plural, differentiated, and conflicted' (Honig 1996: 272).

## Relating Equality, Difference and Diversity

Having mapped out the archetypal equality, difference and diversity perspectives, let us consider how these three work themselves out in the context of political debate. For rarely is any one of the three found in its pure form. Much more frequent is the modified variation or ambivalent negotiation. There are three distinctive ways in which the strategies of inclusion, reversal and displacement are negotiated with reference to the debates concerning equality, difference and diversity. In the first, the difference perspective is modified in the face of the challenge of plural identity differences. In the second, the diversity perspective is modified in the context of the need for strategic endorsements of difference. In the third, the equality perspective is modified in the light of both the difference and diversity perspectives. Before looking at examples of each of these in turn, though, it is worth noting that there is a significant confusion of terminology in these debates.

Endorsements of a pluralized version of the 'difference' side of the equality/difference dichotomy are commonly called a 'politics of identity' (see Evans 1995: 21–2), and the attempt to explode the dichotomy between 'equality and difference' is frequently referred to as a 'politics of difference' (see Grosz 1994a). These conflicting uses of the same terminology add to the complexity of mapping distinct perspectives within this debate. A wide range of political theorists currently claim themselves to be advocating a 'politics of difference', including theorists advocating what I have labelled difference, identity and diversity perspectives (Taylor 1992, Young 1990a: 171). This serves to cloud what is already a complex terrain. It leads to a situation in which we find, within a group of theorists adopting the same methodological frame and proposing the same advocacy project, some criticizing a 'difference perspective' in the name of 'diversity' (Scott 1997) and others criticizing an 'identity perspective' in the name of 'difference' (Grosz 1994a).

## Difference/identity

Many people who argue the need to 'go beyond' the equality/difference dichotomy are motivated more by political events than theoretical disputation. Indeed some of the strongest critics of the abstract theoretical approach of the diversity perspective are themselves responsible for challenging the claims of the difference perspective in practice, thereby weakening the hold of the apparent clear-cut dichotomy between difference and equality. A practical, political and historical reflection on what actually happened to alter the terrain of debate with the development of new political alliances and divisions focuses attention on the importance of 'identity politics'. Here the equality/difference debate is displaced by political activism, not destabilized by theoretical reflection. It was the political challenge of 'lesbians and feminists of color' (Fraser 1997a: 101), placing the issues of sexuality and race firmly on the agenda, that undermined the pertinence of the debate between equality/difference in practice. The displacement of dichotomy emerges, on this account, not from deconstructive theory but from 'identity politics'.

The rise of 'identity politics' in the 1980s placed both the difference and the equality perspectives under intense critical scrutiny and severe strain. But it is the difference perspective that has been most significantly weakened. For identity politics movements adopted the same general approach to cultural differences per se that the difference perspective adopted with respect to gender alone. They extended the difference analysis to a wider range of cultural differences, meaning that the gender issue no longer held the centrality that its advocates had once claimed.

The idea that there might be a single 'woman's perspective', opposed to the dominant 'male perspective', was undermined by the protests of those women who found themselves silenced by such a claim. The 'difference' approach was itself experienced as assimilatory by those women who did not conform to the norm of female identity proposed by those claiming to speak for 'the women's movement'. The conception of 'woman' being affirmed was in reality a particular conception of white, heterosexual, middle-class, educated, Western women. To claim that the experiences of these particular women could be used to define the nature of woman per se was not only inappropriate, but also harmful to the vast majority of women whose experiences were quite other. The response of those excluded by this discourse of 'woman' was to assert the specificity of their own experiences and demand recognition for the particularity of their own identities. The identifications of sexuality, race and class were all highlighted as central to the personal experiences and political identity of most women. Attention shifted from an exclusive focus on gender difference to an exploration of the question of the differences among women.

For if one claims that women have been undervalued as a result of the failure to recognize gender difference, what grounds can there be for not also recognizing similar claims made by all marginalized and subordinate groups? Once one has rejected the equality theorists' commitment to neutrality and impartiality, what is the basis for prioritizing one form of difference, namely gender, as more significant and more worthy of recognition than any other? Does not the assertion that there is a single shared woman's experience and voice itself subordinate other forms of difference and repress the diversity of voices within women? Furthermore, as other forms of difference intersect with gender difference, the grounds for claiming a radical discontinuity between male and female perspectives are clearly weakened.

This pluralized discourse of identity differences shares with the singular discourse of gender difference the commitment to making political activity an expression of one's identity and the political ambition for the recognition of one's identity. Identity politics, Grosz argues, 'is about establishing a viable identity for its constituency, of claiming social recognition and value on the basis of shared common characteristics' which are attributed to the particular social group of an identity (Grosz 1994a: 31). Its project is to establish for its members the rights, recognition and privileges that dominant groups have attempted to keep for themselves. As such, identity politics is a pluralized form of difference politics. The focus is still upon the recognition of difference, but now the identities in question are multiple rather than simply binary: the differences emphasized exist among women as well as between women and men.

Where a difference perspective was premised on a critique of patriarchy, identity politics works with pluralized discourses of marginalization and repression. The initial battles to rank and prioritize the various forms of oppression experienced have largely given way to a pragmatic acceptance of multiplicity. Where difference theorists aimed to realize the recognition of the female, specific groupings of identity theorists each pursue the recognition of their own distinctive identities. As women lose their exclusive status as 'marginalized other', space is not only opened up to explore the marginalized identities of gay, black, working-class and disabled women, it also emerges to explore marginalized masculinities.

Identity politics therefore issues a vital challenge to the hold of the equality/difference debate within gender theory. It represents an approach that is politically, but not methodologically, distinct from a difference perspective. While the deconstructive diversity stance is openly critical of both the politics and the methodological approach of the difference theorists, this identity politics approach uses the basic methodological commitments of the difference theorists to undermine their political claims. In this respect the development of identity politics was made possible by, and emerged in response to, the difference perspective. In focusing attention on the issue of gender and seeking to gain recognition for women's distinctive cultural identities, difference theorists laid the groundwork for the emergence of identity politics. In failing to be attentive to their own assimilatory tendencies, difference theorists also created the backlash, which energized identity politics.

This political and historical account makes it clear that the commitment to the deconstruction of binary dualisms emerges not out of theoretical thin air but at the end of a gradual progression in which the assertion of gender-visibility is a first step towards identity politics and then diversity. As Fraser argues, when the focus on 'gender difference' gave way to a focus on 'difference among women', the equality/difference debate was itself displaced (Fraser 1997a: 101). This inaugurated a new phase of feminist debate in which the deconstructive diversity perspective has come to play a major role, but a role that is often highly critical, or at best deeply ambivalent, about the identity politics which seem to have created the conditions for its appeal.

### Diversity/difference

The difference and diversity perspectives appear, on a theoretical level, to be profoundly antithetical. Politics, for the difference theorist, is a manifestation of one's authentic self. For the diversity theorist, the subject

is constituted by political structures and relations. The former is concerned to make politics reflect authentic identities, the latter to reveal
the extent to which all notions of authenticity are themselves constructed.
Nonetheless a surprising number of theorists committed to the diversity
perspective in principle endorse a difference perspective or some form of
identity politics in practice.

For all its theoretical clarity, the nature of the advocacy project arising from the diversity project is perhaps less obvious than is the case
with equality and difference projects. Given that it is not primarily (or
perhaps remotely) normative, there are no direct political strategies or
policy implications that follow from the endorsement of this archetype.
Those who do view themselves as diversity theorists frequently do not
engage in practical debates or political activism at all. Others do, but
adopt some form of equality and/or difference perspectives in the process. For many, it is not clear that the diversity perspective alone generates a political programme at all.

Take, for instance, the position of Kristeva, who has influentially
argued for a deconstructive approach to gender. She states that one
might categorize feminism, both historically and politically, according
to a threefold schema: women demand equal access to the symbolic
order; women reject the male symbolic order in the name of difference;
women reject the dichotomy between masculine and feminine as metaphysical. These three approaches map directly onto the strategies of
inclusion, reversal and displacement and lead to the endorsement of
equality, difference and diversity perspectives respectively. From the third
position, Kristeva directly critiques the difference politics of the second:
'In this third attitude, which I strongly advocate – which I imagine? –
the very dichotomy men/women as an opposition between two rival
entities may be understood as belonging to metaphysics. What can 'identity', even 'sexual identity', mean in a new theoretical and scientific
space where the very notion of identity is challenged?' (Kristeva 1981:
13–35). However, it is not clear that Kristeva intends to advocate this
third position in isolation from the other two. She also states that she
sees them as simultaneous and non-exclusive.

Commenting upon her work, Moi is clear that to:

> advocate position three as exclusive of the first two is to lose touch with
> the political reality of feminism. We still need to claim our place in human
> society as equals, not as subordinate members, and we still need to
> emphasise that difference between male and female experience of the
> world . . . as long as patriarchy is dominant, it still remains *politically*
> essential for feminists to define women *as* women in order to counteract
> the patriarchal oppression that precisely despises women *as* women. (Moi
> 1997: 249)

This position is fairly representative of one adopted by many who find the deconstructive diversity perspective compelling in theory, but none-theless perceive the difference and equality approaches important in practice. It results in a discontinuity between theory and practice: the rejection of 'difference' as an ideal theoretical type accompanied by the strategic use of difference arguments in political debates.

Many diversity theorists are not happy with this proposal. The retreat to a strategic endorsement of difference is frequently seen as an unhelp-ful capitulation. Fuss, for example, is concerned that: 'deference to the primacy and omniscience of Politics may uphold the ideology of plural-ism, for no matter how reactionary or dangerous a notion may be, it can always be salvaged and kept in circulation by an appeal to "politi-cal strategy"' (Fuss 1989: 106–7). Butler is equally cynical about the claim that the diversity perspective puts 'into jeopardy politics as such', and therefore needs to endorse a difference perspective for strategic po-litical engagement. She argues that this is 'an authoritarian ruse by which political contest over the status of the subject is summarily silenced' (Butler 1995: 36).

There are more sophisticated attempts to negotiate a frame of refer-ence that draws on all three perspectives. For example, in the pursuit of the diversity perspective Young advocates what looks like a combina-tion of equality and identity policies. In order to avoid the risks of each, Young proposes a dual system of rights: 'a general system of rights which are the same for all, and a more specific system of group-conscious policies and rights' (Young 1990a: 174). In contrast to the oppositional conception of difference, Young proposes a more relational conception. Rather than understanding difference as a description of attributes, it is here viewed as 'a function of the relations between groups' (Young 1990a: 171). In this formulation group differences 'will be more or less salient depending on the groups compared, the purposes of the comparison, and the point of view of the comparers' (Young 1990a: 171). Group similarities too will be relational rather than fixed: 'what makes a group a group is a social process of interaction and differentiation in which some people come to have a particular *affinity* . . . for others' (Young 1990a: 172). In other words, rather than using the concept of 'diversity', she tries to 'reclaim the meaning of differ-ence', 'offering an emancipatory meaning of difference to replace the old exclusionary meaning' (Young 1990a: 168).

## Equality revisited

Not everyone who is currently concerned to 'go beyond' the equality/ difference dichotomy is committed to deconstructive methodological principles. For some the need to undermine the hold of the dichotomy is motivated simply by a pragmatic need to recognize actual plurality of people and perspectives. For these theorists the central task is to formulate a perspective that draws on the best insights of both the equality and the difference perspectives. In other words, the project is viewed as a synthetic rather than a deconstructive one. Where Scott provides one of the clearest statements of the deconstructive diversity perspective, one of the clearest accounts of the synthetic approach to equality and difference is to be found in the work of Fraser.

Fraser views neither the difference perspective modified by identity politics nor the diversity perspective (her own labels for these two perspectives being 'multiculturalism' and 'anti-essentialism' respectively) as 'entirely satisfactory'. Both, she claims, rely on one-sided views of identity and difference. 'The anti-essentialist view is skeptical and negative; it sees all identities as inherently repressive and all difference as inherently exclusionary. The multiculturalist view, in contrast, is celebratory and positive; it sees all identities as deserving of recognition and all difference as meriting affirmation' (Fraser 1997a: 103–4). Neither, she claims, can sustain a viable feminist politics. For both 'fail to connect a cultural politics of identity and difference to a social politics of justice and equality. Neither appreciates the crux of the connection: *cultural differences can only be freely elaborated and democratically mediated on the basis of social equality*' (Fraser 1997a: 107). In other words, she claims that current debates about gender politics are characterized by various complex negotiations and confrontations between difference and diversity perspectives. These debates fail to engage with the equality perspective, and yet no resolution is possible until they do. As Fraser argues: 'both approaches repress the insights of equality feminism concerning the need for equal participation and fair distribution' (Fraser 1997a: 107). Fraser would have us construct a new equality/difference debate: one which confronts the relation between cultural difference and social equality.

Fraser's proposed strategy of displacement focuses on the reconstructive, rather than solely the deconstructive, moment. Rather than viewing the distinction between equality and difference as false or absolute, she sees these as complementary strategies pertinent to distinct, but equally significant, aspects of life. This leads to a debate about conceptions of justice: is gender justice about social distribution, cultural recognition or both, and can we – should we – distinguish the two? We will return to the debates about justice in Chapter 5. For now I want simply to indicate that, while recent debates about gender in political theory have been dominated by disputes within and between difference and diversity perspectives, there are some who are now signalling the importance of bringing the equality perspective back in.

## Conclusion

Debates about gender in political theory have long been characterized by a recurrent oscillation and antagonism between equality and difference perspectives. During the 1980s the pertinence or coherence of constructing debate according to these two approaches was challenged. The dichotomy was undermined both by the growth of identity politics and by the turn to deconstructive theoretical perspectives. The emergence of identity and diversity perspectives led to a reformulation of the difference perspective (focusing on differences among women rather than differences between women and men) and to a destabilization of the binary opposition between equality and difference itself. The main focus of debate shifted from one focused on the relative merits of equality and difference to one focused on the relative merits of identity and diversity. Diversity theorists have been concerned to reveal the extent to which identity politics replicates the theoretical partiality and political dangers of the difference perspective. Advocates of identity politics have been keen to highlight the abstract and apolitical nature of the diversity approach. There have, however, been recent moves to recuperate the equality perspective as a framework for pursuing a modified form of difference. The equality/difference debate has certainly been shown to be more complex than originally presumed, but its hold appears to be as strong as ever. As Di Stefano notes, 'the theoretical and political dilemmas of difference are well worth pondering. As yet, they remain stubbornly persistent and elusive, suggesting that gender is basic in ways that we have yet to fully understand, that it functions as "a difference that makes a difference," even as it can no longer claim the legitimating mantle of *the* difference' (Di Stefano 1990: 78).

# 5

# *Justice*

## Introduction

Is moral reason gendered? There are three different sorts of response to this question within the literature on gender in political theory. Moral reason is usually equated in this literature with 'an ethic of justice' (though it is also referred to as the 'ideal of impartiality' or a 'universalistic morality' or 'Kantian ethics'). The first response is that an ethic of justice is the most reasonable and convincing perspective according to 'a view from nowhere' and is therefore in principle neutral with respect to gender. The second response is that the ethic of justice is a product of the male psyche and is intrinsically gendered. The third response is that the ethic of justice is a particularly limited and historically specific form of moral reasoning that has played a significant role in the process of gendering social identities.

This ethic of justice is widely criticized within feminist political theory. The precise nature of the criticism varies according to which of the three perspectives listed above one adopts. From the first perspective gender theorists are critical not of the ethic of justice itself, but of its selective application. They argue that its range of application ought to be extended to encompass those forms of social relations that are characteristic of family and personal life. In other words, they pursue a strategy of inclusion. From the second perspective gender theorists are critical of the dominance, rather than the delimitation, of the ethic of justice. They argue that it is but one form of moral reasoning, and one particular to men. There is, it is held from within this second approach, another form of moral reasoning called an 'ethic of care' which ought also to be recognized. In addition it is said that women are more likely to adopt this ethic of care than are men, and that to privilege only the ethic of justice is to silence women's distinctive moral voice. This, in other words, is the strategy of reversal.

In contrast to this second gender-differentiated conception of moral reasoning, gender theorists approaching this debate from the third perspective are critical of the move to bifurcate forms of moral reasoning and to celebrate the antithesis of the ethic of justice. They argue that the ethic of justice is not simply one of two possible forms of moral reasoning. In its impossible assertion of a single universal form of moral reasoning the ethic of justice actually creates an 'other', subordinate form of moral reasoning as its antithesis. It imposes hierarchical dichotomy upon fluid plurality. The 'justice' model of moral reasoning is therefore not only different to the 'caring' model, it is generative of it. Given that the care model exists only in relation to, and as the remainder of, the justice model, the adoption of either model works to perpetuate the hierarchical dualism of moral debate generated by the ethic of justice. This, then, is the strategy of displacement.

These three positions map roughly onto the equality, difference and diversity approaches respectively. As Ruth Lister points out: 'the counterpoising of the ethic of justice, derived from abstract, universal individual rights, with that of an ethic of care, grounded in specific contextual relationships, parallels and has its roots in the equality versus difference dilemma' (Lister 1997: 100). The three archetypal perspectives to be explored in this chapter, then, might best be summarized as the claim that moral reason is neutral, that it is gendered and that it is gendering.

In order to understand fully the issues at stake in this debate, and their relevance to specifically political as opposed to moral debate, let us first consider the ethic of justice and the ethic of care. We will then contemplate the two subsidiary issues which have been central to the justice/caring debate: the nature of the relation between the two ethics and the two genders; and the nature of the relation between the two ethics themselves. This leads on to a consideration of several distinct strategies adopted for going beyond the justice/care dichotomy. Finally, we will consider attempts to introduce recognition of difference into this debate.

## An Ethic of Justice

What has come, within the feminist theory literature, to be labelled an 'ethic of justice' perspective is actually a certain articulation of moral objectivism. As outlined in Chapter 3, cognitive objectivism is the conviction that there is some permanent, ahistorical framework to which we can ultimately appeal in determining the nature of truth. Moral objectivism applies this conviction to moral reason. Its most distinctive representative, Immanuel Kant, clearly argues for an ahistorical, universal framework for grounding moral claims.

Kant sought to explain and establish the objective foundation of morality. He rejected all attempts to ground morality on experience and worked to establish the existence of a basic, universal, objective moral law for all rational beings. This was his 'categorical imperative'. This conception of morality, also called an 'ideal of impartiality', invokes a form of rationalism (discussed in Chapter 3). Whereas feminist critiques of cognitive objectivism have dominated debates in relation to science, it is the critique of moral objectivism, or impartiality, or an ethic of justice that has been more central to political theory.

Young characterizes the 'ideal of impartiality' as that conception of moral reason that assumes 'that in order for the agent to escape egoism, and attain objectivity, he or she must adopt a universal point of view that is the same for all rational agents' (Young 1990a: 100). The emphasis on detachment from context, as with Cartesian rationalism, is viewed as a means of transcending the particularity of emotional and interested attachments and achieving a universal point of view. Impartiality demands that one abstracts from particular experiences, feelings, desires and commitments and adopts a detached and dispassionate 'view from nowhere'. Tronto labels this form of moral reasoning 'universalistic morality', outlining the same key features: the requirements that 'morality be derived from human reason in the form of universal principles that are abstract and formal' (Tronto 1993: 27).

An important recent rearticulation of this ideal of impartiality can be found in the work of Lawrence Kohlberg, whose psychological theory of moral development has influenced not only psychologists but also political theorists such as John Rawls and Jürgen Habermas. Kohlberg claimed, on the basis of empirical research, that moral reasoning progresses via six sequential and hierarchical stages. Of these, two are pre-conventional (amoral punishment avoidance and action accompanied by an expectation of a response in kind), two conventional (judgements made primarily to please first one's family and friends and then the entire community), and two post-conventional (obeying rules due to recognition that one agreed to their creation and finally universal justice as fairness). (See Tronto 1993: 64–76 for further discussion of this theory.) The culmination of this developmental process is the ability to see all sides of an issue from an Archimedean point of reciprocity and equality. Achieving this stage of moral reasoning involves not only comprehending but also creating the moral world.

Kohlberg's six stages are derived empirically and used descriptively. He estimates that only 5 per cent of people reach stage 6. Critics have noted the lower moral development scores of working-class people, black people and 'more traditional women'. But the stages are also clearly prescriptive. Indeed some critics claim that Kohlberg's theory is an ideological account of contemporary Western liberal society. Others argue that it is a patriarchal account of moral reasoning.

## An Ethic of Care

Many feminists have argued that women commonly adopt a different moral voice to that privileged in the ethic of justice approach. It is argued that an ethic of justice is a manifestation of the male psyche. A more accurate manifestation of the female psyche is to be found in a contextual morality, or an 'ethic of care'. This care perspective is held to be distinctly female, whether in determinist terms of biological mother-hood or – more commonly – in constructionist terms of socially specific forms of childrearing practices.

The care perspective draws most explicitly on the work of Carol Gilligan, who claims that women's experience of interconnection shapes their moral domain and gives rise to a different moral voice (Gilligan 1982: 151–76). Gilligan drew on the earlier work of Chodorow and the object-relations form of psychology in order to develop her own analysis of moral development. Gilligan and Chodorow's work together have been used widely as a basis for endorsing and applying the notion of a moral voice distinctive to women. In criticizing Kohlberg's research into moral development, on the grounds that it privileged an 'ethic of justice' over an 'ethic of caring', Gilligan offers feminists a framework within which they might critique the individualism and universalism of liberal political institutions. As Benhabib notes, 'Gilligan's critique of Kohlberg radically questions the "juridical" or "justice bias" of universalist moral theories' (Benhabib 1992: 146). In other words, although the debate between Kohlberg and Gilligan is carried out within the realms of moral psychology, it has had a huge impact on the thinking about political theories of justice.

Gilligan's work was inspired by a concern that Kohlberg's method-ological research was partial and biased, focusing primarily on male subjects and using only hypothetical moral dilemmas. She undertook her own research, producing results that challenged the Kohlbergian assumption that the highest level of moral development involves the ability to abstract and universalize moral rules. Significantly, where Kohlberg used only young boys as his sample group, Gilligan used only (white, middle-class) girls. On the basis of her research Gilligan argues that we can distinguish two ethical orientations: justice and rights on the one hand and care and responsibility on the other. The latter requires a contextuality, narrativity and specificity not valued in the former.

Gilligan applies the ethic of justice category to Kohlberg's post-conventional stages of moral reasoning, and contrasts this with 'an ethic of care' which focuses on responsibilities and relationships rather than rights and rules, on concrete circumstances rather than abstract principles. The ethic of care, like the ethic of justice, is argued to be developmental, proceeding through 'self-regarding' and 'other-regarding' stages to culminate in a third 'self-in-relationship-to-others' stage.

There are two significant elements to Gilligan's work in addition to the claim that there are two distinct ethics, each with their own developmental stages. One concerns the proposed relation between gender and these different ethics. The other concerns the proposed relation between the ethics themselves. Let us consider each of these issues in turn. Both are contentious issues about which there is little consensus.

## Gendered Ethics?

Consideration of the relation between these two ethics and gender has generated a huge literature. The different, but not inferior, moral voice of the caring ethic has been widely discussed and adopted within feminist literature as a moral voice distinctive to women.

Gilligan and her followers have argued that the two ethics correlate to two conceptions of subjectivity, the abstract individual and the connected self, which are usually manifest by men and women respectively. The feminist defenders of an ethic of care claim there to be a distinctive women's morality characterized by caring and nurturance, the importance of a mother's love and the value of peace. This distinctive form of ethics is variously argued to derive from being female, being a mother or a potential mother, from women's cultural role and exclusion from the marketplace. The claim is echoed in the writings of the 'maternalists', who argue for a feminized version of citizenship and articulate a female political consciousness that is grounded in the virtues of women's private sphere – primarily mothering (Ruddick 1989, Elshtain 1981).

The claim that the ethic of justice is characteristically male and the ethic of care characteristically female has its origins in the writings of Gilligan. Although neither Kohlberg nor Gilligan explicitly claims that the form of moral reason they are proposing is gendered, Gilligan's work was inspired by a concern that girls did less well than boys according to Kohlberg's criteria of moral development. Her samples are almost all female and her work has been taken by most of its commentators as an account of a female moral voice. The central methodological issue here is Gilligan's adoption of object-relations theory (as articulated by Chodorow) to explain the emergence of the 'different voice' adopted by women when engaging in moral reasoning. According to this account, there are – given the particular social structures of childrearing which predominate in contemporary society – highly gendered structural constraints within which we develop our moral voice. This reliance on object-relations theory has proved a controversial move for Gilligan.

Theorists who focus on forms of social cleavage and subordination other than gender have challenged the claim that the ethic of care is a moral voice distinctive to women. For example, Patricia Hill Collins, a black feminist theorist, endorses an 'ethic of care' while criticizing Gilligan for her assumption of commonality between women and the resulting privileging of the experiences of white middle-class women. While she claims the ethic of care as a distinct form of moral reasoning, she denies its exclusivity to feminine thought. For her it also represents an element of African-American culture (Collins 1991). She points out that the 'values and ideas Africanist scholars identify as characteristically "black" often bear remarkable resemblance to similar ideas claimed by feminist scholars as characteristically "female" (Collins 1991: 203). The emphasis on connectedness and the concrete, rather than on separation and abstraction, is to be found in an Afrocentric as well as a women's tradition. For Collins an ethic of caring is grounded in a tradition of African humanism. This claim erodes the polarized male versus female forms of moral reasoning debate. While retaining the notion of a clear and dualistic distinction between two forms of moral reasoning, the correlation between the ethic of care and women is challenged. This makes it possible to value an ethic of care without becoming enmeshed in an endorsement of women's essential voice, or an assertion of a unity among all women.

Joan Tronto offers one of the most sustained accounts of the need to disentangle clearly the ethics of justice and care from deterministic notions of gender (Tronto 1993). She introduces factors other than gender to reveal the extent to which the ethic of care might be common to all marginalized social groups, not just women. This works to locate the caring form of moral reason with subordination rather than essential voice. There is, she argues, empirical evidence which indicates the existence of differences of moral reasoning discernible between working and middle classes and between whites and ethnic minorities. Among groups that are not so privileged, gender differences are not so prominent. For example, African Americans use both care and justice arguments with little divergence between genders. Indeed Gilligan herself offers evidence that the ethic of care might be a manifestation of a subordinate status rather than anything more specifically related to gender.

Gilligan states that her research into women's moral reasoning reveals a 'sense of vulnerability that impedes these women from taking a stand . . . which stems from her lack of power and consequent inability to do something in the world . . . The women's reluctance to judge stems . . . from their uncertainty about their right to make moral statements or, perhaps, the price for them that such judgement seems to entail' (Gilligan 1997: 554). This passage suggests that, whatever psychological dimensions there might be to explain women's moral differences, there are also social causes. This particular moral voice might be a function of a subordinate social position that is not common among, or exclusive to, women. Tronto's claim is that, if moral difference is a function of social position rather than gender, the morality Gilligan has identified with women might be better identified with subordinate or minority status (Tronto 1993).

How then, asks Tronto, might we explain the continuing force of Gilligan's association of gender with an ethic of care? Here she pulls no punches in arguing that the supposed relation between women and the ethic of caring has nothing to do with a radical commitment to social change. The continuing force of Gilligan's argument resides in its fit with object-relations theory (the prevailing psychoanalytic paradigm in American clinical practice), its complicity with traditional sexist notions of gender roles (where women are nurturing) and the quasi-scientific grounding it provides for essential difference arguments (Tronto 1993: 84–5). In short, there are deeply conservative, rather than radically progressive, reasons which sustain the claim that the ethic of caring is the distinctive moral voice of women. Catharine MacKinnon makes a similar claim. She is 'troubled by the possibility of women identifying with what is a positively valued feminine stereotype' (MacKinnon 1985: 74).

Tronto's claim is that 'changing the kinds of questions that are centrally important in moral life will change how and what constitutes moral theory' (Tronto 1993: 35). There is nothing inherent in women, Tronto claims, that associates them with moral sentiments rather than with reason, with the particular rather than the universal. One need only look at the writings of the Scottish Enlightenment to find men deemed capable of morally delicate feelings (see also Baier 1987a). Her argument is that the eighteenth century was a period of social transformation requiring people to think differently about morality. Kantian disinterested and disengaged moral theory was best able to answer the most pressing questions of the day and therefore gained dominance over contextual sentimental morality. Pure sentiments were increasingly located within the private household, as were women. So, while universalistic morality could conceivably have accommodated women as rational moral beings, it could not accommodate those aspects of life associated with women as a result of eighteenth-century developments, and therefore excluded both. Historical circumstances led to the containment of both women and moral sentiments within the domestic sphere. It was then only one short step to naturalize this by claiming women to be essentially caring. 'To have imposed upon women the essentialist view that con-textual, moral sentiments morality *is* women's morality was an import-ant accomplishment of anti-feminists of the 18th and 19th centuries' (Tronto 1993: 56).

By emphasizing the historical specificity of an ethic of justice in rela-tion to wider social developments, Tronto focuses attention on the fact that, even if Kantian moral objectivism is a manifestation of a contem-porary male psyche, it has not always been so and is not exclusively so. The ideal of impartiality might be understood as the form of moral reasoning appropriate to the hegemonic masculinity of nineteenth-century liberal states, but it is overly simplistic, if not politically danger-ous, to claim that it is male per se. This is an important insight in that it allows one to explore the precise way in which the ethic of justice necessarily creates hierarchies and inevitably marginalizes subordinate groups, without accepting and championing this marginal status or cel-ebrating it as fundamentally female.

In this spirit Tronto develops an account of elitism in Kohlberg's model which is not specifically gendered. In order to develop morally along Kohlberg's schema, claims Tronto, one must learn how to assume different roles, and for this one needs role-taking opportunities that are afforded only via group or institutional participation. Feeling excluded from the institutions of government and economy will, Kohlberg recog-nizes, hinder one's moral development. This is an external social con-straint upon the full realization of the ideal itself. There is, in addition, a second problem of elitism internal to the model itself.

Kohlberg argues that, to achieve post-conventional moral reasoning, one must first go through the two conventional moral stages. Here one's moral reasoning takes the form of making judgements that will gain the approval of one's family, friends or community. To be conventionally moral is to conform to the group's norms. This depends on the existence of 'others' not in the group, the creation of which results in 'objectifica-tion'. Having created a category of otherness, anyone moving on to post-conventional moral reasoning must then generalize his or her moral judgements such that they apply not just to the group but to everyone. In other words, 'they reincorporate those others, who they have previ-ously excluded, by assuming that they are the same as themselves' (Tronto 1993: 73). First one objectifies others, then one assimilates them.

Given the above, straightforward claims about the gendered nature of the ethics of justice and care look dubious. A direct correlation between the two ethics delineated by Gilligan and the male and female genders has been widely endorsed within feminist literature. Presumptions about the femaleness of the ethic of care and the maleness of the ethic of justice resonate with commonly held beliefs about the gendered nature of moral reason. They also provide a useful theoretical basis for a politics of difference. Nonetheless, there have been many empirical studies that question the simplicity of the equation of justice and care with men and women. Some have revealed class and race to be equally, if not more, significant variables. Others have argued that there are no measurable gender differences (see Tronto 1993: 82–4). On the basis of even contemporary empirical research there would seem to be little consensus that we can plausibly claim an ethic of care to be distinctively or exclusively female. When considered historically it becomes even more difficult to sustain the claim. These facts have, however, not worked to undermine its political influence.

## Between Caring and Justice

Given the widespread influence of Gilligan's writings on the existence of two distinct moral voices, it is perhaps surprising that there is so little consensus as to what the relation between these two ethics is understood to be. Some commentators argue that the lack of agreement on this question arises from the fact that Gilligan was herself not consistent in her characterization of the relation between the two ethics.

It is claimed that Gilligan vacillates between three possible articulations of the relation between the two ethics. The first is that the two ethics are incompatible alternatives to each other but are both adequate from a normative point of view. The second is that they are complements of one another involved in some sort of tense interplay. The third that each is deficient without the other and that they therefore ought to be integrated (Flanagan and Jackson 1990: 38–40). It is interesting to note that, notwithstanding the significant differences between these three accounts, each represents an attempt to negotiate both ethics. Gilligan nowhere endorses the rejection of the ethic of justice in favour of an ethic of care. This is worth commenting on because it is frequently presumed that the feminist assertion of an ethic of care entails the rejection of the ethic of justice.

Nel Noddings is perhaps one of the few theorists who has advocated a fully fledged ethic of care and rejection of all forms of impartiality (Noddings 1984). Noddings uses the figures of Abraham and Ceres as ideal types representing the justice and care perspectives respectively. Abraham is willing to sacrifice his own child for a principle. Ceres would sacrifice any principle for her child. These, she argues, are conceptions of morality typical of the father and the mother generally (Noddings 1984: 40–3), and are fundamentally incompatible moral frameworks. Her ideal would appear to be a society adopting only that latter moral perspective.

Most theorists have stopped short of this position, attentive to the negative implications of relying exclusively upon an ethic of care. The overwhelming majority of feminist theorists have actually been keen to reconcile the two ethics in some way. Overextension of the value of caring is widely recognized to be unhelpful, even to the pursuit of an ethic of care itself. As Diemut Bubeck argues, 'the choice between care and justice is a false choice . . . considerations of justice have to form part of an ethic of care if it is to be acceptable at all' (Bubeck 1995a: 13). It has been pointed out that unconditional care is not in the best interests even of the recipient of care, and Sevenhuijsen draws attention to the importance of distinguishing between an ethic of care and 'compulsory altruism' (Sevenhuijsen 1991). Lister also argues that, if such altruism is to be avoided, the ethic of care must be 'tempered by the more conventional ethic of justice or rights to which it is frequently opposed' (Lister 1997: 102).

In other words, if there is a distinctive form of moral reasoning adopted by women rather than men, it arises in the context of particular social structures of childrearing which generate two distinct senses of self in men and women (see Chapter 2 for a discussion of this point in relation to Chodorow). This bifurcation of identity formation is a cause of concern rather than celebration. Women's claimed interconnectedness and men's claimed autonomy are both a product of inequality. Both are distortions of a more rounded sense of self. Any celebration of interconnectedness must therefore be limited by the acknowledgement that it is a product of inequality and is to be balanced with an autonomous sense of self, not pitted against it.

In this vein Tronto, who is keen to unmask the essentialist account of women's morality and reveal the socio-historical circumstances which generate this separation of justice and caring, seeks to include caring within a commitment to rights, laws and political procedures (Tronto 1996). She accepts that one explanation as to why society currently devalues care, seeks to contain it within the private and associates it with the powerless is the enormous real power of care. Ironically, it is the power of care-givers that makes it essential that society devalue care: 'the rage and fear directed toward care givers is transformed into a general disgust with those who provide care' (Tronto 1993: 123).

Bubeck also emphasizes the significance of care *as a practice* in this debate. The reason why so many feminists have been so keen to revalue caring *as a moral perspective* is that they view this as part of a political strategy of combating women's exploitation as carers. However, most recognize that an effective critique of such exploitation will require a complex synthesis of the ethics of justice and caring in theory.

This trend towards explorations of compatibility is hindered by the conviction that there are certain articulations of an ethic of justice which simply cannot accommodate considerations of caring (see, for instance, Bubeck 1995a: 13). The ethic of justice, as articulated by Kohlberg, is felt by many to be too narrowly conceived to provide a fully adequate conception of morality or to allow for incorporation of elements of a caring perspective. However, as Noddings is atypical of advocates of an ethic of care in her assertion of incompatibility between the two ethics, so Kohlberg is atypical of advocates of an ethic of justice.

Brian Barry, one of the most bullish contemporary defenders of an ethic of justice, or 'justice as impartiality' in his own terminology, is uncompromisingly critical of Kohlberg's methodology, conclusions and influence (Barry 1995: 237–66). He points out that Kohlberg subscribes to a kind of pseudo-impartiality that 'leaves no room for the moral significance of prior commitments, institutionally derived obligations, or personal relations' (Barry 1995: 247). This is because, when considering the claim that people who are alike in morally relevant respects should receive similar treatment, Kohlberg adopts a highly restrictive understanding of what counts as morally relevant. For him a moral rule must be universal in the sense that it defines the rights for anyone in any situation. But, as one commentator notes, she does 'not know of any impartialists who believe that our conduct should meet this test' (Baron 1991: 851). In other words, the rejection of this narrow definition of moral relevance is not specific to feminists, but is also to be found among mainstream theorists defending impartiality. As Barry notes in relation to feminist debates about justice: 'it is strange that so much passionate invective has been poured on ideas so infrequently advocated' (Barry 1995: 256).

The feasibility of reconciling the ethics of justice and caring within a single account of morality requires the jettisoning of both Noddings's articulation of caring and Kohlberg's articulation of justice. To adopt an overly narrow conception of justice is necessarily to render it incompatible with a caring perspective. For this particular form of justice reasoning is so narrowly defined as to generate dichotomy instead of unity. The narrow conception of the ethic of justice which most infuriates its care critics is one that generates hierarchical dualism. The problem, then, is not justice thinking, but dichotomous thinking.

This insight moves the debate away from one polarized between male justice and female caring towards an exploration of the construction of this apparent dichotomy. As the diversity perspective refuses the terms of debate in which the equality and difference perspectives are rendered mutually incompatible, so we find an increasing number of theorists determined to refuse the apparent dichotomy between the ethics of justice and caring. Once again it is the case that an overly restrictive concept of the dominant norm necessitates the creation of an oppositional 'other', which is then defined as specifically female.

'Cartesian anxiety' (discussed in Chapter 3) is manifest in the overly restricted conception of justice proposed by Kohlberg and those who adopt similarly restrictive conceptions of justice. Their narrow conception of justice creates a constitutive outside regarded as a threat. This propels the endorsement of fixed, permanent constraints that generate either/or oppositions. This is classic dichotomous thinking (Prokhovnik 1999). The insistence on the narrow conception of justice creates an opposition between two ethics and a hierarchical ordering of the pair. It further generates the idea that, between them, the ethics of justice and caring span the entire field of possible forms of moral reasoning. The two ethics appear to be mutually exclusive and mutually exhaustive. This appearance is itself generated by the dominant ethic of justice that requires a subordinate other, the ethic of caring. The ethic of justice is dependent upon its exclusion of the ethic of caring, which is a condition for the possibility of justice. In this context, the celebration of an ethic of caring, deemed incompatible with any rendering of an ethic of justice, represents not a rejection of the justice thinking, but an articulation within its terrain.

In order to move beyond such dichotomous thinking it is helpful to distinguish between those articulations of justice which require hierarchical dualism, and those which do not. Here Barry's distinction between first- and second-order impartiality is useful. First-order impartiality is a requirement that one is not motivated by private considerations: 'to be impartial you must not do for one person what you would not do for anybody else in a similar situation – where your being a friend or relative of one but not the other is excluded from counting as a relevant difference' (Barry 1995: 11). Second-order impartiality, in contrast, pertains not to individual motivation, but to social principles. It generates a theory of justice, not an account of individual morality. 'What a theory of justice as impartiality calls for are principles and rules that are capable of forming the basis for free agreement among people seeking agreement on reasonable terms' (Barry 1995: 11). Far from being synonymous with first-order impartiality, second-order impartiality is a procedural mechanism for reaching general agreement as to when and where first-order impartiality might or might not be appropriate.

Universal first-order impartiality is not compatible with an ethic of caring – 'it fills up the whole moral space and thus leaves no room for any other basis of moral judgement to be combined with it' (Barry 1995: 249). The attempt to integrate an ethic of caring into a first-order form of impartiality will require either the adoption of both antithetical ethics by each individual (who will then have to determine how and when to adopt one or the other), or a moral division of labour, in which one group of people adopt one ethic and another group the other. Both strategies assume the continued existence of two rival ethics. However, if one were to adopt a second-order impartiality one would be able to pursue a single morality in which justice and caring were complementary. On this model, caring would fit into, rather than stand in opposition to, a structure of rights and duties. In short, it is entirely possible to reject the Kohlbergian depiction of justice, identified as the two highest stages of moral development (which are crude versions of utilitarianism and Kantianism respectively – each of which entail universal first-order impartiality), without jettisoning the commitment to impartiality altogether.

The concrete demands of those who would revalue an ethic of care by giving caring greater social recognition and material support, and by spreading the burdens of caring more equitably, are entirely compatible with an endorsement of justice as impartiality. Indeed, it could be argued that a properly conceived justice as (second-order) impartiality would demand that caring be more publicly and equitably recognized.

## Justice and Care as Political Principles

The debate about the relative merits of the ethics of justice and caring has played an important role within feminist political theory. Here it is not the form of moral reasoning adopted by the individual that is under scrutiny, but the moral reasoning appropriate to the political realm and adopted by the citizen. Ferguson notes that 'many people have criticized Gilligan for failing to mention that the notions of rationality and identity in her "men's voice" sound a lot like classical liberalism, and that "women's voice" could be attributed to all groups excluded from that dominant paradigm' (Ferguson 1993: 199 fn 26). The fact that the ethic of justice sounds 'a lot like' liberalism has encouraged many people to apply the justice/care debate directly to the literature about liberalism. Notwithstanding Gilligan's own silence on questions of political theory, it is common to find an untheorized shift from discussing individual moral reasoning to discussing principles of political justice adopted by the state.

When the justice/care debate gets transposed from developmental psychology to political theory, the ethic of justice is more commonly referred to as 'an ideal of impartiality' (second-order rather than first-order impartiality in Barry's categorization) or 'justice as fairness'. This latter term derives from the most influential articulation of justice as impartiality to be developed in recent years, John Rawls's *A Theory of Justice* (1971). Rawls's theory of 'justice as fairness' rests on the idea of an 'original position' which is intended to exclude information that might bias the process of deliberation about principles of justice. However, when the ethic of justice (as defined by Kohlberg) is taken to be synonymous with justice per se, or even with justice as fairness (as defined by Rawls), the distinction between first- and second-order impartiality (as defined by Barry) gets overlooked. As Barry argues, what is appropriate for the design of major social institutions should not be confused with what is appropriate for deciding about particular problems that arise within them (Barry 1995: 266). Impartiality is crucial in the former and should be used to determine when it is appropriate in the latter.

Notwithstanding the presumption within much feminist theory, few theorists advocate universal first-order impartiality. Yet the inadequacies of a narrowly conceived ethic of justice are frequently held against, and used as a basis for rejecting, theories of justice more broadly conceived. The feminist literature on justice has been significantly and unfortunately limited and skewed by its focus upon Kohlberg's impoverished representation of what a 'mainstream' conception of justice entails. Critics of maternalist politics have felt compelled to defend Kohlberg's position (Jones 1993a), and vice versa (Noddings 1984). This has done little to encourage a more complex engagement with more refined perspectives.

Feminist theorists have challenged the political ideal of justice in several distinct ways. Some have challenged delimitation of the impartial point of view. It is argued that impartiality has been inappropriately applied only to the public realm, leaving the operation of the private realm and the family unaddressed. In *Gender, Justice and the Family* (1989) Susan Moller Okin argues that the neglect of the family in theories of justice ought to be rectified by extending the requirement of impartiality to the private sphere. Others have challenged not the delimitation, but the dominance of the impartial point of view. Drawing on Gilligan's work, many feminists argue that impartiality is a specific form of moral reasoning, rather than moral reasoning per se. It corresponds poorly to family and personal life, where engagement rather than detachment is called for. These theorists call for the recognition of the importance of an 'ethic of care' as well as (and occasionally even instead of) an 'ethic of justice'.

In contrast to both these critiques, which valorize impartiality and particularity respectively, there is a third that undermines the pertinence of the dichotomy itself. In her *Justice and the Politics of Difference* (1990), Iris Young argues that the ideal of impartiality generates a dichotomy between universality and particularity that masks the particular perspective of dominant groups and marginalizes people associated with the body and feeling, notably women. Impartiality denies difference in that the aspiration towards universality reduces differences to unity. The stance of detachment that is supposed to produce impartiality is attained only by abstracting from the particularities of context, feeling and body. This challenge to the overly constrictive conception of justice as impartiality creates space for an attempt to theorize justice as second-order impartiality that incorporates the insights of the ethic of caring. Benhabib, for example, proposes a synthesis of impartial with contextual forms of moral reasoning (Benhabib 1992). She adopts a model of communicative or discourse ethics which, she maintains, subverts the distinction between the two.

In other words, we find the recurrent dynamic or debate emerging. The strategy of inclusion results in a concern to extend the ethic of justice. The strategy of reversal leads to an assertion of the value of the ethic of care, and the strategy of displacement generates an interest in exploring and unsettling the relation between the ethics of justice and care.

## Extending the ethic of justice

Okin provides the clearest endorsement of justice as impartiality from within feminist theory. The amount of intellectual energy that has gone into the claims that justice is a masculine way of thinking about morality, and one that feminists should eschew or radically revise, is thoroughly misplaced, she argues. The empirical evidence that men and women have different moral voices is far from clear. There is certainly no evidence that such a difference, if it does exist, is natural or unalterable. To claim a distinct women's moral voice is to play into the hands of reactionary forces, which would confine women to motherhood on the basis of their special capacity for caring.

Moreover, the distinction between an ethic of justice and an ethic of care has been overdrawn. The best theorizing about justice, Okin argues, has 'integral to it the notions of care and empathy, of thinking of the interests and well-being of others who may be very different from ourselves' (Okin 1989: 15). It is simply misleading, she maintains, to draw a dichotomy as though these were two contrasting ethics. It is more helpful to suggest that theorizing about justice 'is not good enough if it does not, or cannot readily be adapted to, include women and their points of view as fully as men and their points of view' (Okin 1989: 15). Intriguingly, nearly ten years later, this point still needs to be rearticulated in the face of an ever-expanding literature which continues to presume that justice as impartiality necessarily takes the reductive form ascribed to it by Kohlberg.

Okin applies her insight to the work of Rawls. Her claim is that Rawls's theory, as currently articulated, fails to include women and their points of view as adequately as it might, but that it nonetheless has the scope to be adapted such that it does. The point is that the basic theory of justice is not held to be at fault. The object of her critique is not the impartiality of the model, but the failure to extend this impartiality to the family. Rawls's theory of justice entails a role for the capacity for empathy, which allows it to be adapted and applied in a manner that entails rather than denies caring. However, Rawls himself fails to articulate the full potential of his theory by remaining silent about issues within the family.

Okin's ambition is to apply the principles of distributive justice as manifest in Rawlsian liberal theory to the family. She does so on the grounds that justice in the private sphere is a prerequisite for the realization of equality in the public sphere. If women are to develop their capacities to allow them to be equal to men they must be equal within the family as well as in the economy and polis. Furthermore, she argues, it is within the family that children learn the principles of social interaction. If family relations are just, children will be better able to internalize the principles of justice themselves and abide by them within the public sphere in later life.

Okin therefore modifies Rawls's theory of justice as fairness to apply to relations between men and women in the family. This would have the effect, she claims, of eliminating the sexual division of labour that allocates primary responsibility for housework and childrearing to women. And this would in turn require not only fundamental cultural change, but also significant changes in state policies regarding childcare provision, parental leave provision and the balancing of family and work commitments.

This analysis, while clearly radical in implication, remains within the justice as impartiality framework of Rawlsian liberalism. Okin's claim is that women suffer injustice because they 'benefit less from the benefits and are burdened more by the burdens in the distribution of social goods than are men' (Okin 1989: 114). As such, she argues for the endorsement of justice as fairness with an extended frame of vision and application. She also suggests that the best theorizing of justice 'has

integral to it the notions of care and empathy, of thinking of the interests and well-being of others who may well be very different from
ourselves' (Okin 1989: 15). In other words, her argument for the extension of justice thinking is premised on the assumption that it does not
exclude considerations of caring.

### Extending the ethic of care

Social justice, care theorists retort, is not sufficient to generate a morally
acceptable polity. We also need to adopt the maternal mode of caring as
a basis for public interactions. The claim is that women's experiences as
mothers within the private sphere provides them with certain insights
and concerns which are valuable to the public sphere but currently
absent from it. Rather than suggesting that social institutions should be
altered such that women might be equally able to proceed to the highest
levels of abstract moral reasoning, these advocates of the ethic of caring
argue that women's voice should be recognized publicly and used as a
basis for a distinctively female political presence.

Many have found the ethic of care articulated in this form largely
unappealing as a basis for a reformulated politics. The illusion of cohesion and unity, of consensus and collectivity, can all too easily become
dangerous rhetorics which seek to repress fragmentation and difference.
As Jones asks: 'how far can we extend these moral categories, derived
from intimate relations, into the arena of political discourse and public
action?' (Jones 1993a: 150). Ferguson's answer is not very far at all. It
is, she says, 'a warm, mushy and wholly impossible politics of universal
love' (Ferguson 1984: 172). Jones too argues that there are limits on the
adaptation of mothering practices to the political realm. The mother/
child relation is not one of equality, and there are proprietary dimensions of mothering which do not provide a basis for a politics of equality
(Jones 1993a: 151).

It may be difficult, Jones allows, to apply Kohlbergian moral reasoning, but 'how much more difficult and fraught with controversy will it
be to attempt to develop this intensity of feeling about and obligation to
those who are distant?' (Jones 1993a: 154). Jones points to Arendt's
concern that the attempt to found authority on compassion is likely to
deteriorate into pity and so to lead to domination and violence. It
'abolishes distance, the worldly space between men where political matters, the whole realm of human affairs, are located, it remains, politically speaking, irrelevant' (Arendt 1963: 81).

There are, though, more sophisticated defences of an ethic of care,
which are not so susceptible to these critiques. Tronto argues that we

need to switch from talking of 'women's morality' to talking of 'a care ethic' which comprises: 'a vision for the good society that draws upon feminist sensibilities and upon traditional 'women's morality' without falling into the strategic traps that have so far doomed this approach' (Tronto 1993: 2). While recognizing that 'it would be very easy for non-democratic forms of care to emerge' (Tronto 1993: 171), Tronto none-theless insists that care can contribute to the process of democratizing political life. The political implication of this is that, while it might make sense to speak of women's interests (challenging their presumed containment within the family, for example), it does not make sense to speak of a female perspective. While one might usefully aim to incorpo-rate an ethic of care into our political discourses along with rights-based commitments, it does not make sense to seek to replace a male with a female morality.

## Synthesizing justice and care

Despite the continued pitting against each other of care and justice perspectives, advocates of both positions actually argue that their posi-tion entails elements of the other. Tronto's defence of a modified care ethic and Okin's defence of a modified form of justice as impartiality are clearly similar, differing in emphasis rather than in kind.

Happily, recognition that a continued polarization of justice and care is largely unhelpful is now increasingly prevalent. Tronto argues that a standard of justice is needed to assess the distribution of care tasks and benefits in the context of power imbalances. Similarly Virginia Held holds that caring relationships need to be underpinned by a 'floor of justice' (Held 1993: 76). Meanwhile Okin incorporates elements of car-ing and empathy into her thinking. The continuity between the two approaches is increasingly apparent. As Lister comments, when consid-ering the conception of justice developed by Flax, 'her conceptualisation of justice as a process, incorporating reconciliation of diversities; reci-procity; recognition of others' standpoints; and judgement, bears some resemblance to the qualities associated with an ethic of care by Tronto and Sevenhuijsen' (Lister 1997: 104). That this is surprising is a product only of the unhelpful and simplistic conception of justice adopted within the ethic of care versus the ethic of caring debate.

Overcoming this bifurcation, Lister argues that, rather than setting care and justice against each other as mutually exclusive ethics, they need to be seen as potentially complementary, each reinforcing and thereby transforming and strengthening the other (Lister 1997). This is a clear example of the identification and resolution of one of the many false dichotomies that feminists have viewed as paradigmatic of mas-culine Western thought. As Lister notes, identification of such false dichotomies can 'all too easily slip into a simple reversal of the value attached to the two sides of the binary divide' (Lister 1997: 115).

Other theorists currently arguing for the need to synthesize these two perspectives in some way include Sevenhuijsen (1991), Bubeck (1995a), Bacchi (1990), Phillips (1993) and Benhabib (1992). Benhabib's pro-posed resolution has been particularly influential, and is distinct in that the particular form of impartial moral reasoning that she seeks to modify is that developed by Habermas.

Habermas's theory of moral reason shares, with liberal theory, a com-mitment to impartiality. As with all advocates of moral objectivism, Habermas endorses the features of cognitivism, universalism and for-malism 'which make it possible to identify the structure of moral thought in abstraction from any particular aim or conception of the good life' (Meehan 1995: 3). His theory is formal in that it is focused on the form, not on the content, of moral reasoning, cognitivist in that he holds that moral conflicts can be resolved through argument, which is a cognitive skill acquired through a developmental process, and universalist in that he claims that there are criteria of moral reasoning which hold univer-sally. In other words, Habermas adopts a notion of morality that is closely related to (indeed directly influenced by) Kohlberg's conception of moral reasoning. 'The making of norms', he suggests, 'is primarily a justice issue and is gauged by principles that state what is equally good for all. And unlike ethical questions, questions of justice are not related from the outset to a special collective and its form of life' (Habermas, 1996a: 25).

However, while Habermas adopts Kohlberg's basic conception of moral reasoning, his account is distinctive in its emphasis on the role of com-munication and discourse in the establishment of moral norms. He rejects 'monological reflection' as inadequate for the identification and justification of norms (Meehan 1995: 4). In other words, the Kantian view of moral subjects as those who give the moral law to themselves, through independent and abstract reflection, is jettisoned. This follows from his understanding of the subject as socially and linguistically con-stituted. Opting for a social constructivism rather than an abstract indi-vidualism, Habermas places great emphasis on language as the medium in which identity is constituted. He therefore makes an appeal to both the abstraction of the impartiality perspective and the embeddedness of an account of the inter-subjective constitution of identity.

Nonetheless, his commitment to maintaining a clear distinction be-tween abstract questions of justice and more contextual forms of ethical reasoning makes many sceptical about the possibility of integrating an ethic of care into Habermas's framework. For example, Peter Dews put it to Habermas that the 'ethics of care relates to concrete others, not to the generalised other. It demands a contextualizing rather than a formal-abstract way of seeing. It keeps in mind social relations, not fixed roles, and it traces moral questions back to conflicting interests, not opposing rights. How can all these differences be subsumed under formal justice?' (Dews 1986: 250). In response Habermas says that the impression that 'a deontological ethics such as that of Kant requires us to neglect the concrete other, and his or her particular situation, arises only from a one-sided concentration on questions of grounding, which is avoidable' (Habermas 1986: 251). In making a clear distinction between 'grounding' and 'application', Habermas endorses a distinction similar to Barry's distinction between first- and second-order impartiality. He claims that, once one is clear about the complementarity of grounding and application, 'then one sees how discourse ethics can do justice to those reservations which you [Dews] share with Carol Gilligan, and also with Seyla Benhabib' (Habermas 1986: 251).

Although Habermas claims that his model of discourse ethics is itself able to incorporate the form of moral reasoning that Gilligan is concerned to articulate, Benhabib proposes that discourse ethics be modified in the light of the ethic of care. She offers a feminist revision of Habermas's work, which concentrates on a synthesis of 'generalized others', considered as equal moral agents, and 'concrete others', individuals with irreducible differences.

The dichotomous model of justice and the good life presumes the existence of two distinct ways of interacting with others. The standpoint of the 'generalized other' 'requires us to view each and every individual as a rational being entitled to the same rights and duties we would want to ascribe to ourselves' (Benhabib 1992: 158). The standpoint of the 'concrete other' 'requires us to view each and every rational being as an individual with a concrete history, identity and affective-emotional constitution' (Benhabib 1992: 159). In other words, commonality and individuality are polarized. Benhabib shares the common feminist scepticism about the privileging of the generalized other: the self, she argues, 'that is restricted to the standpoint of the generalized other becomes incoherent and cannot individuate among selves' (Benhabib 1992: 163). But she is equally clear that a political theory of justice that does not appeal to the standpoint of the generalized other is 'unthinkable' (Benhabib 1992: 164). She therefore proposes that we adopt a form of universalism that acknowledges that 'every generalized other is also a concrete other' (Benhabib 1992: 165).

Benhabib interprets Gilligan's work not as a wholesale rejection of universalism 'but as a contribution to the development of a non-formalist, contextually sensitive and postconventional understanding of ethical life' (Benhabib 1992: 158). Universalism is interpreted by Benhabib procedurally, as a test of the validity of moral judgements, principles and maxims – applied equally to issues that Habermas (and Kohlberg) would want to distinguish as 'evaluative questions of the good life' and 'moral matters of justice' (Benhabib 1992: 187). Her post-conventional understanding of ethical life challenges the presumption that the ethics of justice and caring can be clearly located within distinct spheres of life. The feminist tradition of deconstructing the operation of the public/ private dichotomy leads her to be suspicious of the move to locate the ethics of justice and caring within the public and private spheres respectively. Despite the claims of many feminist critics that Habermas's theory is 'the male particular posturing behind the veil of the universal' (Landes 1995: 98), Benhabib believes that we can pursue a universalist ethical perspective which incorporates Gilligan's insights. She challenges the notion, prevalent in political theory, that autonomy and nurturance are incompatible.

Contrary to Habermas's own insistence that discourse ethics must clearly distinguish between justice and the good life, or morality and value, Benhabib claims that discourse ethics offers an articulation of the ideal of impartiality which is able to move beyond these dichotomies. She claims that Habermas conflates the standpoint of universalist morality (which she endorses) with a 'narrow definition of the moral domain as being centred around "issues of justice"' (which she rejects) (Benhabib 1992: 185). Universalism is not antithetical to an ethic of care. It provides the constraints within which such an ethic must operate.

This project has certain affinities with the proposals of Okin and Tronto. But Benhabib is keen to differentiate Okin's suggestion that Rawlsian theory is compatible with emotional and empathetic relations from her own modification of the ideal of impartiality. Rawls and Habermas offer two different articulations of this ideal. Rawls's model is constructed as a hypothetical thought process. Habermas's model is constructed as an actual dialogue. Okin modifies the former by emphasizing the role of empathy. Benhabib contrasts empathy, which works through projection, with dialogue, which requires a more active self-definition on the part of the other. Notwithstanding these differences, a shared concern to synthesize the justice and the care perspectives emerges among these theorists.

## Justice, Caring and Difference

There are some theorists, such as Young and Coole, who are concerned that the various syntheses of justice and caring surveyed above remain inadequately attentive to difference, or alterity. Notably, Young is equally critical of the model of the self-interested, autonomous self proposed in the ethic of justice and the empathetic, connected self proposed in the ethic of care. Her concern is that both the ideal of impartiality (justice) and the ideal of shared subjectivity (caring) deny difference.

The ideal of impartiality, which offers a conception of the self as 'dispassionate, abstracting from feelings, desires, interest, and commitments that he or she may have regarding the situation' (Young 1990a: 100), denies difference in three ways. It denies the particularity of the situation. It seeks to 'eliminate heterogeneity in the form of feeling'. It reduces 'the plurality of moral subjects to one subjectivity' (Young 1990a: 100). On the other hand, the ideal of community or shared subjectivity also denies difference. On this conception people 'become fused, mutually sympathetic, understanding one another as they understand themselves. Such an ideal of shared subjectivity, or the transparency of subjects to one another, denies difference in the sense of the basic asymmetry of subjects' (Young 1986: 10). Neither option is adequate. Both are generated by an ideal of impartiality, which dichotomizes reason and feeling.

Although Young and Benhabib's arguments are fairly similar in this regard, they differ in the detail of their proposals as to how one should move beyond this false dichotomy. Young criticizes Benhabib's characterization of the 'concrete other'. Discourse ethics is not sufficiently distinct from the ideal of shared subjectivity for Young's liking. Both, Young claims, 'express a similar ideal of social relations as the *copresence of subjects*. Whether expressed as common consciousness or as mutual understanding, the ideal is one of the transparency of subjects to one another' (Young 1990a: 231). Benhabib's careful distinction between an endorsement of an ethic of care, without the contextualizing frame of the ideal of impartiality and her own position, is collapsed by Young, who rejects both as proposing an ideal of transparency of subjects to one another that denies difference.

Benhabib responds to this charge. She argues that 'Young's claim that mutual care and responsibility must presuppose a "transparency" of understanding is exaggerated' (Benhabib 1992: 197). She suggests that Young does not heed her distinction between 'consensus' and 'reaching understanding'. The latter, which is endorsed by discourse ethics, presumes 'the infinite revisability and indeterminacy of meaning' (Benhabib 1992: 198) because of its commitment to conversation, in which agreement and disagreement will always be intertwined.

The significance of this dispute between Benhabib and Young is that it focuses attention on the possibility that the ideal of impartiality (in its various articulations) excludes not only an ethic of care, but also recognition of difference, or alterity. Habermas, Young argues, 'has gone further than any other contemporary thinker in elaborating the project of a moral reason that recognised the plurality of subjects' (Young 1990a: 106). But 'even Habermas seems unwilling to abandon a standpoint of universal normative reason that transcends particularist perspectives' (Young 1990a: 106). He is, Diana Coole suggests, 'unable to attribute any emancipatory potential to alterity, or otherness, . . . because his basic ideas concerning communicative reason and an emancipatory project of modernity are predicated on its exclusion' (Coole 1996: 221).

Habermas is overtly hostile to the school of thought, which he labels postmodern or 'young conservative', that has its origins in Nietzsche and which privileges alterity. Advocates of postmodernism are accused by Habermas of making mystical appeal to something prior to reason and immune to it yet retrievable through transgressive experiences which would extinguish the rational subject. He characterizes them as equating alterity with some pre-discursive referent that precedes reason. Alterity, suggests Habermas, is viewed as 'some unspeakable and undifferentiated excitement which, he remarks, is now fashionably labelled feminine' (Coole 1996: 223).

Coole rightly points out that, for Habermas, the effects of alterity are resolutely non-emancipatory. He argues that in modernity the pre-discursive, mystical forces of alterity have been contained within religion and art, which are dismissed as apolitical. Coole is more sympathetic to Derrida's position. For Derrida recognition of alterity is not some mystical Other, but exists in the fault-lines and ruptures which structure language itself. And, if this is the case, the project of discourse ethics is undermined. To allow that even the most rational discourses will remain charged with alterity implies that to deny such alterity is to engage in a 'violent metaphysical project'.

Habermas's politics, formulated in the name of critical theory and an emancipatory project, excludes otherness and thereby particularly affects groups who are associated with it, or who forge their identities and life forms along these lines: groups marginalized by pre-discursive processes. The central question, for Coole, is whether one can afford to turn one's back on this politics, since it affects, even constructs, the capacities and opportunities of actors who would participate in the free and equal manner that discursive democracy requires.

Similarly, Young's dispute with Benhabib emerges out of her concern to recognize this alterity. She states that the 'ideal of impartial moral reason corresponds to the Enlightenment ideal of the public realm of politics as attaining the universality of a general will that leaves difference, particularity and the body behind in the private realms of family and civil society' (Young 1990a: 97). Contra this ideal, she argues that the meaning of the 'public' should be transformed to exhibit the positivity of group differences, passion and play. She suggests that 'the ideal of the civic public as expressing the general interest – the impartial point of view of reason – itself results in exclusion. By assuming that reason stands opposed to desire, affectivity and the body, this conception of the civic public excludes bodily and affective aspects of human existence' (Young 1990a: 109).

Intriguingly, Young does not reject discourse ethics altogether, as her earlier critique of the ideal of impartiality might have indicated. Instead, she suggests two modifications to discourse ethics: a weakening of the conditions of participation in conversation, and an extension of what is to count as dialogue. There are, she allows, conditions required to reach a just decision (which Young declines to label a revised ideal of impartiality), but these are weaker than those proposed in discourse ethics. They are simply a recognition of significant interdependence, a commitment to equal respect for one another, and agreement on procedural rules of fair discussion and decision-making (Young 1996a: 126). These conditions are, she claims, much thinner than that of shared understanding.

Secondly, Young recommends that the forms of communication considered significant in debates about justice be extended to include greeting, rhetoric and storytelling. Greeting entails non-linguistic gestures, such as smiles and handshakes, which bring bodies into communication. Rhetoric entails humour, wordplay, images and metaphors, which bring desire into communication. Storytelling entails narratives that exhibit subjective experience and evoke sympathy, which brings experience into communication (Young 1996a: 129–32). In short, her claim is that there is an alternative to moral theory founded on impartiality, which is communicative ethics. Whether this ideal of communicative ethics really stands in opposition to impartiality, or simply articulates a form of impartiality that attempts to be attentive to both caring and alterity, is, however, worth pondering.

## Conclusion

The debate about moral reasoning within feminist theory has been dominated by consideration of two distinct ethics: an ethic of justice and an ethic of caring. An ethic of justice (as presumed within liberal distributive justice) is contrasted with an ethic of care (as presumed within maternalist visions of politics). These have frequently been claimed to be male and female perspectives respectively, usually thought to result from differing social locations rather than from essential identities. But they have also been depicted as two distinct and incompatible perspectives manifest by dominant and subordinate groups. These groups are held to be more diverse than the universalized categories of gender alone can account for.

Feminist responses to the perceived dichotomy between justice and caring have overwhelmingly involved a renegotiation of the two ethics. The motivation for and form of this renegotiation varies. Some theorists, adopting a strategy of inclusion, propose that we extend the ethic of justice in the interests of women. Others, adopting a strategy of reversal, propose that we extend the ethic of caring in recognition of women's distinctive perspective. Many propose that we synthesize the two ethics in order to produce a more adequate morality for all. Finally some, pursuing a strategy of displacement, argue that the dichotomy between justice and caring reduces a plurality of ethical perspectives to two hierarchical opposites and that it is more useful to celebrate heterogeneity.

The justice/care debate has largely resolved itself into various attempts at resolution of what now seems to be widely viewed as an unhelpful false dichotomy. Nonetheless, it is important to recognize that the dichotomy between justice and care was accentuated within feminist theory itself and has proved particularly appealing to many feminists. The feminist literature on the ethic of care might itself have worked to reinforce the symbolic association of woman with caring. It certainly worked to mask the diversity of perspectives within mainstream political conceptions of justice. As the genealogical theorists remind us, one can never be sure that discourses claiming to be liberatory are not actually working to constrain us. Yet, as the interpretative theorist might well retort, one cannot begin to undermine a false dichotomy until one has uncovered and gained recognition for the subordinate term in the pairing. For example, although Lister proposes that we go beyond the dichotomy between justice and caring, she nonetheless endorses the idea that reversal might have been a necessary phase in the process of deconstruction. For the process has to start 'from within the very binary categories it aims to subvert' and needs 'to illuminate the hierarchical relations involved' (Lister 1997: 115). Whatever one's assessment of the rather reductive move to claim a distinctive female morality, this strategy of reversal has now largely been displaced in favour of more heterogeneous negotiations of justice, caring and alterity.

It does appear that the justice/caring debate as characterized within feminist theory has at times been an 'ill-joined battle', in that 'what the opponents are attacking is not what the supporters are defending' (Barry 1995: 191). From the perspective of second-order impartiality, the core contentions of both camps are equally valid. What the critics of impartiality are criticizing is first-order impartiality. What the defenders of impartiality are defending is second-order impartiality. To recognize that valuing the ethic of care need not also entail a rejection of impartiality per se goes some way to resolving an apparent impasse within gender theory, which arises from the too hasty rejection of impartiality. With this in mind, we will turn in the next chapter to consider how the justice/caring debate gets articulated within the literature on citizenship.

# 6

# *Citizenship*

## Introduction

Is citizenship gendered? The weight of historical tradition, the impact of contemporary political events and the preoccupations of current normative debates have all conspired to make citizenship a ubiquitous presence in most political debates. There are widespread but contradictory appeals to the concept. Citizenship is presented as both an undesirable anachronism and as a yet-to-be-realized ideal of immense political value: it has been most things to most people.

The malleability of the concept arises from its complexity. Judith Shklar defines citizenship as: 'the legal recognition, both domestic and international, that a person is a member, native-born or naturalized, of a state' (Shklar 1991: 4). Debates about citizenship are largely assumed to be debates about what it is to be a member of a state. This is necessarily a complex and multifaceted question, involving negotiation of several distinct issues.

## Complex Citizenships

Rights-based conceptions of citizenship construct membership as entitlements (focusing on the formal prerequisites for participation rather than its substantive realization and its accompanying responsibilities) granted to individuals (rather than groups) by the state (not the people directly). Each element of this liberal conception of citizenship presents its own benefits and burdens. It is formal, universalistic and statist.

One particularly influential definition of citizenship, provided by T. H. Marshall, which focused on the rights granted to the individual by the state, categorized these rights into three distinct groups: civil (liberty of the person, freedom of thought and faith and the right to justice); political (the right to participate in the exercise of political power); and social (the right to economic welfare and security, the right to live the life of a civilized being according to the standards prevailing in the society) (Marshall 1950: 10–11). Marshall's definition of citizenship proved particularly influential and still structures contemporary debate. His definition was, however, never a neutral description: it represented a dream of a post-war welfare settlement that was never realized, and the moment of which has long since been eclipsed.

Since Marshall's 1950s discussion of citizenship the concept was left largely untheorized, seeming to carry no particular contemporary weight or do much important political work. However, by the 1980s citizenship again become a central political term, focusing attention on the shifting relations between state and civil society: from the erosion of the welfare state and local democracy to the growth of European integration and global interconnectedness (Held 1991c: 19). In contemporary political debates the notion of citizenship has been reinvoked as an 'escape-route for both the right and the left', allowing the right to speak of responsibilities and the left of rights (Andrews 1991: 12).

In other words, citizenship is a concept that has a long and complex history, which has not always been conceived, as in Shklar's and Marshall's formulations, as a legal relation to the state. It has also been understood more generally as the notion of membership in the community in which one lives one's life. If one adopts, as does Held, this broad conception of citizenship as involving 'the struggle for membership and participation in the community' (Held 1991c: 20), one is able to use citizenship as a means of examining the nature and composition of 'the community' and the terms of inclusion. The nation-state is clearly but one form of community, legal inclusion but one form of membership.

The difference between these two perspectives is pivotal in current citizenship debates. The formal, universalistic and statist conceptions are pitted against the participatory, embedded and social conceptions. The issues at stake within these citizenship debates coalesce into three broad areas. Firstly, there is the question of rights versus responsibilities, involving dispute about not only the relative importance of rights and responsibilities but also the appropriate form of each. Secondly, there is the question of the universal versus the particular, focusing on the merits of transcending or recognizing cultural differences within the polity. And thirdly, there is the question of the geographically bounded state versus the commitment to universal moral norms, exploring the centrality of the sovereign nation-state and the territorial dimensions of the concept.

The gender literature on citizenship had tended to focus on the first two of these issues, usually highlighting the limitations of the rights-based, universalistic vision (usually labelled 'liberal'), but also frequently acknowledging the contrasting dangers of the responsibility-based, particularist vision (usually labelled 'communitarian'). These two conceptions of citizenship tend to be perceived as articulations of the equality and difference perspectives within feminism respectively and usually get labelled as 'equality' (or liberal) and 'maternalist' conceptions of citizenship. Although much of the feminist literature on citizenship has been shaped by a polarized opposition between these two, the trend is now towards rejecting both positions as falsely dichotomous, and exploring synthetic perspectives which draw on both traditions in the pursuit of a 'radical democratic' vision of citizenship. The central controversy here is whether such a democratic vision ought to be gender-differentiated or gender-neutral. There are also important gender concerns arising from the territorial aspects of citizenship debates which tend to be overlooked in many of these synthetic conceptions of democratic citizenship, but which are more commonly considered in world politics discourses.

Let us look at each of these debates in turn. Firstly, let us consider the debates about rights and responsibilities, universality and particularity and cosmopolitanism and territoriality. We can then look at the feminist debates for and against 'maternalist' and 'equality' conceptions of citizenship, the various attempts to move beyond this opposition via critical synthesis and, finally, thoughts on the role of territoriality in relation to these feminist conceptions of citizenship.

### Rights and responsibilities

There is a long-standing debate about how best to define citizenship, arising from whether one understands membership of a community as a status or an activity: whether one possesses citizenship rights (the liberal perspective) or participates in citizenship responsibilities (the civic republican, and latterly the communitarian, perspective). Citizenship conceived as status is realized through the acquisition of rights. These rights can be civil, political or social (Marshall 1950). Citizenship conceived as obligation is realized through activity within the community, either social or political (some conservative forms of contemporary communitarianism stressing social obligation, more radical appeals to civic republicanism stressing political participation).

The liberal model of citizenship, conceived as a set of rights enjoyed equally by every member of the society in question, embodies the ideal of justice as impartiality. Everyone has a common set of political entitlements whatever their social, cultural and economic status. Marshall, who provided perhaps the classic articulation of this position, presumed that the precise substance of these rights would be a matter of common agreement. The primary focus of concern here tends to be the relation between citizenship and economic inequality, requiring a minimum level of redistribution to overcome the pressures of social exclusion. Citizenship is conceived as a political identity working to mitigate other (primarily economic) identities.

The civic republican model of citizenship, in contrast, 'conceives the citizen as someone who plays an active role in shaping the future direction of his or her society through political debate and decision-making' (Miller 1993: 14). It augments the liberal conception of citizenship as rights with a correlative stress on responsibilities, specifically a responsibility to promote the common good of the political community through active participation in its political life. Reacting against the perceived atomism and passivity of the liberal model, the civic republican tradition emphasizes an active, collective politics as the essence of citizenship. Where the liberal conception of citizenship is overtly based upon the fact of pluralism, the civic republican one more directly presumes the common traditions and heritage of a culturally homogeneous society. It aspires to a substantive rather than a formal conception of citizenship, jettisoning the liberal attempt to distinguish the right from the good.

This model of citizenship also gets articulated in a communitarian form, which sits within this broad civic republican tradition, but which tends to emphasize social obligation rather than political participation as central to the individual's relation to the community. Communitarian critics of liberalism argue that the liberal conception of the self, and the vision of citizenship that arises from it, are inadequate. Theorists such as Michael Sandel have argued that subjectivity is socially constructed and the self must therefore be understood as contextual and inter-subjective. This has political consequences in that it is argued that the attempt to conceptualize citizens as abstract and disembedded individuals both misrepresents reality and commits liberals to an impoverished understanding of political community, or citizenship. The communitarian conception of citizenship is collective, responsibility-based, communal and embedded in particular traditions. The communitarian agenda is the remoralization of social life. The project is to enable communities to articulate and sustain a set of moral values, which will require greater attention to parenting and socialization and continual social control in the form of public shaming backed up by legal sanctions. The object of this remoralization is to produce disciplined citizens: 'citizens and community members need self-control so that they will not demand ever more services and handouts while being unwilling to pay taxes and make contributions to the commons' (Etzioni 1994: 91).

There are clearly problems attendant upon adopting either the liberal or the civic republican conceptions of citizenship. If one defines citizenship narrowly in relation to formal rights only, one is open to the charge of failing to understand the embedded nature of identity, of omitting discussion of civil society and remaining too firmly wedded to the institutions of the state. If extensively defined, citizenship becomes open to the charge that it is overly assimilatory, demanding too high a degree of conformity of its citizens, presenting a single model of the active citizen, which is actually partial and therefore substantively exclusionary. This is particularly so with the communitarian articulations of citizenship which, in emphasizing social obligation, make it more likely that many will feel themselves to be 'second-class citizens', granted formal rights of residence, but not meeting the more extensive criteria of inclusion. There is, then, a concern that citizenship can become an overly moralized discourse used to discipline a recalcitrant population into cultural conformity (Phillips 1991b: 77).

## Universality and particularity

Critics of the universalist pretensions of citizenship discourse argue that citizenship has been conceived in such a way that it claims to be inclusionary and universalist while actually and inevitably working in an exclusionary and particularist manner. Proponents of a particularistic citizenship criticize both the liberal and republican forms of citizenship, shifting the focus from the differences between them to their shared characteristics. Despite the long history of dispute between these two camps, there is a recent trend to challenge both (sometimes interchangeably) as failing to recognize the cultural particularity of social groups. Both traditions of citizenship are criticized for being 'falsely universalistic' in their portrayal of the citizen: the liberal tradition, it is argued, transcends particularity and the civic republican one suppresses it. Both are charged with 'imposing a false homogeneity' (Taylor 1992: 44), generating assimilationist and integrationist manifestations of universalism respectively (Parekh 1991: 189–90).

The assimilationist approach to citizenship requires that citizens think and behave in certain ways. It demands that they positively identify with the political community to which they formally belong and that they are actively committed to promoting its common good through participation in its political life. Its theoretical roots lie with Rousseau, for whom 'the sovereign people embodies the universal point of view of the collective interest and equal citizenship' (Young 1990a: 109). The universalism of citizenship here takes the form of a commitment to unity and cultivation of a shared notion of the common good or general will. The public realm is conceived as unified and homogeneous and stress is placed on the importance of education, shared civic traditions and celebrations to foster such unity. The critics of this assimilatory form of universalism argue that the attainment of such unification has always been, and always will be, bought at the price of the exclusion of the actual heterogeneity of society and the public denial of cultural pluralism.

In contrast, and specifically claiming to take differences seriously, the integrationist approach to citizenship requires that all citizens are formally but not substantively equal. It explicitly welcomes cultural differences and recognizes the fact of pluralism. It has in practice involved equal opportunities, coupled with cultural diversity, in an atmosphere of mutual tolerance (Parekh 1991: 190). Its theoretical roots lie with the Kantian categorical imperative and take the more recent form of the Rawlsian reflective equilibrium. Here the citizen pursues an ideal of impartiality by abstracting from all the particularities which characterize individual persons and reasoning from an Archimedean point a transcendental 'view from nowhere' (see Chapter 5). In order to engage in such reasoning, the citizen must regard their private aims and attachments as contingent and open to revision; they must be able to distinguish between personal commitments and political principles and to give priority to the latter. In other words, the citizen must adopt a form of moral reasoning and a language of liberal citizenship which, while claiming to be formal rather than substantive, actually render certain substantive positions ineligible because non-universalizable.

Despite the severity of the critiques of universalism, many are still wedded to a reformulation of citizenship as ideal and practice, reluctant to forgo the political and moral power of appeal to the ideals of equality and universality (Phillips 1992). Rather than rejecting universalism altogether and opting for particularism, many theorists actually seek to develop a differentiated universalism as opposed to the false universalism of 'traditional citizenship theory' (Lister 1997). The paradox is that those who would replace traditional citizenship theory with a more differentiated vision of social and political inclusion want to critique universalism while recognizing that it is precisely in the universality of citizenship that it gains its political force for subordinate social groups.

## Cosmopolitanism and territoriality

Although the pursuit of a critical synthesis between these two traditions of citizenship theory (universal rights and particular responsibilities) is hugely valuable, one should retain a continued sense of the partiality of the debate itself. In focusing on the differences between these perspectives, the discourse of political theory has tended to occlude their similarities. Notably, each assumes citizenship to exist within a territorially bounded nation-state and aspires to a form of inclusion within its boundaries.

Formal citizenship status is granted by the state. Citizenship claims are claims made against the state. Citizenship debates, though internally complex, do nonetheless tend to presume a shared territorial boundary. They focus primarily on the relation between people and the state, where these people have basic legal citizenship. However, given the increasing number of people who are not able to issue entitlement claims against any state, many theorists are increasingly drawn to an exploration of the potential for a conception of citizenship that transcends national boundaries, usually located in the notion of international human rights.

The central question here is whether one could or should disentangle citizenship status from the state. There are pressing practical reasons that propel many to consider the possibility of formulating a discourse of 'global citizenship' that might prefigure the establishment of an institutional framework to secure such global citizenship rights. As Narayan points out, 'many countries have substantial numbers of immigrants who are legally part of its ongoing workforce but who are not eligible for citizenship and lack political, social and civil rights as non-citizens' (Narayan 1997: 61). If one is to attend to the immigrants, refugees, exiles, guestworkers and other moving groups that constitute an essential feature of the contemporary world, it is possible that the state-based conception of citizenship stands in need of either reformulation or augmentation.

While some suggest citizenship may be rendered anachronistic by the globalization process, others counter that globalization has had not one but two effects on the state in relation to citizenship. The state's autonomy is eroded, but its gate-keeping role is intensified (Hirst and Thompson 1996: 190). As Lister notes, 'in an era of extensive migration across an economically polarised world, the boundary-staking functions of citizenship as a legal status have become more prominent' (Lister 1997: 43). In this context, the right to enter or remain in a country is a critical issue for citizenship which is completely outside the agenda of Marshallian theories of citizenship but crucial to contemporary citizenship debates (Narayan 1997: 61).

Marshall argued that citizenship had incrementally come to include not only civil and political rights but also social rights. This brought about an active conception of citizenship where citizenship required not only formal access but also material conditions to enable substantive participation. The transformations in the global economy are such that states are now increasingly reprivatizing these responsibilities, re-emphasizing the civil aspects of citizenship and downplaying the social aspects. Given the changing form of the state, the current concern is whether one can take seriously the rights of non-citizens while using citizenship as a strategy for improving the rights of existing citizens.

It has become increasingly clear that to contemplate citizenship from the standpoint of particular group identities is to confront the presumed universality of traditional citizenship theory. The very factors that propel such a wide range of theorists to make appeal to 'citizenship' as a common status which might provide a framework for a just and peaceful co-existence also seem to expose citizenship as an impossible and even oppressive discourse. The simultaneous desirability and impossibility of the neutral state and universal citizenship becomes the increasingly pronounced paradox that haunts these debates.

## Feminist Perspectives on Citizenship

Feminist theory has focused critically on the role of hierarchical dichotomies within political theory: dichotomies such as public and private (discussed in Chapter 1), reason and emotion (discussed in Chapter 3), equality and difference (discussed in Chapter 4), justice and caring (discussed in Chapter 5). As Susan James points out, the 'first terms of these pairs characterize the public sphere, while the second serve to limit it by showing what it excludes' (James 1992: 48). And, as this public sphere has been cast as male and defined in opposition to the private sphere of women, 'women lack full membership of the political world and are not full citizens' (James 1992: 48).

It has been shown that, despite the universalist rhetoric on which they were based, civil, political and social citizenship were granted to different social groups within a given territory at differential rates (Walby 1997: 171). Moreover, not only did different social groups gain access to citizenship at differing rates and times, they also gained these rights in divergent progressions. Walby notes that, 'in the case of British women, political citizenship was at least as often the power base from which women were able to win civil citizenship, as vice versa' (Walby 1997: 172). Movement towards the acquisition of social citizenship came later again, with the development of the welfare state. Full social citizenship is argued to elude women still, as access to social citizenship rights (such as state pensions) are largely derived from being in paid employment and fail to recognize the long-term care work undertaken within the family by many women. Given this historical experience, numerous feminist theorists have focused on uncovering, explaining and challenging the disparity between the claims of liberal citizenship and the reality of women's exclusion.

The manner in which the concept of citizenship has been considered within feminist theory has followed the general pattern of moving from inclusion to reversal to displacement: from an attempt to add women into existing citizenship structures; to a rejection of the dominant conception of citizenship itself; and on to an assessment of the extent to which discourses of citizenship have worked to construct gendered identities themselves. This general schema is, however, complicated in citizenship debates by (at least) two factors. Firstly, there is clearly no single dominant conception of citizenship into which one might seek inclusion. The liberal and the civic republican traditions, each of which is rich and complex, offer two distinct understandings of what inclusion might entail. This fact has not always been fully recognized within recent feminist debates.

The second thing that complicates the schema is the distinction between civil, social and political citizenship. The strategies of inclusion, reversal and displacement have been applied to three, largely discrete, debates about civil, social and political citizenship. The civil debate focuses on issues of legal status and rights; the social on care work versus paid employment; and the political on questions of democratic practices and constitutional guarantees. The social aspects of citizenship have been the focus of extensive feminist critique (Lister 1990, Lister 1997, Bubeck 1995a, Glendinning 1990, Nelson 1984). Indeed, feminist considerations of citizenship have tended to concentrate on the sphere of social citizenship almost to the exclusion of considering 'the kind of politics that citizenship implies' (Phillips 1993: 79). The rejection of the narrow focus on the political (discussed in the Introduction) has led to the political aspects of citizenship being somewhat underdeveloped.

Feminist political theorists have recently begun to address this lack. For example, Mouffe states that, 'far from being a sign of political maturity', the absence of a political frontier 'is the symptom of a void that can endanger democracy' (Mouffe 1993: 5). Phillips too notes that, in contrast to that vision of citizenship that stresses social responsibilities, she finds citizenship 'most useful and meaningful when it is considered as a primarily *political* term' (Phillips 1991a: 77). This, she tells us, marks a distinct shift within the terms of debate about gender and citizenship, which in previous decades tended to use the claim that the 'personal is political' to side-step the political and instead 'concentrate on transforming and democratizing the economic and social spheres' (Phillips 1993: 85). In contrast, this recent feminist move to affirm a specifically political citizenship works to reaffirm the significance of the boundary around a public political sphere.

Whether focused on the civil, social or political aspects, the central feature of feminist debates on citizenship has been the opposition between gender-neutral and gender-differentiated visions of citizenship, and the attempt to displace the apparent opposition between the two. As Walby says, 'whether women are intrinsically different from men and should value this difference, or are basically the same and should claim the same rights on the basic of this similarity, is a key philosophical, theoretical and political division in feminist analysis and practice' (Walby 1997: 175). The gender-neutral vision of citizenship can take either a liberal or a civic republican form. This reduces the focus on the differences between these two and emphasizes their similarities in relation to the gender-differentiated model. As with the debates about equality and difference, and about justice and caring, a third position has emerged which aims to displace the apparent dichotomy between these two. So, in relation to social citizenship, for example, there is debate as to whether women should campaign for inclusion within social citizenship via entry into the labour market (the strategy of inclusion) or via a revaluing of women's position as carer (the strategy of reversal). Theorists such as Lister, who suggests both the entry of women into the public labour market and that their presence in the private sphere of caring be acknowledged, seek to synthesize the two (Lister 1990: 464).

## Maternalist citizenship

Arguments for the inclusion of women as equal citizens are widely assumed to be a necessary initial corrective to women's historical exclusion, but one that ought to lead on to a more fundamental consideration of the criteria of inclusion themselves. Maternalist visions of citizenship are specifically conceived so as to counter the impoverished vision offered by the individualist, rights-based conceptions of citizenship proposed by liberal theorists.

Elshtain, who is widely held to be one of the key advocates of this position, states: 'no substantive sense of civic virtue, no vision of political community that might serve as the groundwork of a life in common, is possible within a political life dominated by a self-interested, predatory, individualism' (Elshtain 1982b: 617). In direct contrast to the ideal of a formal, universalist and statist conception of citizenship (which is claimed to justify, in reality, a conflictual and instrumental practice), this maternalist vision is informal, particularist and communitarian. It stands in direct opposition to the liberal conception: 'for the maternalist', Dietz suggests, 'such a notion is at best morally empty and at worst morally subversive since it rests on a distinctly masculine conception of the person as an independent, self-interested, economic being' (Dietz 1998: 386). The shift from working towards inclusion to celebrating reversal is clear.

The maternalist version of citizenship, which proposes the feminine values of the private sphere as the basis for a new model of citizenship, is usually attributed to Ruddick and Elshtain (Ruddick 1983, Ruddick 1989, Elshtain 1981). It draws substantially on an ethic of care (as discussed in the previous chapter). It is, in effect, a version of the communitarian vision which prioritizes community as the basis for politics, a community which shares not only a spirit of benevolence and certain shared final ends but also a common vocabulary of discourse (Sandel 1996). This maternal citizenship is based on the values of the private sphere, emotional rather than rational relations, the recognition of difference rather than the aspiration to equality. Maternal thinking, Elshtain suggests, 'requires paying a special sort of attention to the concrete specificity of each child; it turns on a special kind of knowledge of this child, this situation, without the notion of seizure, appropriation, control or judgement by impersonal standards. What maternal thinking could lead to ... is a wider diffusion of what attentive love to all children is about and how it might become a wider social imperative' (Elshtain 1998: 375). Here the community is conceived as a community of women and the conception of the good a feminized one. Maternalists seek to reject the dominant terms in the dichotomous pairings generated by liberal political theory and to revalorize the subordinate pairings as the basis for a reconceived citizenship.

Maternalist citizenship manifests the same strengths and weaknesses as the communitarian responsibility-based vision. Its strengths *vis-à-vis* the liberal conception are that it encompasses more than the reductive notion of individualist rights-based contractual citizenship and offers a vision of a substantive good which might mobilize a sense of loyalty, belonging and caring in members of a community. Its weakness is that its vision of community is often nostalgic and cohesive, actually working to exclude all those who do not conform to its particular conception of the good.

Both its strengths and weaknesses can be witnessed in the practical developments of feminist political action within Britain throughout the 1970s and 1980s. The women's movement did much to generate new models for citizenship participation. One of the defining characteristics of much second-wave feminist activism was the extent to which it challenged the procedural conception of citizenship and inspired the active participation of women in small informal action groups: hierarchy was shunned, the rotating of responsibilities was instituted, expertise and authority were divided and shared. Meetings were perceived, not primarily as decision-making mechanisms, but as spaces for sharing experiences and ideas. The political become personal on all levels, the agenda for debate changed, the procedures for discussion altered. The association of politics and friendship was valorized (Phillips 1991a). In short, the participatory, informal aspects of citizenship were fostered and celebrated within these feminist practices, while the formal, statist aspects were roundly rejected.

This form of direct democratic participation was clearly invigorating and emancipatory (for some), but it was not without its political problems. As Phillips observes, it was not long before people noted the limits of friendship: 'the most serious being that it is impossible to include everyone in the circle of your friends, and that it is hard to disagree without more fundamentally falling out' (Phillips 1991a: 125). This recognition of the failings of friendship as the basis for politics highlighted some of the problems inherent in the too-hasty rejection of the universalist rights-based conception of citizenship in favour of a total embrace of a particularistic responsibility-based model. To demand that political actors are also personal allies was to demand too much: it undermined the possibility of affinity despite differences, of debate without pre-given consensus, of understanding despite opacity.

In recent years the trade-off between the intensity of commitment among those involved in the women's movement, and the ability of the movement to extend its appeal, has become clear. It has also become clear that the definition of a 'we' implies the delimitation of a 'frontier' and the designation of a 'them'. The creation of a cohesive community requires the simultaneous creation of a 'constitutive outside', exterior to the community and a precondition for its existence. The realization that all forms of consensus are by necessity based on acts of exclusion was experienced, often painfully, within the day-to-day operation of the women's movement, which ultimately fragmented under the strain of the assertions of marginalization from women who were not part of the community. The bitter reproaches levelled at the primarily white, middle-aged, middle-class and heterosexual women involved in the women's movement by women who were not shattered the illusion of cohesion and unity. As Young tells us, the 'striving for mutual identification and shared understanding among those who seek to foster a radical and progressive politics, can and has led to denying or suppressing differences within political groups or movements' (Young 1990a: 312). To demand such cohesion, she argues, is to deny the possibility of a fully inclusive citizenship. The fragmentation of the women's movement was therefore a practical warning of the impossibility of achieving fully inclusive cohesive communities as the basis for citizenship. In the light of this experience, both feminist practice and theory moved away from the search for unity and the celebration of a single maternal, caring, vision of citizenship.

## Feminist civic republican citizenship theory

Dietz has been one of the most influential critics of the maternalist conception of citizenship (which she believes Elshtain to advocate). She argues against maternalism not only because the maternalists 'threaten to turn historically distinctive women into ahistorical, universalized entities' (Dietz 1998: 389), but also because they are mistaken in their conviction that maternal thinking is, or could be, political.

Dietz suggests that maternalists offer a choice between an impoverished conception of citizenship as impersonal, representative government and an apolitical conception of citizenship based on the intimate bond between mother and child. 'The problem for a feminist conception is that neither of the above will do, because both leave us with a one-sided view of politics and therefore citizenship. What we need is an entirely different conception' (Dietz 1998: 389). Dietz's point is that feminists 'should turn to the virtues, relations, and practices that are expressly political and, more exactly, participatory and democratic' (Dietz 1998: 390). Her conception of the political as participatory and democratic differs (she claims) from both the liberal model of representative government and the maternalist model of mothering in that it emphasizes the 'collective and participatory engagement of citizens in the determination of the affairs of their community' (Dietz 1998: 390). As such, she invokes the civic republican tradition of citizenship theory.

Democratic citizenship, Dietz asserts, should not be confused with the liberal politics of pressure groups and representative government. A democratic vision and a feminist citizenship must be more than this; it entails engaging in public debate and sharing responsibility for self-government (Dietz 1998: 391–2). Dietz feels that this vision of democratic citizenship is one that feminists are particularly well placed to resuscitate, given the feminist commitment to 'spontaneous gatherings and marches, diverse and multitudinous action groups, face-to-face assemblies, consensus decision making, non-hierachical power structures, open speech and debate' (Dietz 1998: 393).

Here Dietz's argument is similar to that of Elshtain, who also contends that women's exclusion from full citizenship has paradoxically granted them a freedom from the prevailing orthodoxy of efficiency and control and allows them space for critical reflection and challenge (Elshtain 1992a: 119). The difference between these two insights, though, is that, whereas Elshtain speaks of women's moral insights, Dietz speaks of feminists' political practices. Dietz also insists on the need for a comprehensive theory of citizenship: feminist political practice, she states, 'will not in some automatic way become an inspiration for a new citizenship. Instead, feminists must become self-conscious political thinkers' (Dietz 1998: 393).

Pateman also invokes the civic republican tradition of citizenship and argues both liberal and maternalist conceptions of citizenship to be a product of the same problematic bifurcation of life into two contrasting realms. If, she notes, ' "motherhood" represents all that excluded women from citizenship, motherhood has also been constructed as a political status' (Pateman 1992: 18–19). This second insight is lost in the maternalist celebration of all that has been excluded from liberal conceptions of citizenship. The maternalist approach invokes only half of the story. It emphasizes that women's distinctive capacities (to become pregnant, give birth and suckle their infants) have been directly opposed to those characteristics deemed necessary for participation in full citizenship relations, and that citizenship gained its meaning through the exclusion of women. What is largely overlooked is the fact that women were not only excluded, but also included 'on the basis of the very same capacities and attributes' (Pateman 1992: 19). Women were incorporated, but differently from men: they were included as mothers. In other words, the power of this masculine citizenship discourse was productive as well as repressive.

Such arguments have been central to the move to develop a citizenship theory that displaces the apparent dichotomy between liberalism and maternalism. The civic republican tradition offers a frame from which both the impoverished formal, rights-based citizenship and a cohesive familial maternal citizenship appear overly restrictive in their contrasting ways.

## Rejecting Both Maternalism and Universalism

There is disagreement, however, as to whether these twin critiques of maternalism and liberalism ought to entail the invocation of the civic republican tradition. While Dietz argues that they should, Chantal Mouffe and Iris Young argue that they should not. Dietz's position is that the civic republican tradition prioritizes democratic participation in its stress on collective action and the transformation of individual interests and identities into shared ideals through democratic engagement (Dietz 1998). Mouffe, on the other hand, equates civic republicanism not so much with active political participation as with a communitarian 'insistence on a substantive notion of the common good and shared moral values'

(Mouffe 1992b: 378). In other words, for Mouffe, civic republicanism implies not political participation but social obligation. She therefore differentiates her own position from both of these: citizenship, she tells us, 'is not just one identity among others, as it is in Liberalism, nor is it the dominant identity that overrides all others, as it is in Civic Republicanism' (Mouffe 1992b: 378).

Similarly, Young finds the liberal and the civic republican traditions equally guilty of projecting 'an ideal of universal citizenship' (Young 1998: 401). She too warns against simply replacing an impoverished conception of liberal citizenship with a civic republican conception, which provides the notion of the general will. The civic republican tradition may stand in 'critical tension' with individualistic contract theory, but shares a common commitment to universalism. And this commitment necessarily entails the exclusion of all groups that threaten to explode the unity of the polity (Young 1998: 404–5).

Mouffe offers a resolution of the rights-based and participatory approaches to citizenship, stressing the centrality of the notion of rights complemented by a more active sense of political participation and belonging (Mouffe 1992b: 378). Mouffe, like Dietz, endorses the participatory vision of citizenship, but is clear about the centrality of rights for citizenship and the dangers of a substantive notion of common good. She distances herself from the communitarian renderings of participatory visions of citizenship by clearly differentiating between social and political communities. The only notion of community which is acceptable as the basis for citizenship is, she argues, an ethico-political community – a community which accepts the procedural mechanisms of democracy. Arguing that all other communities are partial and exclusionary, the only community that Mouffe allows as the basis for political action in a political community is a group 'bound by their common identification with a given interpretation of a set of ethico-political values' (Mouffe 1992b: 378). The community of women is an identity-based community, which ought not to be a basis for political action.

Mouffe shares Dietz's sense that we need to replace the specifically liberal, male conception of modern citizenship not with a specifically maternal, female conception of future citizenship, but with a radical democratic conception of citizenship (Mouffe 1992b: 377). From this perspective a concern with gender in relation to citizenship entails an endorsement of neither a male nor a female form of citizenship, but a rejection of the notion of a gender-differentiated citizenship model altogether. In the context of citizenship (though not necessarily in terms of all aspects of life) gender is pertinent only to an analysis of what has been, not to a theory of what could be. Mouffe's argument is that sexual difference is a product of particular social discourses, which can be subject to change. There is no reason why all social discourses should draw distinctions of sexual identity. She favours making citizenship one particular discourse in which sexual difference is non-pertinent.

For this reason Mouffe is unable to accept Pateman's claim that 'motherhood and citizenship remain intimately linked' (Pateman 1992: 29). Pateman's proposal for a differentiated citizenship that recognizes the specificity of womanhood rests, Mouffe claims, 'on the identification of women *as* women with motherhood' (Mouffe 1992b: 375). Mouffe and Pateman share the same basic critique of the universalist pretensions of liberal citizenship practices to date. Mouffe accepts Pateman's argument that the individual has been constructed 'in a manner that postulates a universalist, homogeneous "public" that relegates all particularity and difference to the "private" and that this has very negative consequences for women' (Mouffe 1992b: 376). What she does not accept, however, is the claim that the remedy to this state of affairs entails advocating a sexually differentiated citizenship. In Mouffe's view, Pateman's assertion of the political value of motherhood is a mistaken endorsement of an essentialist politics that generates an inadequate conception of democratic citizenship.

Whether this is indeed the case is a highly contentious point. What is significant, though, is that Mouffe's scepticism about the universalism of the liberal conception of citizenship leads her not to contrast it with a maternalist citizenship, but to balance it with the participatory vision of the republican conception of citizenship. In other words, although Mouffe explicitly engages with the discourses of 'feminism, citizenship and radical democratic politics', her project is best characterized as a proposal that particular elements of both the liberal and the republican traditions of citizenship be synthesized to generate a radical democratic politics. It is not to develop a specifically feminist theory of citizenship.

The central problem with the liberal conception of citizenship, Mouffe argues, is that it has 'reduced citizenship to a merely legal status, indicating the rights that the individual holds against the state' (Mouffe 1992b: 377). She notes, as generations of republican thinkers have noted, that notions of public-spiritedness, civic activity and political participation have been excluded by this overly narrow rights-based approach. However, she also notes, as an equally long tradition of liberal theorists have noted, that the communitarian insistence on a substantive notion of the common good and shared moral values is incompatible with pluralism (Mouffe 1992b: 378). A 'modern pluralist democracy' would, in Mouffe's estimation, negotiate both of these potential dangers by casting citizenship as a political identity that consists in the identification with the assertion of liberty and equality for all.

Whereas liberalism evacuates the idea of a common good, and republicanism (and maternalism) reifies it, a radical democratic approach views the common good as something that we constantly refer to but that can never be reached. This is so because a radical democratic vision of citizenship requires recognition of the numerous relations of domination that deny people liberty and equality and necessitate that people articulate their differences, but also requires that these differences be articulated as 'relations of equivalence'.

So far the arguments of Mouffe are very similar to those proposed by Young. Young also criticizes modern conceptions of citizenship as asserting a claim of homogeneity and universality, which has the effect of relegating differences to the private sphere. She also accepts that these differences are numerous (and not only gendered). Like Mouffe, she proposes a vision of citizenship that is participatory without demanding an overly cohesive conception of the common good. She too is concerned to create a form of democratic citizenship that is able to recognize diversity within the polity. But, unlike Mouffe, she proposes a form of 'group-differentiated citizenship'.

Although Young is overtly critical of the liberal ideal of citizenship, she, like Mouffe, is also sceptical about the republican vision of the responsible citizen. The problem arises, she feels, from the interpretation of responsibility 'as transcendence into a general perspective' (Young 1998: 414). Given the existence of social groups with different experiences and perspectives, such a general perspective simply does not exist (the discussion of interpretation in Chapter 3 is relevant here). The impossibility of any one social group being able to speak for them all requires that all such groups be specifically represented in the public sphere.

Young claims that the 'modern' or 'Enlightenment' ideal of impartiality seeks to reduce differences to unity 'by abstracting from the particularities of situation, feeling, affiliation, and point of view' (Young 1990a: 97). The ideal entails a vision of the public realm as attaining the universality of a general will by jettisoning all particularity to the private sphere. In practice, this was achieved by the exclusion from the public realm of those groups perceived to embody particularity, 'especially women, Blacks, American Indians, and Jews' (Young 1990a: 97). In the pursuit of a single, universal set of principles to govern the public realm, complex difference is necessarily repressed, paradoxically creating dichotomy instead of unity. If the citizen is understood to be a 'universal reasoner', detached and impartial, he or she must abstract from the 'partiality of affiliation, of social or group perspective, that constitutes concrete subjects' (Young 1990a: 100). The result is that members of minority social groups are either excluded from citizenship or included only to the extent to which they are able to repress the particularity of their identity. Given that the universalist ideal 'continues to threaten the exclusion of some', argues Young, 'the meaning of "public" should be transformed to exhibit the positivity of group difference, passion and play' (Young 1990a: 97).

Structures of group representation are required if all people are to be fully granted citizenship status, which requires 'the full and free expression of concrete needs and interests' (Young 1998: 415). However, this articulation of group interest is then assessed according to criteria of public justice. By incorporating a Habermasian conception of communicative ethics (as discussed in Chapter 5) into her model of group representation, Young aims to distinguish her vision of citizenship from both interest-group pluralism and universalist civic republicanism.

Group differences are understood not only in terms of different needs and interests, but also in terms of different values and modes of expression. A differentiated vision of citizenship requires that each social group 'affirms the presence of the others and affirms the specificity of its experience and perspective on social issues' (Young 1998: 416–17). In other words, her conception of citizenship differs from interest group pluralism in two ways: it entails special representation for oppressed social groups (defined in Young 1990a: 48–63) only, which are characterized by identities rather than interests (Young 1990a: 42–8); and it promotes rather than forestalls the emergence of public discussion (Young 1998: 418–19). In other words, the particularities that this proposal seeks to recognize are social identities, not economic interests: recognition of such particularities is intended to provide the basis for public debate, not a replacement of it. So, although it differs from interest-group pluralism, it also differs from civic republican conceptions of citizenship in that it rejects the aspiration to transcend the particularity of social experience in political debate.

A differentiated citizenship, Young argues, requires mechanisms of group representation. (We will consider what sort of structures of representation this conception of a differentiated citizenship implies in Chapter 7.) Any real commitment to increasing political equality must grapple with the fact that 'the equality of citizenship makes some people more powerful citizens' (Young 1998: 410). This 'paradox of democracy' can be solved only by providing institutionalized means for 'the explicit recognition and representation of oppressed groups' (Young 1998: 410). The group representation envisaged implies institutional mechanisms and public resources being structured so as to support the self-organization of group members; the voicing of their analysis of how policy proposals affect them; and the granting of veto power regarding specific policies that affect the group directly (Young 1998: 413). Young is keen to point out that these groups should be understood in relational, not essentialist, terms. The social groups she would positively recognize in her vision of differentiated citizenship are products of social relations and are therefore fluid and intersecting.

Although they share so much in common, Mouffe finds Young's proposals for group recognition unappealing. The problem with Young's approach, Mouffe argues, is that it is actually indistinct from an interest-group pluralism in which the interests and identities of group members are presumed to be given prior to their engagement in politics. This means that politics ceases to be about the construction of new identities, and becomes simply a matter of satisfying existing identities. Mouffe contrasts this with her own vision of democratic citizenship, which aims at the construction of a common political identity that cannot be achieved without the transformation of existing identifications (Mouffe 1992b: 380).

Young argues that, as a social group, women are subject to four of the five faces of oppression (exploitation, powerlessness, cultural imperialism and violence) and therefore require group representation (Young 1990a: 64). Mouffe, in contrast, specifically reasons that 'the limitation of the modern conception of citizenship should be remedied, not by making sexual difference politically relevant to its definition, but by constructing a new conception of citizenship where sexual difference should become effectively non-pertinent' (Mouffe 1992b: 376). These two visions of citizenship endorse qualitatively different mechanisms of political representation. We will consider the implications, and merits, of these proposals in the next chapter. And, though their critique of the liberal, the civic republican and the maternalist visions of citizenship are in many regards similar, they conclude by endorsing very different proposals regarding gender-neutral and gender-differentiated citizenship.

*Liberal citizenship reconsidered*

One of the central differences between Mouffe and Young in this debate emerges from the disparity between Young's insistence that we reject both liberal and civic republican models as unacceptably universalist and Mouffe's determination to articulate a viable form of political liberalism, incorporating elements of a civic republican tradition. This disagreement is significant because it points to the tension surrounding two distinct responses to liberalism within this subgroup of feminist perspectives on citizenship. The first offers a vision of the liberal (formal, universal and statist) conception of citizenship as a single coherent entity, to be accepted or rejected as a whole. The second proposes instability within liberal thought and the need to reconfigure its elements in a renewed fashion.

For example, James argues that 'it is a mistake to see the oppositions around which liberal theory is organised as lined up like two rows of dominoes, each male term facing its inferior female counterpart with implacable hostility. The relations within and between pairs are . . . much more diverse' (James 1992: 49). This perception, clearly adopting a strategy of displacement and proposing the deconstruction of false dichotomies, is an archetypal example of the diversity perspective. The political consequences of embarking on this project are, as is usually the case with the genealogical method, to undermine the clear-cut distinction between the mainstream and the feminist positions and to destabilize the political opposition between oppressive and liberatory discourses. There is, James states, 'more continuity between liberal and feminist conceptions of citizenship than is generally appreciated' (James 1992: 49). Similarly, Nash argues that the relation between liberalism and feminism is ambivalent rather than simply unhappy (Nash 1998: 1). And Phillips maintains that the 'preoccupation with liberal democracy as a totalizing system we must be either "for" or "against" proves relatively unhelpful, for it attributes to liberal democracy a greater theoretical fixity than is confirmed by its subsequent history' (Phillips 1993: 105).

It is important to recognize, Phillips tells us, that liberal democratic citizenship has already evolved, under the pressure of labour and social democratic parties and also of feminism, in ways that have altered the boundary of the public and changed the character of citizenship. Given this, it is unhelpful to assume that it is not capable of further modification in order to deal with the differential treatment of women (Phillips 1993: 109). Nash too considers different historically specific forms of liberalism in detail and shows how feminism has used liberal categories counter-hegemonically. Feminists, she claims, have been able to use liberalism in distinctively feminist ways because of the undecidability of the category of women in liberal political thought (Nash 1998: 140). So, for instance, the continued characterization of women as both rights-holding individuals capable of entering into contracts in the public sphere and subordinate mothers needed to care for others in the private sphere allows women to draw on these conflicting roles in a potentially disruptive way. Nash embraces a strategy of displacement rather than inclusion, but nonetheless argues that liberalism offers invaluable resources for feminism – precisely because of its ambivalence about the nature and role of women.

Feminist critiques of liberal conceptions of citizenship should not, then, be interpreted as necessarily requiring the rejection of liberal citizenship, but rather as a call for further democratization within the framework of liberal democracy itself. As Phillips says: 'A richer and more equal democracy may still be possible within the broad framework liberal democracy implies' (Phillips 1993: 114). Or, as Nash says: 'the feminist project – which aims for equal rights for women – must be part of a wider project, that of radical democracy – which is concerned with equal rights for all, including men' (Nash 1998: 146). It is this characterization of the feminist project, rather than the maternalist one, that tends to predominate in current theoretical literature.

In some authors' work, even the concern about its universalism becomes muted. The rejection of universalism and the celebration of particularity represents such a significant strand within second-wave feminist theory that a substantial sea-change in theoretical mood is marked if the merits of universalism are rearticulated. Notably, Phillips asks: 'When people query the universalizing pretension of previous traditions, do they thereby limit their radical potential and blunt the edge of any critical attack?' (Phillips 1993: 58). Phillips's sense is that they do – that 'ditching all the abstract universals and putting concrete difference in their place' is not progress (Phillips 1993: 65). The truly important project is to build unity without denying social difference. The pursuit of this project will require that feminists avoid overstating the opposition between these two: 'presenting the orthodoxy as more straightforwardly abstract and universal than is in fact the case' (Phillips 1993: 70). In short, the requirement that one must choose between inclusion and reversal comes to look questionable.

Capturing the mood for going beyond dichotomous thinking perfectly, Phillips feels that feminists who challenge the universalism of traditional citizenship theory are at 'their most persuasive, not in counterposing the particular to the general, the sexually specific to the universal, but in emphasizing the interplay between the two' (Phillips 1993: 70). Similarly Lister tells us that: 'rejecting the "false universalism" of traditional citizenship theory does not mean abandoning citizenship as a universalist goal. Instead we can aspire to a universalism that stands in creative tension to diversity and difference' (Lister 1997: 66). Neither Phillips nor Lister underestimates the extent of the challenge posed in negotiating such a differentiated universalism as the basis for a feminist formulation of citizenship, but both see the tension as a creative one.

### Beyond binaries

The most significant trend in recent feminist writing on citizenship is definitely towards the displacement of the false oppositions upon which a liberal conception of citizenship is understood to have been based.

Both inclusion and reversal are widely held to be inadequate responses to the dilemmas of women and citizenship, and displacement is now a favoured project. This entails undermining, rather than accepting, the opposition between the liberal and the maternalist conceptions of citizenship and working to reveal internal ambivalences within, and shared ambitions between, the two.

Although most theorists now claim to be negotiating a distinctive position which avoids the constraints of narrow liberal, republican or maternalist visions, most are nonetheless perceived by other theorists as advocates of one or other of these positions (despite their own denials). There is a rather disconcerting tendency within this citizenship debate to argue for the need to move beyond binaries via a strategy of criticizing others as located within an unhelpful binary, while positioning oneself as beyond it. We can see this in the exchanges between Elshtain, Dietz, Pateman, Mouffe and Brown.

Dietz calls Elshtain a maternalist and rejects her position (Dietz 1998: 386–9), while Pateman calls Dietz an equality theorist and rejects her position (Pateman 1992: 21). Pateman is then cast as a difference theorist by Mouffe, who argues that Pateman's critique of liberal citizenship, though more sophisticated than maternal thinking, 'shares some common features' with it (Mouffe 1992b: 374). Despite all Pateman's provisos intended to distinguish her position from a maternalist one, Mouffe still finds it unsatisfactory. In other words, Dietz categorizes Elshtain as a maternalist and herself as offering a republican 'participatory' theory, Pateman categorizes Dietz as an equality theorist and herself as integrative, and Mouffe categorizes Pateman as a maternalist and herself as offering an integrated 'radical democratic' citizenship model.

Mouffe is then herself cast, despite all her own critiques of liberalism and attempts to distinguish her vision of radical democracy from classic liberalism, as problematically liberal by Brown. What is difficult to discern about Mouffe's radical democratic vision, Brown states, is precisely where the radicalism lies. 'What constitutes the ostensible departure from liberal democracy', she asks, 'and from the forms of domination liberalism both perpetuates and obscures?' (Brown 1995: 11). Brown's particular concern is that in this vision of radical democracy, as with the liberal one, the political is assumed to have relative autonomy from the economic.

Despite this apparently antagonistic series of exchanges, all these theorists appear, when one looks at their positive conceptions of citizenship, to be advocating a very similar thing: participatory democracy. For instance, despite Dietz's characterization of her as a maternalist, Elshtain actually argues for the need to move beyond thinking boringly in inherited categories and to reject binary opposites (Elshtain 1992a: 119).

She, like Dietz, feels that: 'reversals and the valorization of that which was marginalized proffer short-term satisfaction but little by way of concrete, political engagement and an incitement to social change and commitment' (Elshtain 1992a: 124). She, like Dietz, believes that 'equality remains a powerful term of political discourse and an instrument for social change and justice, one of the strongest weapons the (relatively) powerless have at their disposal in order to make their case and define their claims' (Elshtain 1992a: 124). She, like Dietz, adopts a conception of politics as an inter-subjective interaction towards communal goals; a mode of activity which cannot be defined by the gender of its actors, and which is characterized by 'public speech and principles' (Elshtain 1981: 168–9). In other words, Elshtain's vision of citizenship appears to have rather more in common with Dietz's, and rather less in common with the vision of maternalist citizenship rejected by Dietz, than one might imagine.

Similarly, despite Pateman's characterization of her as an equality theorist, Dietz actually argues that the apparent opposition between equality and maternal politics is specious (Dietz 1998: 389). She, like Pateman and Elshtain, feels that 'both leave us with a one-sided view of politics and therefore of citizenship' (Dietz 1998: 389). She, like Pateman and Elshtain, argues for a vision of politics that is participatory and democratic, which takes politics 'to be the collective and participatory engagement of citizens in the determination of the affairs of their community' (Dietz 1998: 390). In other words, all three would seem to endorse a vision of democracy that brings us together as citizens and 'gives us a conception of ourselves as "speakers of words and doers of deeds" mutually participating in the public realm' (Dietz 1998: 390). In short, despite all the apparent hostility and opposition, all the theorists considered here endorse the notion that a genuinely democratic citizenship would require that 'both sexes are full citizens and that their citizenship is of equal worth to them as women and men' (Pateman 1992: 28).

## Territoriality Reconsidered

The recent move to theorize an explicitly and distinctly political form of citizenship offers invaluable resources for considering issues of political participation and representation. But it can also work to refocus citizenship debates back on the state. The political focus illuminates questions regarding the criteria of inclusion within the nation-state, but does little to address the continuing issue of exclusion from the nation-state.

We have, to date, focused in this chapter on feminist approaches to citizenship theory. But it is also worth briefly considering citizenship discourses as constitutive of feminist practice and theory itself. As Jones points out, 'current versions of debates about difference in feminism rest upon a particular discourse about citizenship' (Jones 1993b: 8). Jones's claim is that a particular territorial rhetoric of citizenship (based on a politics of identity and exclusion) has been used to structure arguments about feminist action and theory. The particular understanding of citizenship that constructs boundaries and requires the exclusion of aliens comes to define discourses about the feminist community, creating contested boundaries around the territory of feminism (Jones 1993b: 9–15). In other words, the adoption of an exclusionary territorial conception of citizenship operates, when applied at the level of feminist discourses, to generate an identity politics (see Chapter 4). The assertion of identity and the lobbying for access to an existing system of power then become the political goal.

In an attempt to find a less exclusionary model of citizenship Jones contrasts the status of the 'native-born' and the 'naturalized' citizen, and relates the two to debates about essentialism and mobile subjectivities (see Chapter 2). The naturalized citizen presents a challenge to the pure territorial exclusionary conception of citizens by bringing within the political community 'lingering elements of the foreign' (Jones 1993b: 16). The identity of the naturalized citizen (belonging fully to neither the community of origin nor the adopted community) offers a metaphor for the forging of a new configuration of political identity: a metaphor for a kind of 'citizenship-without-walls' (Jones 1993b: 16). Where the discourse of essential identities generates an exclusionary conception of citizenship, a discourse of mobile subjectivities generates a more cosmopolitan conception of citizenship.

From a perspective which endorses a notion of subjectivities as mobile, Jones proposes that we replace exclusionary citizenship with 'civic-minded world-protection' (Jones 1993b: 21). This form of feminist theory, she claims, suggests models of political action that reject the 'nationalistic and antagonistic parameters' of citizenship theory. The stress on cross-cultural diversity has led to an emphasis on the importance of building international feminist networks of world protection. Consequently, feminists have shifted the boundaries of citizenship away from seeing citizenship as a relationship between the state and its subject and towards a model of political and public space which stresses coalitional, non-statist, pluralist strategies (Jones 1993b: 22).

From such a position, Haraway proposes that we replace the concept of citizens with that of cyborgs, and speak not of citizenship but 'affinity groups'. She intends these terms to capture the constructed, partial and temporary nature of both identity and political coalitions (Haraway 1990: 196). The image of the cyborg displaces the stories of origins and identities and subverts the central myths of Western discourses of citizenship. It threatens to displace not only the dominant masculine myth of citizenship as formal, universalistic and statist, but also the oppositional feminine myth of citizenship as informal, female and organic. There is no 'available original dream of a common language or original symbiosis promising protection from hostile "masculine" separation' and we are freed 'of the need to root politics in identification, vanguard parties, purity and mothering' (Haraway 1990: 218). The global cyborg citizen adopts a strategy of displacement, which stands in opposition both to the strategy of inclusion adopted by those feminists who would gain access to an exclusionary citizenship and to the strategy of reversal adopted by those who would replace a masculine citizenship model with a female one.

How it relates to the other recent trend within feminist political theory to reconsider citizenship in terms of mechanisms of political representation is less than clear. As Jones points out, one of the most serious questions left underdeveloped in Haraway's essay 'is how to establish networked mechanisms of policy-formation that would enable the realization of a progressive political agenda' (Jones 1993b: 18). Others have taken up this challenge, though, and addressed the concept of the global citizen in more expressly political terms.

Notably Lister argues that the pressures upon the nation-state are such that 'our understanding of citizenship can no longer be confined within the boundaries set by nation-states' (Lister 1997: 55). We need, she states, to consider the potential for a conception of citizenship that transcends national boundaries. This potential is dependent on the possibility of transcribing at the international level those features thought central to citizenship at a national level, whether these be civil, political or social: structures granting and guaranteeing individual rights, practices of political participation, or shared values of social responsibility.

The transcription of a liberal conception of citizenship to a global context would require recognition of human rights outside the context of the state. As citizenship rights are commonly understood as enforceable claims against a particular state, global citizenship rights make appeal to mechanisms of global governance. Whether the recent feminist articulations of the appropriate structures for political citizenship might be applied at the level of an infrastructure for global governance is as yet a largely undeveloped area of theorizing.

The transcription of a civic republican conception of citizenship to a global context would require the creation of a global civil society in which shared traditions and common conceptions of the good might develop. This in turn would require the creation of a global public sphere in which all could engage in participatory political debate. In this context feminists have pointed to the effectiveness of UN summits, and also to the extensive network of international women's organizations as the beginnings of a global feminist civil society (Lister 1997: 62–3). Although these issues are now being considered within feminist international relations discourses, they are as yet largely absent from the feminist political theory literature. Yet, as Lister argues, a 'feminist praxis of citizenship committed to the principle of inclusion cannot stop at the borders of individual nation-states' (Lister 1997: 203).

As Narayan notes, the term citizenship has been used in struggles by marginalized groups to secure greater participation within the nation-state, but has also '*simultaneously functioned* to justify the exclusion of other members of the national community' (Narayan 1997: 49). Feminist uses of the term have, she notes, often replicated the tendency to focus on strategies of inclusion rather than issues of exclusion by failing to consider the plight of those who still do not have citizenship status. In other words, by relying too heavily on citizenship discourses as the sources of respect, rights and resources, feminists perpetuate the nation-state as the locus of power.

The concern with the territoriality of citizenship debates, and with the fate of non-citizens, is particularly urgent for feminists. This is so not only because immigrant women and their dependent children are particularly vulnerable if denied rights to welfare and medical care, but also because the acquisition and denial of citizenship status remains a gender-differentiated process. Narayan notes that in the context of the United States women often automatically lose their citizenship rights when they marry foreign nationals and cannot confer their nationality on their children or spouse, yet the same does not apply to men (Narayan 1997: 62).

Interestingly, while Narayan indicates that the procedures and criteria for acquiring citizenship are problematic because they actively discriminate on the basis of gender, she argues that refugee policies operate unjustly with regard to gender because of the failure to discriminate. She notes that criteria for political asylum often require proof that one has personally engaged in political activity that makes one a target of political repression in one's country. However, women are often subject to torture and political intimidation because they are family members of politically active men. Narayan herself does not note the contradiction here. She wants to criticize both the legal strategy of treating women differently in one instance and the strategy of treating them similarly in the other.

This apparent paradox is made particularly acute in relation to the acquisition of citizenship status, because people by and large want citizenship not as individuals, but as members of families. Nonetheless, once one is a citizen, all discourse becomes about individuals. The paradox, arising once again from women's particular relation to the family, generates the recurrent ambivalence as to whether a feminist conception of citizenship should pursue a strategy of gender-neutrality or gender-difference, or perhaps both.

The basic point, however, is that feminists need to consider issues of territoriality in their reflections on citizenship. To focus only on relations within the nation-state is to exclude from consideration all those who are excluded from it: it is to privilege the terms of inclusion of a particular group of women at the expense of the structural exclusion of others. This strategy leads to exactly the sorts of marginalization and 'cultural imperialism' within feminist discourses that led so many to reject the difference perspective and its assumption of a unified category of women (see Chapter 2). Indeed the relation might not be coincidental.

## Conclusion

There are some feminist theorists who are suspicious about any continued use of the concept of citizenship (see Lister 1997: 1–7). Sources of concern are twofold. Firstly, given the stress on the individual's relation to the state as contractual and rights-based, the concept of citizenship is held to be too firmly located within a particular social-contract theory to serve as a tool to critique this model. Secondly, given the assumption within this social-contract model of a territorially distinct nation-state, the forces of globalization and migration of persons make citizenship increasingly unable to deal with important issues of rights beyond territorial boundaries. Of these, it is the first that has dominated the feminist literature on citizenship to date, though the second is coming to be seen as increasingly significant.

Notwithstanding these various arguments for jettisoning the concept of citizenship, it is the strategy of reconceptualization that has clearly predominated, and there is now an extensive literature within feminist political theory that seeks to reconsider citizenship from gendered perspectives. Here three strategies emerge. There are those who would reclaim traditional liberal or civic republican citizenship traditions and hold them more accountable to their own professed ideals of universality and equity. There are the maternalists, who emphasize the importance of friendship as a basis for political action, an ethic of caring rather than justice and maternal rather than universal citizenship. And there are various participatory or radical democrats, who reclaim the formal and universal aspects of citizenship theory in modified form. This last camp argues the case for representative democracy, a distinct political realm and universal citizenship rights, while remaining sceptical about the individualism and gender-neutrality that have usually underpinned these aims. The ambition of such theorists is to displace unhelpful oppositions within the literature, to synthesize the best insights of feminist and mainstream citizenship theories, and to draw these together in a practical agenda for change.

That this leads many feminists to explore again the potential of liberal citizenship theory may seem surprising. Indeed many such theorists are themselves taken aback: 'Until recently', says Phillips, 'no feminist in her right mind would have thought liberal democracy could deliver the goods' (Phillips 1991a: 61). In even bothering to discuss the representation of women, she acknowledges that she goes against the grain of much contemporary feminism, and not only because of the theoretical challenges that have been levelled at liberal democracy, but also because of the strong presumption in favour of direct democracy within feminist practice to date. Nonetheless, it is to considerations of political representation that feminist political theorists are now turning and which we shall consider in the next chapter.

# 7

# *Representation*

## Introduction

Is the under-representation of women important and why might it matter? Should the mechanisms of representative democracy aim to represent women as women and, if so, what would representatives be representing – women's ideas, interests or identities?

In order to consider these questions, let us look first at the historical tension within feminism between representative and participatory forms of political engagement and the growing recognition that the two are inextricably linked. This recognition generates a desire to integrate the apparently opposing strategies of, on the one hand, making the existing representative structures more inclusive of women versus, on the other, rejecting formal, representative politics altogether in favour of more informal, participatory forms of political engagement. The move beyond inclusion and reversal towards displacement gives rise, in this context, to a renewed perception of the need both to extend democratic practices and to place constitutional limits upon these practices in the form of specific mechanisms of representation and accountability.

A central feature of these debates about the potential for modifying the structures of formal, representative politics is the question of whether, and in what ways, it is desirable to increase the political representation of women. In order to understand the range of issues at stake in these debates it is worth considering the complexity of the concept of representation itself, focusing on the distinction between functional, social, ideological and geographical representation. This will be followed by a look at the under-representation of women and arguments in favour of gender parity in the realm of representation, including those relating to role models, justice, women's interests and a concern to revitalize democracy. Proposals for fairer representative mechanisms include arguments for functional and social representation; modified defences of group representation; and genealogical rejections of group representation altogether. Although they have been far less central to these debates, it is also worth reflecting finally on ideological and geographic representation. For, while these have not been central to feminist considerations of representation to date, there are indications that they could be so in the future.

## Participatory and Representative Conceptions of the Political

Historically women have been excluded from participation in the formal institutions of politics by states limiting citizenship in various ways that privileged the hegemonic form of masculinity at that time. At differing periods the performance of military duty, property ownership and the capacity for rationality have all been deemed preconditions for the granting of full participation rights. Under these conditions most women have been structurally excluded from formal political participation (Brown 1988).

In response to women's exclusion from formal politics, feminist campaigns have taken two distinct forms. The first aims to increase women's participation within formal institutional politics, the second to extend the definition of the political in such a way as to reveal and valorize women's extensive political participation outside the formal institutions. During first-wave and early second-wave feminism these strategies tended to map closely to the liberal and radical strands of the feminist movement respectively. Nineteenth-century feminists campaigned for the right to vote and also the right to stand in elections. In so doing, they concentrated on formal equality before the law within the institutions of mainstream party politics. These goals are now largely realized within Western liberal democracies (women having secured the franchise between 1906 in Finland and 1975 in Portugal). Women are now entering the corridors of power as state actors and participating in state-based politics, though the barriers to their entry have proved to be rather more intransigent than those advocating formal equality before the law might have hoped.

In Britain, since 1918 when women over 30 won the vote (it being extended to women over 21 in 1928), the parliamentary political system has not formally excluded women. Yet in practice the interests and voices of women have remained marginal to mainstream debates, and women have notoriously failed to enter parliament in anything like 'representative' numbers. It is generally assumed that women are less interested in politics than men. The statement of the government's Central Statistical Office report on women, that 'women are not particularly interested in politics' (Stephenson 1996: 15), appears to be supported by empirical research. A recent government survey showed that only 7 per cent of women claimed to be 'very interested' in politics, and a MORI poll to accompany the 75th anniversary of women's rights showed that 76 per cent of women were not involved in any form of party political activity. There would seem to be a clear 'gender gap' regarding interest in and identification with mainstream party politics.

But it is not just that the female electorate is less engaged than the male in party politics in terms of levels of voting and membership. When women do engage, they do so differently. A 'gender gap' exists not only in relation to interest expressed and knowledge claimed, but also in voting intentions, political priorities and perspectives. Since 1945 opinion polls have recorded a difference in voting between men and women, with women more likely to vote Conservative, and less likely to vote Labour, than men (though this does reverse with the 18 to 34 age group) (Stephenson 1996: 4). Also, a recent poll revealed clear gender differences regarding political priorities. Women were more likely to be concerned with balancing work and family life, flexible working hours, low pay and part-time work than were men, who prioritized 'being out of work' as a concern (Stephenson 1996: 15).

How one interprets these facts depends on whether one inclines to see women as having a less developed interest in and knowledge of politics, or as holding a distinctive perspective on and conception of politics. The argument that women simply have a less developed interest in politics leads one to be concerned primarily to assist women to find their voice within the political system as currently conceived. The argument that they show a different perspective on the political might on the other hand lead to a concern to learn more about this political perspective and to allow for its concrete articulation by changing political structures themselves.

If women are more undecided, less interested and less knowledgeable about parliamentary politics than men, this could be read not as a failing, but as a positive statement of disillusionment and discontent. It is worth being attentive to recent research that reveals that women find the current form of party politics particularly unappealing, since it fails to represent their concerns or priorities (Stephenson 1996: 15). Such findings have provided useful resources for those who wish to challenge a traditional political science presumption that explanations of women's relative absence from politics should be sought by addressing the failings of women. The notion that this might reflect a considered cynicism arising from a realistic perception that their policy priorities are not adequately reflected in mainstream party agendas requires that one shifts one's attention away from the failings of women towards the failings of mainstream party politics itself. As the authors of a recent think-tank report suggest: 'Since the agenda of politics is defined and articulated primarily by men, many women are bound to be disconnected from traditional politics' (Wilkinson and Diplock 1996: 10).

Women's attempts to gain greater participation in government, either in a legislative capacity or within its administrative machinery, have met with varying degrees of success (Bashevkin 1985, Dahlerup 1986, Stetson and Mazur 1995). Various strategies have been adopted for increasing the number of women in the legislature, ranging from the purely rhetorical encouragement of women to enter into the system as it is, through positive action such as training, to positive discrimination and the adoption of quotas. Party reforms, including new systems of candidate selection, new means of policy-making, and the establishment of new structures of government (such as ministries for women) have all been adopted. Party ideology is a significant factor in determining which, if any, of these strategies are adopted. Social democratic and green parties are far more likely to justify positive discrimination, while parties of the right and centre are more likely to rely upon rhetorical strategies (Lovenduski and Norris 1993). There is some evidence to show that the most significant factor influencing women's success in entering national politics is the electoral system itself, specifically the operation of proportional representation, multi-member constituencies and party lists (Lovenduski and Norris 1995).

However, to concentrate on formal political participation alone is arguably to reproduce those masculine assumptions that have worked to blind us to women's informal political participation for centuries. The slogan 'the personal is political', which arose to challenge orthodox definitions of the political, acted as a rallying cry for a whole generation of feminists and is often perceived to be the key statement of second-wave feminism. Implicit in this statement is the claim that women *are* political actors, where the political is held to include all power-structured relations from the interpersonal to the international. If we adopt this broader notion of the political, it becomes evident that women have long been key political actors.

Many women typically organize outside of state structures in such things as women's peace and ecology movements, as in the numerous women's anti-nuclear groups that existed throughout the 1980s such as those at Greenham Common in the UK and Puget Sound in the United States (Mies and Shiva 1993). Many of their activities are concentrated below the level of the state, and are often aimed against oppressive state structures and policies, as with the Mothers of the Plaza de Mayo in Argentina and Mothers of El Salvador, who organized to bear witness to brutal regimes that had made their children 'disappear'. Women have also tended to be involved in issues and movements that cut across state boundaries (Peterson and Runyan 1993).

During the peak of the second-wave movements there were a large number of protest strategies adopted, generally involving spontaneous action such as gatherings with singing and impromptu speeches. But there were also a large number of well-organized campaigns, sit-ins, marches and demonstrations, as with the 'Reclaim the Night' actions in the UK and West Germany in 1977 and in Italy in 1978. In addition, women initiated and staged one-off activities that were assured to maximize publicity, such as the act of laying a wreath at the monument of the unknown soldier in Paris – a wreath for his unknown wife. There were also numerous acts of civil disobedience: in Iceland over 90 per cent of all adult women twice went on strike, including housewives who refused to mind children and cook dinner; and in France in 1972 three hundred women signed an open letter and published it in a daily paper containing the confession 'I have aborted' at a time when such an act was illegal and punishable by law. Yet perhaps the most common form of protest at this time comprised actions of the written word. The prolific number of journals, magazines and books of women's issues is an important manifestation of women's political participation over this period.

All these forms of political protest were 'movement events', working outside the formal mechanisms of party politics. Throughout the 1960s and 1970s many feminists were cynical about mainstream party politics and argued that women's energies should not be devoted to existing political institutions and electoral politics. The political participation advocated during this period by many within the women's movement was direct participation in women's autonomous organizations. These organizations aspired to be open to all, non-hierarchical and informal. Issues of participatory democracy became central, with great attention paid to organizational practice (Rowbotham, Segal and Wainwright 1979).

The explicit goal of a radical equality of participation for all women was pursued via mechanisms of rotating responsibilities, which aimed to avoid hierarchies, and consciousness-raising, which validated personal experience as a mode of political expression. In short, women's political participation during this period was characterized by the extraparliamentary activity of radical and socialist groups. Seeking no collaboration with government, these feminist groups repudiated the idea that change could be orchestrated from within formal arenas of political power and purposely stayed away.

However, for many the experiences of the radical participatory democracy of the women's movement became paradoxical (Phillips 1991a). Although claiming to be open to all, women's groups were largely unrepresentative. The absence of formal structures often worked to create an insularity that left many women feeling excluded and silenced. The emphasis on participation was too difficult for those who were juggling many other demands on their time, and the lack of representative structures raised serious questions of accountability. Perhaps because of these developments, there has been a notable shift of focus back towards the more conventional forms of political participation for many women. By the 1980s many feminists became more centrally concerned with the importance of mainstream politics, working to increase the numbers of women present within parties and legislatures, and to pursue policies in the interests of women.

The concern with a more extensive notion of the political has not, however, diminished with the waning of the cohesive women's movement. Rather, it has transmogrified into new, contemporary forms. Notably there is a current focus on particularly aesthetic forms of political expression (Wilson 1997: 368–70). Where the difference politics of the early women's movement affirmed collective acts of sisterhood, struggle and transformation, the diversity politics that underpin the current political mood affirm individual acts of dissidence, subversion and resistance. But, despite the hostility between the difference and diversity schools of thought within feminism, they share a tendency to extend the boundaries of the political beyond the institutions of the state, or indeed of civil association.

There is, then, still a suspicion regarding engagement with the state and an ambivalence towards policy formation based on a radical scepticism about the patriarchal and enlightenment discourses concerning justice, equity and emancipation. But recent reflections on the question of women and political representation have attempted to integrate the insights arising from the difference and diversity perspectives into a renewed articulation of the primarily equality-based discourse about the formal mechanisms of political representation. Rather than rejecting the formal arena of political representation, the primary thrust of current feminist writing about women's political participation is focused on ways of reconfiguring representation such that it is more responsive to, and integrated with, women's informal political activities. For example, Narayan stresses the connections between formal and informal political activities. She argues that it is in negotiations with a partner over domestic chores that one develops an awareness of issues which can be carried into the realm of public political activity (Narayan 1997: 59). Similarly, Lister emphasizes the importance of distinguishing between women's political representation and women's political activity. If we simply read one off from the other we reinforce the conventional wisdom that women are less interested than men in fulfilling their potential as political citizens (Lister 1997: 147). Lister therefore affirms the centrality of informal as well as formal politics, claiming that the former is a central feature of women's political citizenship.

However, despite her emphasis on the importance of recognizing the worth of women's informal political activism, Lister nonetheless notes that 'it can only be part of the full citizenship equation for, on its own, a *different* politics runs the risk of being marginalised as an *unequal* politics' (Lister 1997: 154). She recognizes that political empowerment through informal politics is not synonymous with gaining power in the wider society, and that both are needed (see Chapter 1 for a discussion of the distinction between the capacity-based and conflictual conceptions of power alluded to here). Lister therefore concludes that any citizenship which promotes women's equality, as well as their difference, will need to engage with the formal as well as the informal political system (Lister 1997: 155). It is not clear that informal participatory politics alone can address the complex questions of individual liberty and social justice. To engage with these adequately, one needs also to contemplate placing limits on democratic processes themselves.

Citizenship, Held claims, 'requires some specification, and some institutional and political protection, separate from and beyond the simple extension of democracy' (Held 1991c: 23). In other words, rather than pitting informal, participatory democratic practices against formal, institutional structures, they should be seen as requiring the latter. The pursuit of an inclusive political democracy necessitates a constitutional political framework, but a modified one. As Lister says, a 'more inclusive formal politics will require changes in the formal political system itself so as to make it more open both to individual women and the kinds of informal modes of politics in which many women will probably still prefer to participate' (Lister 1997: 155). The apparent dichotomy between formal and informal political activity, between representative and participatory conceptions of the political, is displaced in favour of a reconsideration of the inter-relation between the two.

The attempt to synthesize representative and participatory political activities echoes the move to go beyond equality and difference (see Chapter 4), to integrate the ethics of justice and caring (see Chapter 5) and to develop a conception of citizenship that embodies neither maternalism nor abstract universalism, but a 'differentiated universalism' (see Chapter 6). As Phillips notes, this trend marks 'a substantial shift from the anti-statism that characterized much of the earlier years of the women's liberation movement in Britain' (Phillips 1993: 86). It signifies not a return to an unmodified liberalism, but a recognition of the importance of the representation of women in the institutional political arenas in which decisions are made, 'with implications for the routes into and the organisation and conduct of those arenas' (Lister 1997: 166). Formal political equality within the representative structures of the polity is here recognized as a necessary, though not sufficient, precondition for a more substantive political equality. The importance, frequently overlooked in the more informal understanding of politics, of formal, constitutional frameworks within which participatory democracy must be located, is recognized. There is a renewed recognition of a need for procedural and constitutional mechanisms, coupled with a sense that these mechanisms will need to be modified to make them less individualistic. It is in this context that we witness the rise in debates about the need for a modified theory of representation.

## The Conception of Representation

Does it matter who our political representatives are? Should our elected representatives represent their supporters, their ideological allies within their party, their own conscience, their constituents . . . or some combination of the above? Are these compatible or contradictory roles? Much of the muddle surrounding the nature of representation can be traced back to the historical tension between various distinct forms of representation which have developed alongside, but not replaced, pre-existing representative mechanisms.

Medieval roots within our representative systems can be witnessed in the notion that parliaments function as a geographic forum where representatives speak for districts. Then again, immediately before the late eighteenth century it was commonly assumed that government represented not districts but property owners. The mass suffrage movements, demanding working-class and then women's suffrage, challenged this notion of representation, ushering in the adoption of the party system in which representatives stand for ideological perspectives and class interest. In short, there has been no clear unchanging conception of what it is that we require our 'representatives' to represent. For as long as representation has been a key feature in our model of liberal democracy, the issue of what it is that is to count as being politically worthy of representation and who is to be deemed able to represent others has itself been the object of political battle. Britain, with its emphasis on stability and tradition, manages to assume a particularly confused cluster of working definitions of what representation is.

So, before looking at the particular insights and proposals emerging from feminist theory regarding a more just representative system, a brief clarification of the analytically distinct conceptions of representation may be helpful. There are four questions worth considering: 1) when claiming to be a representative what is one representing? 2) how does one represent it? 3) where does one represent it? and 4) what is the purpose of representation? Theoretical exploration and clarification of the what, how, where and why of representation will bring the key normative issues at stake into clearer relief.

In answer to the first question – what is one representing? – there would seem to be four distinct sorts of answer: beliefs, constituencies, interests and identities. According to which of these one chooses to prioritize, one will advocate ideological, geographic, functional or social representation respectively. In answer to the second question – how does one represent it? – there are generally thought to be three means: symbolic, microcosmic and principal–agent. In answer to the third question – where does representation take place? – the traditional response of local and national arenas has been supplemented by the new site of Europe. The answer to the fourth question – what is the purpose of representation? – is actually very complex, but hinges on the issue of justice.

We can therefore distinguish between distinct conceptions of representation according to what is being represented, how, where and why. Each of these factors will have a significant impact on the form of representative mechanisms. Take, for instance, the fourfold distinction between ideological, geographic, functional and social representation, which arises in relation to the question of what is being represented (Marsh and Norris 1997). Firstly, the representation of beliefs generates a conception of ideological representation that involves collective representation via parties. It is the 'responsible party government' model, which requires disciplined parties with alternative programmes on major issues facing the country, voter choice on the basis of evaluations of government record or policy platforms, and free and fair elections. This is 'representation from above' in that there is a highly centralized, party-led decision-making structure (Marsh and Norris 1997: 154). Collective responsibility and party discipline work to ensure that representatives do not represent differences other than those of belief – be they based on geography, interest groups or identity.

Secondly, the representation of constituencies generates a conception of geographic representation that involves district-based delegates. Here representatives are to act in ways consistent with the opinions of citizens from areas that elect them. This is 'representation from below', with low levels of party discipline and minimal ideological manifestos (Marsh and Norris 1997: 155). Thirdly, the representation of interests generates a conception of functional representation, which involves representatives acting as spokespeople for interest groups and new social movements. Interest-group members are distinct from both party supporters and constituency dwellers. This understanding of representation generates a model of interest-group pluralism. Fourthly and finally, the representation of identities generates a conception of social representation, which involves representatives reflecting the social composition of the electorate in terms of presence. Here representatives speak for social groups of which they are a part, sharing common experiences and therefore holding common commitments and values. This understanding of representation gives rise to proposals for quota policies or reserved places for oppressed social groups. In other words, a representative could be considered to be speaking on behalf of, and accountable to, a political party, constituents, a specific interest group or a social group, depending on which of the ideological, geographic, function or social forms of representation predominate.

There are three distinct sorts of answer to the question of 'how' representation takes place: microcosm, symbolic and principal–agent (Pitkin 1967, McLean 1991). The microcosm conception is used to indicate that a person shares some of the characteristics of a politically significant group, usually assumed to be age, sex, class and racial divisions. This is the sense of representation at play when we speak of 'a representative sample', and demand that the legislature, if it is to be representative, should be a 'mirror' of the nation. Symbolic representation indicates that a person symbolizes the identity or qualities of a class of persons. This sense of representation is invoked in claims that 'a queen represents her people' and does not require, as the microcosm conception does, shared experiences between represented and representative. The third significant conception is that of representation as 'acting for': the representation of interests where a 'representative' denotes an agent who acts on behalf of his or her principal. When we speak of 'a lawyer representing her client' it is this third conception of representation that is being adopted. Principal–agent representation occurs when one person acts on behalf of one other, or when the agent acts in the principal's interests. Microcosm representation occurs when a group includes the same proportion of each relevant subgroup as the population from which it is drawn. The key difference here is whether one looks at the composition of parliament to determine its representativeness, or whether one looks at the decisions made.

Clearly the 'what' and the 'how' of representation are closely related. If one aspires to represent the beliefs of party members or the interests of interest groups one will adopt a principal–agent conception of representation. If, on the other hand, one seeks to represent one's constituents or members of particular social groups, one is more likely to be concerned to endorse a microcosm conception of representation. Endorsement of the symbolic form is more of a problem in a democratic representative system given the lack of emphasis placed on mechanisms of account-ability within this model.

Though helpful, there are also complexities within this basic schema. Take, for example, the case of interest representation. Here one might endorse either principal–agent or microcosm forms of representative-ness, depending on how one understands interests. If one believes, as Edmund Burke did, that interests reflect 'an objective, impersonal, un-attached reality', one is also likely to endorse a principal–agent model, given that these interests could be represented by any sufficiently intelli-gent and trustworthy individual (Pitkin 1967: 168). If, on the other hand, one suspects, as Phillips does, that interests are 'varied, unstable, perhaps still in the process of formation', then it will be far more difficult to 'separate out what is to be represented from who is to do the representation' (Phillips 1998: 234–5). In these circumstances it may make sense to endorse a microcosm model of representation. The com-plexity of this relation between interests and identities becomes particu-larly significant in debates about the under-representation of women.

## The Representation of Women

Which of these notions of representation is being invoked when people claim that women are under-represented within existing political institu-tions, and that a just and democratic system would require gender-parity in terms of representation? Which form of representation would be most sensitive to the interests or identities of women and/or which most likely to secure the presence of women in our decision-making bodies? There is of course no consensus on this issue. Current theoreti-cal debate is focused around the question of whether, as women, we want our identities or our interests represented; whether we want social or functional representation; and whether it is politically acceptable to continue invoking the 'we' of a single category of women at all.

There are, Phillips argues, four distinct arguments for women's equal participation in formal politics: the argument about role models, the argument concerning justice, the argument concerning women's inter-ests and the argument concerning the revitalization of democracy (Phillips 1995: 62–3, Phillips 1998: 229–38). The first is based on the belief that the existence of women representatives will encourage others to gain the confidence that they too can aspire to this role. The second implies that numerically equal representation of women and men in legislatures is itself a sign of parity, regardless of the beliefs of those present or the policies enacted. The third holds that women need to enter formal politics to work for women's interests; thus it is not presence alone, but the decisions made and policies formulated that matter. And the fourth proposes that women should enter into positions of power because they will engage in politics differently, thereby improving the nature of the public sphere.

The role models and justice arguments appeal to concerns about the just distribution of social resources. Positions of political influence are held to be a particular social resource, which ought to be fairly distributed and to which everyone should have equal access. The unequal distribution of positions of political power indicates that there are structural barriers to entry operating to deny particular social groups access to these scarce resources. These approaches, Phillips notes, treat the under-representation of women in politics 'as akin to their under-representation in management or the professions' – they depict politics as simply one profession among many and women's claim to political equality as nothing more than an equal opportunities claim to an interesting job (Phillips 1998: 230–1). There is, she claims, something rather unsatisfying about this approach in that it fails to capture the distinctive role of political representatives as participants in a democratic process. This is the weakness of these two, individualistic, arguments for women's increased representation.

In contrast, the other two arguments focus more directly on the political process itself. The argument from women's interests focuses directly on the function of representative democracy. The claim here is that women 'occupy a distinct position within society' and share common experiences that give them specific needs and interests. The needs and interests peculiar to women will be better represented by other women. Where the argument from justice focuses on women as individual citizens, this argument focuses on women as members of a group (Sapiro 1998a: 162). In other words, it is claimed that 'women have a distinct and separate interest as women; that this interest cannot be adequately represented by men; and that the election of women ensures its representation' (Phillips 1998: 234). The first of these claims is clearly contentious, among both feminists and their critics. The move from difference, to identity and then to diversity politics renders such a claim highly problematic. Very few people would be willing to defend the idea that there is anything like a constant and clearly defined set of experiences and interests that all women share equally. And, even if they could, it is not clear, given the current mechanisms of political representation, that representatives who happen to be women will be able to represent women. For they are elected to act as representatives of their constituents and parties first and foremost. As Phillips notes, 'in the absence of mechanisms to establish accountability, the equation of more women with more adequate representation of women's interests looks suspiciously undemocratic' (Phillips 1998: 235). Given these concerns, it is not clear that the argument from women's interests actually makes a strong case for numerically equal representation.

The argument concerning the revitalization of democracy is one that Phillips proposes as a way of dealing with some of the inadequacies of the other two. It is an argument that views representatives as more than well-paid employees or mandated delegates. Here the argument for increasing the number of female representatives is based on a belief that such representatives will actually participate in the political process differently: be less beholden to party agendas and more engaged in a radical reworking of the political system itself (Phillips 1998: 237–9). On this basis, the argument for the fair representation of women is simultaneously an argument for a more participatory form of democracy.

There are, then, four distinct normative bases to the claims for women's increased representation. There are also many distinct proposals as to how this increased representation ought to be realized. These can be schematically divided between those that endorse mechanisms of group representation and those that do not. Each of the normative bases for women's increased representation (role-models, justice, interests and democracy) can be used to argue for group representation. Each offers a different rationale for the adoption of such a policy and is subject to distinct critiques. As most of the recent debates within feminism have centred on the arguments from interests and from democracy (variously conceived), it is to these that we now turn.

Let us consider the arguments for treating women as an interest group (and for considering gender-parity as an issue of fair functional representation) versus those which perceive women to be an identity group (and gender-parity to be an issue of just social representation). We can then look at attempts (specifically those developed by Phillips and Young) to develop arguments for group representation that synthesize the two, while avoiding the problems of each, before turning to the genealogical scepticism about the project of group representation per se.

### Interests, identities and group representation

Most forms of feminist activism during the 1990s asserted an explicit claim for an increased presence of women in decision-making structures. These demands are often based on a presumption that women have interests that are best represented by women. Yet, as Lovenduski notes, 'that understanding has been fiercely contested by feminists, their sympathisers and their opponents in a continuing and sometimes acrimonious debate' (Lovenduski 1996: 1). Given that women, even those claiming the title feminist, currently articulate such distinct political positions, it is hard to judge what might be an accurate representation of their interests.

Sapiro explores the claim that women share particular experiences and have common 'representable interests' (Sapiro 1998a: 164). To assess whether women are an 'interest group' and, if so, what interests they have, Sapiro claims that one needs to consider both women's 'objective situation' and their consciousness of their own interests. For saying 'that women are in a different social position from that of men and therefore have interests to be represented is not the same as saying that women are conscious of these differences, that they define themselves as having special interests requiring representation, or that men and women as groups now disagree on policy issues on which women might have a special interest' (Sapiro 1998a: 167).

This is politically significant because, contrary to the Burkean notion of paternalistic representation of the interests of others, political systems are – Sapiro notes – not likely to represent previously underrepresented groups 'until those groups develop a sense of their own interests and place demands upon the system' (Sapiro 1998a: 167). Moreover, if the interests in question are not clear and pre-formed, but are still in the process of being uncovered via processes of consciousness-raising, it will then be more difficult, as Phillips noted, to distinguish between the represented and the representative. In these circumstances women would seem to be best placed to advocate the interests of women.

And yet, beyond these divergent perspectives as to whether women will best represent the interests of women, there lies a fundamental critique of this entire approach. Diamond and Hartsock argue against casting women as simply another interest group among many, and against claiming that fairness requires that women promote their interests within the existing political system equally with all other such interest groups. For this, they maintain, underplays the distinctive and radical challenge posed by the recognition of women's experiences and political ambitions. It also overlooks the new political and methodological questions raised by their position: 'if the inclusion of women into politics threatens the most basic structures of society, one cannot fit their concerns into the framework of interests' (Diamond and Hartsock 1998: 193). They propose (adopting an interpretative methodology and a difference perspective) that, in order to understand the interests that women have in common, one must develop a systematic analysis of the sexual division of labour. They use Chodorow's theory to claim profoundly different social understanding between men and women (see Chapter 2).

Attention to the sexual division of labour 'calls into question the appropriateness of the language of interests for understanding political life' (Diamond and Hartsock 1998: 196).

The very language of interests, according to Diamond and Hartsock, emerges with and then perpetuates the division of labour that creates the ideal of rational economic men seeking to maximize their satisfactions. They propose that it be replaced by more encompassing categories of analysis which more adequately capture the range of human emotions, such as needs. Their basic resistance to Sapiro's focus on interests is that it implies that the issue of women's fair representation is an issue of inclusion: that women are seeking to catch up with men (Diamond and Hartsock 1998: 197). In direct contrast, what they seek is a strategy of reversal: recognition that female experience inverts that of the male and forms a basis on which to expose masculine values as fundamentally flawed (Diamond and Hartsock 1998: 195). Women's demands cannot simply be integrated into the system. Including questions of reproduction and sexuality in the political process will transform the very concept of the political, eroding the public/private distinction and, presumably (though they do not state this directly), undermining the current system of representative democracy in favour of a more participatory one. Nonetheless, within the confines of the current representative system they are clear that 'only women can "act for" women in identifying "invisible" problems affecting the lives of large numbers of women' (Diamond and Hartsock 1998: 198). In short, they reject Sapiro's strategy of inclusion in favour of a strategy of reversal.

### Modified defences of group representation

This debate between strategies of inclusion and reversal (between the more effective representation of women's interests within interest-group pluralism and the transformation of the representative system itself) is, as with the other debates considered thus far, now subject to various feminist strategies of displacement. Notably, Phillips adopts an integrative position, synthesizing the interest-based and identity-based approaches in a manner which she claims offers a less problematic basis for arguing for the group representation of women.

Phillips's 'rather commonsensical' solution is to use both the terms 'interests' and 'needs' together (Phillips 1995: 73). There is a long history to this tension, as Phillips notes (Phillips 1995: 72). Both positions, she claims, have their strengths and weaknesses. 'Interests can sound rather grasping and competitive, but it does at least serve to remind us that there may be conflicts between different groups. Need has more obvious moral resonance, but it originates from a paternalist discourse which lends itself more readily to decision by experts on behalf of the need group' (Phillips 1995: 73). Considered in the context of the debates about equality and difference, one can see that this insight echoes the widely held perceptions about the relative merits of these two positions: the first may be overly individualistic, but there are contrasting worries that the second may be overly assimilatory. In an attempt to synthesize the best of these approaches and provide a firmer normative basis from which to consider the arguments for the increased representation of women, Phillips proposes a negotiation of a different pair of categories: the politics of ideas and the politics of presence.

A politics of ideas is Phillips's term for a politics that focuses on policies and a representation that focuses on people's beliefs and interests. Fair representation is, on this ideas-based model of politics, realized in the ongoing responsiveness of representatives to those they are representing. The accountability of representatives to their electorate is therefore paramount. As long as they are responsive, it matters little who the representatives are: 'the messages will vary, but it hardly matters if the messengers are the same' (Phillips 1995: 6). A politics of presence, on the other hand, is Phillips's term for a politics that focuses on the messengers themselves, and a representation that concentrates on people's identities. Fair representation, on this conception of politics, requires that the overly cerebral concentration on beliefs and interests be extended to recognize the normative and political significance of the identity of the representatives. The descriptive similarity of the representatives in relation to their electorate is paramount. It is the degree of shared experience that indicates representativeness on this identity-based politics.

Where a politics of ideas privileges accountability as the central measure of representativeness, a politics of presence privileges authenticity. Fair representation, from the perspective of a politics of presence, regards the gender (and any other social identity deemed politically significant) of the representative to be 'an important part of what makes them representative' (Phillips 1995: 13). In other words, where a politics of ideas invokes a notion of ideological or functional representation, a politics of presence invokes a notion of social representation. The interest-based and identity-based arguments for group representation are different versions of a politics of presence. They offer different bases for the claim that the presence of women in the decision-making bodies is significant, but share a sense that the identity of the messenger matters.

These endorsements of a politics of presence are controversial. Phillips lists three central objections. The first two originate from within the interest-based model of politics and the third from the participatory democracy model of politics (there being internal divisions within these camps as to whether group representation is the best way forward). Firstly there is the argument that such a politics poses a threat to national unity and leads to a 'Balkanization' of the polity, or a politics of the enclave, in that it encourages intransigence rather than cohesion. Secondly there is a concern that it undermines the basis for political accountability in that it is much harder to define clearly what a social group, as opposed to an interest group, really wants (what its interests are and whether they are being pursued). The third objection, made not by advocates of interest-based politics but by civic republicans and deliberative democrats, is that this is yet another capitulation to representative politics (albeit group-based rather than individualistic) which detracts from the pursuit of a truly inclusive and participatory politics of the common good (Phillips 1995: 21–4). We could also add a fourth objection, which arises from a more genealogical concern that any institutionalization of group identity will work to reify and normalize identities in a manner that might then be used to resubordinate the group in question.

It is the second concern about accountability that Phillips takes to be the most serious in relation to debates about the political representation of women. As accountability 'is best understood in relation to the politics of ideas', it is essential that a politics of ideas is not jettisoned altogether in any move towards a politics of presence (Phillips 1995: 56). Accordingly, she argues that: 'It is in the relationship between ideas and presence that we can best hope to find a fairer system of representation, not in a false opposition between one or the other' (Phillips 1995: 25). She also takes the third concern about participatory democracy seriously, holding that arguments for group representation are at their strongest when placed in the context of wider arguments for participatory democracy (Phillips 1995: 145–65). The fourth objection, arising from the deconstructive approach to gender issues (see Chapter 2), is one that Phillips does not consider in detail.

What Phillips proposes is a particular synthesis of the politics of ideas and presence as the basis for arguing for 'active intervention to include members of groups currently under-represented in politics' (Phillips 1995: 167). She distinguishes such arguments from the more reductive interest-based and identity-based arguments for group representation. For although she claims that changing the composition of the legislature in terms of presence will make a difference, she also wants to avoid a simple endorsement of a politics of presence which proposes group representation on the basis of the representation of either women's interests or their identities. 'The politics of presence is not about locking people into pre-given, essentialized identities; nor is it about just a new way of defining the interest groups that should jostle for attention' (Phillips 1995: 167). The project is to enable those currently excluded from politics to engage in political debate and decision-making.

If anything, this modified defence of group representation (drawing on a politics of both presence and ideas) is closer to the tradition of civic republicanism. Indeed, Phillips claims that proposals to modify the mechanisms of representative democracy in order to secure a greater parity of presence for women 'move in close parallel with arguments for more participatory democracy' (Phillips 1995: 190). Theorists grounded in a tradition of deliberative and participatory democracy are, she feels, best placed to develop arguments for a politics of presence and for group representation, which avoid the pitfalls of the overly narrow arguments for group representation based on the traditions of interest-group pluralism or identity-based politics. Notably, Phillips thinks that Young's particular vision of group representation 'avoids most of the pitfalls in appealing to shared experience as an automatic guarantee . . . it makes no claims to essential unities or characteristics; it recognises the potential diversity and disagreement within any social group; and it provides some basis for the accountability of representatives to those they might claim to represent' (Phillips 1995: 54). There are feminists in the republican and deliberative democratic camps who find group representation significantly less appealing than do Young or Phillips, due to the fear that group representation might generate essentialism (Voit 1992). But let us consider Young's arguments for group representation in more detail.

Young claims that existing electoral and legislative processes are 'unrepresentative' in the sense that they fail to reflect the diversity of the population, leading her to demand that a certain number of seats in the legislature be reserved for the members of marginalized groups. This call is made on the assumption that under-representation can be overcome only by resorting to guaranteed representation and that representing difference requires constitutional guarantees of group participation within the parliamentary system. Groups who have suffered oppression need guaranteed representation in order that their distinct voice can be heard.

Young's claim is that a just polity requires the participation and inclusion of all groups, secured only by the different treatment for oppressed groups. This rejection of the assimilationist ideal is based on a belief that attachment to specific traditions, practices, language and other culturally specific forms is a crucial aspect of social existence. Young argues that 'a democratic public should provide mechanisms for the effective recognition and representation of the distinct voices and perspectives of those of its constituent groups that are oppressed or disadvantaged' (Young 1990a: 184). These mechanisms will involve three distinct features. Firstly, the provision of public resources, which will be used to support the self-organization of group members, 'so that they achieve collective empowerment and a reflective understanding of their collective experiences and interests in the context of the society' (Young 1990a: 184). Secondly, the provision of public resources to enable the group to analyse and generate policy proposals in institutionalized contexts, and the formal requirement that decision-makers show that they have taken these perspectives into account. Thirdly, group veto power regarding specific policies that affect a group directly, 'such as reproductive rights for women' (Young 1990a: 184).

Young, like Phillips, refers to the importance of representing both needs and interests and endorses group representation while sharing widespread concerns about essentialism (Young 1990a: 185). She proposes that the groups in question be given the resources to develop and the institutional mechanisms to articulate their own specific voice. Her vision of group representation thereby avoids the potential dangers of paternalism or cultural imperialism – where people feel empowered to define the needs and perspectives of others purportedly sharing the same group identity. Not only does she seek to avoid charges of essentialism, she also refuses to endorse a simple microcosm vision of representation, which requires that representatives would be proportional to their numbers in the polity. While she is clear that the voice of women (and all other oppressed groups) ought to be heard within decision-making institutions, she does not believe that this requires strict microcosm representation given the structures proposed to facilitate accountable mechanisms for the articulation of such a voice. 'Allocating strictly half of all places to women . . . might be more than is necessary to give women's perspective an empowered voice, and might make it more difficult for other groups to be represented' (Young 1990a: 188). Interestingly, Young is not then endorsing the microcosm conception of representation that one might expect from a difference theorist. But neither is she endorsing a symbolic conception, for there are structural mechanisms of accountability built into her proposals. If anything, she is endorsing a form of principal–agent representation, but one based on groups rather than individuals.

These two moves clearly distinguish Young's defence of group representation from more directly identity-based forms of difference politics. But, in making these proposals, some critics feel that she moves too close to an interest-based form of equality politics. The embrace of group-based principal–agent representation leads some critics to argue that Young's vision is actually nothing more than a rearticulation of interest-group pluralism (Mouffe 1992a: 369–85). But this is a charge that Young rejects. She claims that her vision of group representation is fundamentally different from interest-group pluralism in two ways: it operates with a concept of social groups, not interest groups, and it promotes public discussion and decision-making rather than the pursuit of group interest (Young 1990a: 186–90). Intriguingly, both of these distinctions appear to invoke an appeal to precisely the impartiality that Young, in most of her writings, is keen to reject (see Chapters 4 and 5). In other words, she avoids the problems of essentialism and unaccountability of an identity-group politics only to be charged with adopting a form of interest-group pluralism that is itself problematic. Her attempts to distinguish her position from interest-group pluralism, then, propel her to invoke norms of just deliberation that arise from a deliberative democracy framework, which she has, on other occasions, criticized for being overly universalistic.

Young's first claim is that it is social groups, not interest or ideological groups, with which she is concerned. Social groups are neither 'any aggregate or association of persons who seek a particular goal, or desire the same policy' nor 'a collective of persons with shared political beliefs' (Young 1990a: 186). A social group is 'a collective of people who have affinity with one another because of a set of practices or way of life; they differentiate themselves from or are differentiated by at least one other group according to these cultural forms' (Young 1990a: 186). Her second claim is that interest groups simply promote their own interests in a political marketplace, with no reference to a conception of social justice or the common good. The social groups argued by Young to require special representation are, on the other hand, defined with reference to a specific vision of justice which generates criteria for assessing social oppression and hence criteria for establishing which groups require such representative guarantees. This vision of justice offers guidance not only as to which groups require special representation rights, but also as to how they should act in the political realm. A distinction is made between demands stemming from self-interest and those stemming from justice: 'the test of whether a claim upon the public is just or merely an expression of self-interest is best made when those making it must confront the opinion of others who have explicitly different, though not necessarily conflicting, experiences, priorities and needs' (Young 1990a: 186). In other words, the engagement in deliberation with other social groups marks a just political dialogue as opposed to a simple expression of instrumental interest.

As republican theorists have noted, this attempt to distance herself from the individualism and instrumentalism of interest-group pluralism actually propels Young towards an endorsement of a form of impartiality and deliberation that she finds unacceptable in republicanism (Miller 1993: 16). Indeed, as Phillips notes (Phillips 1995: 147), whereas Young's initial formulation of her argument for group representation relied on heavily criticizing deliberative democracy, she now uses this framework, in a slightly modified form that she labels communicative democracy, to defend her own vision of group representation (Young 1996a: 120–36). Whether she can do this without invoking a notion of impartiality is open to question.

For example, Young's response to the question of how interest-seekers will be transformed into citizens who attend to the claims of others is sketchy. She addresses the dilemma by quoting a passage from Pitkin, who argues that interest-group competition draws us into politics because: 'we are forced to find or create a common language of purposes and aspirations ... we are forced to transform "I want" into "I am entitled to", a claim that becomes negotiable by public standards' (quoted in Young 1990a: 107). Young then goes on to add: 'In this move from an expression of desire to a claim of justice, dialogue participants do not bracket their particular situations or adopt a universal and shared standpoint. They *only* move from self-regarding need to recognition of the claim of others' (Young 1990a: 107; italics added). The crucial question of precisely how this transformation occurs, and whether it does not actually constitute an appeal to impartiality, is not directly considered. Nonetheless, it is clear that, of the three models conventionally proposed within political theory – the appeal to transcendental Archimedean positions, to embedded communal bonds or to ethics which derive from the structure of undistorted communication – it is the third, deliberative, option that Young appears to find the least unacceptable.

Let us briefly reflect on the central elements of these modified defences of group representation. The form of group representation proposed by both Phillips and Young rests on a politics of ideas, modified by recognition of the importance of a politics of presence. The politics of presence is used as a basis for arguing not for absolute gender-parity, but for constitutionally guaranteed special representation rights. Both Phillips and Young seek to synthesize models of functional representation with apparently antithetical models of social representation. In other words, they propose that the apparently dichotomous options of representative or participatory politics be displaced, and further that the apparently dichotomous options within representative politics, of functional and social representation, also be displaced.

### Representation and contingent identities

A genealogical perspective focuses attention on the ways in which any mechanism for political representation works to constitute and/or entrench identities which may themselves come to be constraining or even oppressive. Any mechanism for representing women will, if adopted, also become a mechanism for constituting the category of woman. The representative structures we adopt and operate not only determine the inclusiveness and justice of the political system with respect to existing marginalized groups, they also work to construct future groups' identities.

Representative politics does not simply re-present what we are. It is not simply a mechanism for more or less accurately capturing and articulating pre-existing identities and/or interests. It is never solely a means of voicing 'authentic' selves. Politics is also performative and constituting (Honig 1993). In engaging in the political we actually gain identities and interests. Clearly, it is a function of representative politics to express what already exists. But this should not blind us to the significant role that politics, including representative politics, plays in *perpetuating* certain identities and interests while denying others, and actually *creating* that which does not yet exist. The selection of future mechanisms of representation entails not only the pursuit of a pure expression of authentic selves, but also the modification of the art of government in which subjects are shaped. Rethinking the boundaries of political representation might well allow for a more inclusive politics, but it will also generate a new set of criteria as to what is to be deemed politically pertinent, which identities and interests perceived as authentic. We would do well to reflect on this and consider which exclusions are implicit in the new forms of inclusiveness proposed.

When, Brown provocatively asks, 'does legal recognition become an instrument of regulation, and political recognition become an instrument of subordination?' (Brown 1995: 99). To pose this question is to shift attention away from the social positioning of existing identities towards the processes of the construction of subjectivities themselves. Specifically, it focuses attention on that role representative mechanisms play in constructing, as well as reflecting, social identities. Identity occurs, Brown tells us, 'at the point where these touch, where the particulars of subject formation intersect with vectors of social stratification such as race and gender' (Brown 1995: 119). If subjects are not only positioned by power, but are also the effects of power, then the study of women and representation must be attentive to both of these dynamics.

Perhaps because of these concerns, most diversity theorists do not discuss representation (in its formal political sense) at all. When they do, they argue that representation doesn't stand for something, it is constitutive of the subject of representation: political representation is not solely instrumental or expressive but productive of power relations, constituting the subject (Seitz 1995, Redner 1994). Mouffe stands out, among the theorists who adopt a deconstructive account of gender and a genealogical approach to theorizing, in that she directly engages in debates about representative politics. Unlike most theorists whom one might locate within the diversity school of thought, she considers the virtues of political liberalism (Mouffe 1993). She shares the genealogical approach in that she argues that representative democracy should be understood as a regime: 'it concerns the symbolic ordering of social relations and is much more than a mere 'form of government'. It is a specific form of organizing human coexistence politically' (Mouffe 1996: 245–6). But this insight does not lead her to reject representative politics; indeed, she finds the pluralism characteristic of representative democracy to be profoundly important.

Pluralism is conceived by Mouffe as an ideal rather than as simply a description of existing relations (the 'fact of pluralism' considered by Rawls). She defines pluralism as the central feature of the political order, in that it legitimates conflict and division (Mouffe 1993: 51). Mouffe argues that, from a diversity (or as she terms it anti-essentialist) theoretical perspective, 'pluralism is not merely a fact . . . it is taken to be constitutive at the conceptual level of the very nature of modern democracy and considered as something that we should celebrate and enhance' (Mouffe 1996: 246). This, she claims, is what it is to be a radical democrat. The type of pluralism she is advocating 'gives a positive status to differences and . . . refuses the objective of unanimity and homogeneity which is always revealed as fictitious and based on acts of exclusion' (Mouffe 1996: 246). In contrast to straightforwardly genealogical approaches, Mouffe recognizes the limits to pluralism, invoking the need to construct a collective identity in the face of antagonism and subordination. 'To deny the need for a construction of collective identities and to conceive democratic politics exclusively in terms of a struggle of a multiplicity of interest groups or of minorities for the assertion of their rights is to remain blind to the relations of power' (Mouffe 1996: 247).

Mouffe's model of representative democracy is not simply instrumental – it is not about the articulation and representation of pre-formed interests. It is about the constitution and contingent negotiation of identities and interests within the political itself. This, she argues, will always be an antagonistic process: 'To negate the ineradicable character of antagonism and aim at a universal rational consensus – this is the real threat to democracy' (Mouffe 1996: 247). And it is here that she is clearly at odds with the type of modified defence of deliberative democracy offered by Young. Despite Young's own scepticism about universality, Mouffe finds her too accepting of the deliberative vision of discourse ethics for comfort.

Mouffe also rejects Young's proposals for group representation, objecting to the idea that sexual difference should be a valid distinction in the domain of politics (Mouffe 1992a: 377). She dislikes the idea of group representation as a positive political strategy. She, like all feminist theorists situated firmly within the genealogical and deconstructive frames, is determined to avoid both instrumental interest-group pluralism and essentializing identity-based group recognition. These theorists highlight the very real dangers of these two approaches. But, unlike in the more integrative and deliberative work of Phillips and Young, the nature of the specific proposals for mechanisms of political representation that emerge from this perspective are largely undeveloped.

## Ideological and Geographic Representation Reconsidered

The debate about the representation of women has so far focused on the question of whether women should be represented *as women*, and, if so, whether this group representation should be based on arguments regarding women's interests or women's identities. In other words, we have considered the various ways in which functional and social forms of representation have been negotiated within recent feminist political theory. Absent from these debates is any sustained reflection on the ideological and geographic elements of representation. Given that it is precisely these forms of representation that currently predominate in the British electoral system, this is perhaps surprising. Let us look at each, focusing specifically on the questions of redistribution and location.

### Representation, recognition and redistribution

To be a radical democrat, claims Fraser, is to appreciate two different kinds of impediment to democratic participation: social inequality and misrecognition of difference (Fraser 1997a: 173). The current structuring of representative mechanisms around ideological differences emphasizes the social inequality aspect of politics, but fails to address the 'misrecognition of difference' aspects.

Feminist theory has in recent years leaned towards the other extreme. If anything there has been a tendency to focus 'one-sidedly on cultural politics to the neglect of political economy' (Fraser 1997a: 174). Preoccupied with debates about functional and social representation, and about group representation rights as an appropriate means of securing such representation, feminists have largely ceased to consider ideological representation and the questions of redistributive justice that are central to it.

The form of party politics that operated throughout most of the post-war period in Britain was based in the social realities and cleavages of

Fordist production and Keynesian welfare economics. Social class, based on one's relation to the production process, was the basis for party affiliation. Political representation was about the representation of economic interests and the object of politics was largely distributive or redistributive. Justice was conceived in terms of a distributive paradigm, with debate focused around whether and to what extent the state should legitimately redistribute social wealth and resources. To the extent that there were politically recognized differences among the electorate and their representatives, they were differences of wealth and ideals.

The feminist shift away from this form of representative politics can be defended in that the current institutional privileging of ideological representation is increasingly at odds with popular conceptions of political identification, turning many away from representative politics altogether. However, attempts to replace this system with one which only emphasizes identity differences by privileging social representation potentially runs into problems associated with essentialism, ghettoization and a politics of 'ressentiment'. Attempts to replace it with functional representation alone potentially runs into problems associated with individualism, instrumentalism and a politics of the marketplace. The old ideological notion of representation may indeed no longer be adequate, but a simple replacement of it with social or functional representation will not suffice. It is therefore worth considering how the functional and the social forms of representation relate to the ideological form.

While the traditional form of redistributive party politics seems increasingly alienating to many, cultural politics and a 'politics of recognition' has emerged as a distinctive and significant factor on the contemporary political landscape. As Fraser notes, the 'struggle for recognition' has become the paradigmatic form of political conflict in the late twentieth century (Fraser 1995a: 1). Schematically, she argues that, insofar as cultural politics engages with the question of justice at all, it is concerned with justice as recognition rather than as (re)distribution, which more conventionally characterized various modernist forms of political perspective. To the extent that people are participating in and theorizing about politics in an innovative and engaged manner, it is based on a politics of recognition that sits uneasily within our existing political structures – built as they were around the old class model of redistributive politics. Most manifestations of identity politics take place outside the party political arena. Those that work within it take the form of the demand for 'presence' and group participation.

This acknowledgement of cultural politics focuses on the emergent claims to positive recognition of identity among constituencies whose previous identifications (along lines of gender, sexuality, nationality, class, race or religion) were experienced as injurious or degrading. As Tariq Modood comments, that many leading political theorists

> come to place diversity, pluralism and multiculturalism at the centre of their theorising, with the emphasis being on the justness of cultural rather than economic transactions, is . . . determined by changes in the political world; by the challenges of feminism, the growing recognition that most Western societies are, partly because of movements of populations, increasingly multi-ethnic and multi-racial, and the growing questioning of whether the pursuit of a universal theory of justice may not itself be an example of a Western cultural imperialism. (Modood 1996: 177)

Recent feminist discussions about group representation can be understood in the context of this general turn to conceiving justice in terms of recognition rather than redistribution. Notably, Young – who has been one of the most important theorists of group representation – explicitly criticizes the narrow focus on a distributive conception of justice. She claims that we need to rethink the meaning of social justice 'beyond the distributive paradigm that dominates in contemporary Anglo-American philosophical approaches to justice' (Young 1996b: 253).

Young defines the 'distributive paradigm' as an approach that assumes that all questions of social justice are about the distribution of social benefits and burdens among individuals and groups. There are, she argues, two reasons why it is a mistake to reduce all issues of justice to issues of distribution. 'First, the distributive paradigm tends either to distort or ignore issues of justice not easily conceived of in distributive terms. Second, the distributive paradigm tends to presuppose institutional structures within which distributions take place as given, without bringing the justice of those institutional structures themselves into question' (Young 1996b: 255). This latter assumption is problematic because justice debates then fail to evaluate the justice of the institutions of distribution themselves. A broader conception of justice takes not fairness but liberation as its ideal (Young 1996b: 257). The former assumption is problematic because, while many of these benefits and burdens are quantifiable and measurable, rendering their distribution clearly ascertainable, others (such as power and self-respect), which are also commonly included in calculation of distributive justice, are intangibles.

Young's claim is that to apply distributive justice to such intangibles 'wrongly reifies relations and processes' (Young 1996b: 254). It focuses attention on that which can be distributed (positions, tasks, economic resources) and perpetuates the silence surrounding issues of sexuality and reproduction. For these entail 'systematic issues of justice that are broadly speaking cultural' (Young 1996b: 225). For instance, sex discrimination that entails the denial of benefits (such as jobs or equal rates of pay) is but one element of the injustice frequently raised by women. Feminists have emphasized the importance of the violence, stereotyping and stigma associated with pornography, prostitution, rape and sexual harassment. They have also placed great emphasis on issues of procreation and parenting. These are issues that Young claims to be ill-conceived in distributive terms.

The issues of child custody, for example, cannot be successfully negotiated from within the distributive justice paradigm. In disputes as to who will have primary custody over their children it makes little sense to think of either the children or the rights to access as the subject of distribution. Whereas the Rawlsian model of justice might imply that we could and should think in this way, in practice such cases are frequently decided on the basis of facilitating the most beneficial set of intimate relationships. The existing system of justice already incorporates elements of a care perspective in practice for pragmatic reasons, based on the sorts of interactions being considered. It is the exclusion of parenting and reproduction issues from abstract theoretical justice thinking that continues to downplay and undertheorize this fact.

Fraser's point is that acknowledgement of the normative significance of the cultural and political importance of recognition should not involve a denial of the normal significance of the economic and political importance of redistribution. Young's critique of the distributive paradigm of justice is, Fraser claims, confused. There are actually three distinct critiques offered by Young: the focus on distribution rather than production; the distribution of the wrong sorts of social goods; and reification. It is Fraser's opinion that, in the end, Young adopts the second of these critiques and therefore operates within the distributive paradigm itself (Fraser 1997a: 191). This is significant because it allows Fraser to argue that we can accept Young's critique of certain forms of redistributive politics without jettisoning a concern with just distribution altogether. This leaves open a space to argue that feminists need to address both recognition and redistribution. Negotiation of the two different agendas will of course be complex. Women are subject to both economic and cultural injustice. Yet the redistribution that responds to the former promotes group dedifferentiation, and the recognition that responds to the latter promotes group differentiation (Fraser 1997a: 16).

This complexity or recognition and redistribution needs to be addressed. For recognition arguments, concerning the revaluation of women's identities versus the deconstruction of gendered identities, are not only partial, they are also unresolvable. While representation is considered only from the terrain of identity politics, and dissociated from political economy, the 'gordian knots of identity and difference' will never be untied (Fraser 1997a: 174). In other words, the debate between difference and diversity theorists will never be resolved until each recognizes the insights of the equality theorists' position that they have repressed. Neither the difference theorists' celebration of women's identities nor the diversity theorists' characterization of all identities as repressive fictions provides a basis for distinguishing 'democratic from anti-democratic identity claims' and, as a result, neither 'can sustain a viable politics or a credible vision of radical democracy' (Fraser 1997a: 182). For this, Fraser argues, we will need to consider which identity claims are rooted in 'the defence of social relations of inequality and domination' and which in 'a challenge to such relations' (Fraser 1997a: 186). In short, both approaches repress the insights of equality feminism concerning the need for equal participation and fair distribution.

Fraser offers a fourfold schema for understanding the possible perspectives available, generated by two intersecting divisions: the redistribution/recognition divide and the affirmation/transformation divide. A stance of affirmation is one that aspires simply to correct the outcomes of existing structures. A stance of transformation is one that aspires to restructure the underlying generative framework itself (Fraser 1997a: 23). An affirmative politics of redistribution and recognition will entail the socio-economic politics of liberal feminism and a cultural politics of difference feminism (advocating a fair share of jobs and education within the existing structures coupled with the revaluation of femininity). A transformative politics of redistribution and recognition will entail socialist feminism and feminist deconstruction (advocating a transformation of the existing economic structures coupled with the replacement of hierarchical gender dichotomies with multiple intersecting differences) (Fraser 1997a: 23–30). It is the second of these pairings that Fraser presumes to be most productive.

If we now return to the issue of political representation, it becomes clear that Fraser's attempt to draw the redistributive back in has the effect of refocusing attention on the ideological conception of representation previously overlooked in recent feminist debates. For it is the ideological forms of representation that have, in the British political system, most directly addressed socio-economic issues of redistribution and engaged with the issue of the just representation of competing redistributive agendas. The failure of recent feminist debates to consider directly the issue of ideological representation arises primarily from the fact that the particular ideological cleavages that predominate in contemporary Western democracies are ones that focus on issues of economic distribution at the expense of social recognition. The need to consider mechanisms for group representation (drawing on functional and social rather than ideological conceptions of representation) is created by the exclusion of the interests and perspectives of women from this particular ideological agenda. The sets of beliefs that one is currently asked to choose between are ones that, while internally distinct, are united in excluding a whole range of issues from the political agenda.

In this context, Phillips candidly recognizes that 'the most persistent structure of political exclusion is surely that associated with inequalities of social class, and this is the one form of social division and inequality that has been remarkably absent from my discussion' (Phillips 1995: 171). Her writing focuses on the ways in which the existing ideological agenda might be extended to include social groups (specifically those of gender, race and ethnicity) currently excluded. As a principle for defining the central cleavages in political parties and the central basis for political representation, Phillips tells us, 'class itself has had an extraordinary presence. For much of the last two centuries, class has operated as the organising symbol for defining the political spectrum, dividing parties and movements according to their stance on competition and co-operation, capitalism and socialism, the free market and planning, private property and social equality' (Phillips 1995: 173). The need to guarantee constitutionally the presence of groups whose particular agenda might be excluded from political debate does not, then, apply to class in the way that it applies to gender, race and ethnicity.

This is significant because the relation between functional, social and ideological representation becomes clearer in this context. The arguments for group representation (drawing on either functional or social conceptions of representation) are arguments for the strategic and limited use of group representation in order to modify and improve the operation of the more fundamental and enduring form of ideological representation. The demands for group representation would, Phillips tells us, 'lose some of their urgency if the political agenda already incorporated the interests and perspectives of these groups' (Phillips 1995: 175). In other words, the fact that justice has been conceived in terms of recognition rather than redistribution, and representation in terms of presence rather than ideas, indicates that these issues need to be drawn to the attention of political theorists and structurally included within mechanisms of representative democracy. It is not because they could, or should, replace the latter. 'The real importance of political presence', Phillips specifies, 'lies in the way it is thought to transform the political agenda, and it is this that underlies the greater priority now accorded to gender and ethnicity and race' (Phillips 1995: 176). Phillips argues that ideological representation makes sense 'when politics is organized around binary oppositions, or when political beliefs and objectives fall into coherent clusters of congruent ideas', a presumption which looked more plausible when class was the central organizing principle defining the political spectrum than it does today (Phillips 1995: 41). If this transformation is to engage with the full range of issues pertinent to gender identity, in all its contingency and complexity, it will inevitably deal with both recognition and redistribution.

## Re-siting the political

What then of geographic representation? Although it is rarely the explicit focus of feminist attention, there is evidence that geographic representation, coupled with ideological representation, works against the incorporation of the functional and social forms of representation, which feminist theorists have been keen to explore if not privilege.

It has been shown that the nature of the electoral process adopted makes a big difference to the actual composition of legislatures. On the basis of comparative empirical research, Norris claims that multi-member constituencies and a 'party lists' system allow greater recognition of difference within one's political structures (Norris 1996: 89–103). Proportional representation allows for a greater inclusiveness of candidates for election by making under-representation in the nomination process both more visible and more accountable. Countries with proportional representation and large numbers of representatives in districts are the leaders among democracies in the proportions of women in parliament. More women are elected in countries with proportional lists electoral systems (Norris 1997: 280).

For the equality and diversity theorists, wary of the consequences of an overly essentialist reliance on social representation, proportional representation may be a vitally important way forward. In allowing for diversification and fragmentation generally, proportional representation systems are able to address the relative absence of women and minorities within the political system without resorting to the entrenchment of such identities within existing party selection procedures. In other words, geographic representation as currently conceived in the form of single-member constituency representation, with its emphasis on the importance of the link between the territorially located constituents and their representative, would appear to work against a more open and inclusive representative system from the perspective of gender.

## Conclusion

What, then, are the practical implications of these theoretical debates? Does the under-representation of women matter, and how should it be addressed? The first point is that there is no single theoretical perspective within the feminist literature to which one might appeal for guidance. The strategy of inclusion endorses a vision of representation as the representation of beliefs and interests (ideological and functional representation). The strategy of reversal endorses a vision of representation as the representation of identities (social representation). The strategy of displacement largely adopts a critical perspective, highlighting the potential dangers of each of these two perspectives, but has few of the theoretical tools necessary to assert a practical alternative.

The strategy for fair representation which most obviously seeks inclusion with the existing mechanisms of representation is manifest in many of the arguments made in favour of equal opportunities for women to engage in ideological or functional representative practices as currently applied. Such strategies are usually accompanied by a direct rejection of both positive discrimination and social representation as an ideal. This leads to a rejection of (social) group representation altogether. The assumption underpinning this strategy of inclusion is that the existing criteria of selection and election are themselves fair and need to be more fully realized rather than structurally amended. Though basically individualistic and interest-based, the strategy of inclusion can, however, be modified to incorporate an endorsement of group representation, if it can be shown that women constitute an interest group. Given the current discrimination against women, women might have interests that are best represented by women (assuming the likelihood of shared experience) but could be pursued by anyone who understood and sympathized with them. The important point is that one engages in politics to pursue interests, not to articulate identities, with the aim to transcend one's female specificity, not emphasize it. Representation is assumed to be about the representation of interests.

Those who advocate a strategy of reversal have, on the other hand, a relatively clear (if highly ambitious) agenda. These theorists argue that women are a discernible identity group; they engage in politics differently. They adopt a care rather than a justice perspective and a maternalist rather than a universal conception of citizenship. The recognition of women's distinctive identities requires political representation of women as women. Representation is assumed to be of the mirror form. This approach directly endorses the 'politics of presence' and group recognition, with quotas as one appropriate mechanism. When pursued in the context of existing structures of representation, this strategy of reversal requires that a form of social representation be introduced into representative structures, which are primarily developed to represent differences of interests and beliefs, not identities. The claim is that there is a 'woman's perspective' which is currently repressed and that requires greater political recognition. The reason why it might be important to have more women involved in the political arena on this account is because women will engage in politics differently. They will transform the style of debate and moral framework underpinning politics. In order to achieve this, women will have to be present themselves: one cannot delegate the task of representing identities in the way one can delegate the task of representing interests. The representation of women is here the representation of women's identities.

Some, like Phillips and Young, advocate a critical synthesis and negotiate the apparent incompatibility between these two forms of representation by developing a modified defence of group representation that draws on notions of both interests and identities. They seek to recognize women as a group, without also positing an essential group identity. In order to achieve this recognition, they draw on the tradition of deliberative democracy.

There is, then, a third significant grouping of theorists, more clearly located within the frames of genealogy and deconstruction, who advocate a strategy of displacement. They argue that these various endorsements of group representation simply fail to escape the pitfalls of representative politics itself. These diversity theorists have a challenging task in negotiating the connection between their abstract theoretical insights and their practical political proposals. There is a tension between constituting political procedures (which inevitably posit some stability of identity and require exclusions of certain differences) and celebrating the fluidity of heterogeneous difference. Given that the project of a diversity perspective is to challenge the normalizing rules that seek to constitute, govern and control various behaviours, to question and denaturalize all that is constative in politics, both individual and group representation look problematic. It is simply not clear what practical proposals might emerge from a strategy of displacement that aims to 'ventilate and supplement' the institutional politics of territorial democracy rather than engage directly with them (Connolly 1991: xi). Theorists such as Mouffe, who have attempted to address explicitly institutional issues from a genealogical and deconstructive perspective, have – perhaps surprisingly – drawn on the model of political liberalism. This might support the claim that the debate between difference and diversity theorists will never be resolved until each recognizes the insights of the equality theorists' position that they have repressed.

# Conclusion

I would like to conclude by drawing out three underlying issues that have emerged in the course of writing this book. All three relate, in various ways, to the current interest in displacing binary dualisms. The first pertains to the theory/practice binary and the relation between feminist theory and institutionally oriented studies of women's partici- pation in politics. The second pertains to the inclusion/reversal binary and the relation between a strategy of displacement and the project of reconstructing political theory. The third pertains to the gender binary and the relation between feminism, gender and political theory.

The strategy of displacement, involving an exploration and critique of binary oppositions, has come to be a central aspect of gender theory. The deconstruction of dichotomies, revealing the ways in which each side of a binary division implies and reflects the other, has become increasingly influential in gender theory. The central features to dichotomous thinking include the notion of an oppositional and hierarchical ordering between two identities, where this pair sum up and define a whole. Thought and debate constructed on this model of binary logic are structured around oppositions between two things held in tension, only one of which can be right. Moreover, the two are not only mutually exclusive, they are also mutually exhaustive. They are held to constitute a whole, not simply parts of an open-ended plurality. Together they comprise all the possible options. Dichotomous thinking adopts an adversarial, zero-sum stance. The current preoccupation with displacing such thinking has various profound implications for the theorization of gender and politics.

The first underlying issue of significance concerns politics. One dual- ism that has structured much of the work surveyed in this book is that between feminist theory and political science. Rinehart commented that these two 'have had unfortunately narrow epistemological grounds, and almost no methodological grounds, in common' (Rinehart 1992: 16). Links between debates within feminist political theory and more institutionally oriented studies of women's participation within politics have been surprisingly weak. Indeed, these two areas of study are normally quite disjunct. Where feminist political theory has been self-consciously inter-disciplinary and has drawn extensively on recent literary and aesthetic theories, institutionally oriented studies of women and politics have tended to draw on a more traditional frame of political science. This has led to a substantial gulf between the two bodies of work. A negative reaction to the overly narrow conception of politics led many feminist political theorists to vacate the traditional arena of government altogether in their research and focus instead on issues of subjectivity. This work has been invaluable, but it is nonetheless a matter of regret that the links between these sophisticated reflections on subjectivity and the more orthodox questions of institutional politics have been left so under-developed. Dietz's claim that feminism 'needs a calling back to politics' (Dietz 1991: 250) signals a justified concern at the disjuncture between these two endeavours.

I have tried in this book to show that these two areas of debate are neither irreconcilable nor interchangeable. This is worth pointing out both because feminist theorists have tended to concentrate on subjectivity, and because, when they have been concerned to engage with the political, they have frequently formulated their attempts to reconstruct the political directly from ontological debates. Critics claim that this has had the effect of characterizing politics as 'the incidental results of gendered standpoints' rather than as linked to 'self-conscious ethical choices' (Grant 1993: 123). There has been, in Taylor's terminology, a tendency to view ontological propositions as synonymous with the advocacy of normative political proposals (Taylor 1991: 159).

Ontological issues are concerned with the question of what 'you recognise as the factors you will invoke to account for social life'; advocacy issues concern 'the moral stand or policy one adopts' (Taylor 1991: 159). As Taylor argues (in relation to communitarian theses about identity), such debates are purely ontological, they do not amount to an advocacy of anything. 'What they do purport to do, like any good ontological thesis, is to structure the field of possibilities in a more perspicuous way. But this precisely leaves us with choices, which we need some normative, deliberative, arguments to resolve' (Taylor 1991: 161). Such arguments have been somewhat lacking of late. The tendency to presume that normative choices are foreclosed by ontological commitments has led to a stultification of debate.

A concern, frequently articulated by those engaged in these debates themselves, is that much recent feminist theorizing has become overly entrenched and antagonistic regarding issues of ontology and worryingly sketchy and inattentive regarding issues of advocacy. As Fraser says, if the politics of the deconstructive theorists have at times been simplistic, it is probably because of the difficulty that arises from trying to deduce a normative politics of culture from an ontological conception of identity and difference' (Fraser 1997a: 183). The relation between the frames mapped out in Part I and the debates surveyed in Part II is, then, one particularly critical issue facing contemporary theorists of gender in political theory.

The second underlying issue that I want to highlight concerns strategies for theorizing gender and politics. I have argued that there are three distinct ways of considering 'gender and political theory'. The first proposes the recasting of political theory in order to realize its non-gendered ideal form. The second proposes the reworking of political theory from gendered perspectives in order to recognize the particularity of women's perspectives. The third proposes the rethinking of gender from a political perspective in order to destabilize dominant discourses of gender. The strategy of inclusion endorses the ideals of equality, justice, gender-neutral citizenship and the representation of ideas. The strategy of reversal endorses the ideals of difference, caring, gender-differentiated citizenship and the representation of identities. The strategy of displacement endorses the ideals of diversity, transgression, heterogeneous citizenship and representation as itself constitutive. This tripartite schema offers one way of categorizing what is a very complex field.

It has been common to find feminist theory divided into categories. Some theorists have focused on the historical distinction between first- and second-wave feminism, others on the geographical distinction between Anglo-American and French feminism. Although some theorists argue that it is mistaken to consider feminist theory in terms of the history of Western thought rather than in terms of feminism itself (Grant 1993: 3), many early typologies tended to categorize according to frames arising from, and pertinent to, existing disciplines and canons. In the context of political theory this has meant a focus upon ideological categorizations. This resulted in the extensive use of the fourfold typology of radical, liberal, Marxist and socialist feminism (Jaggar 1983).

But dissatisfaction with this schema has become increasingly common. Its explanatory use is marred, many argue, by the significant gaps it produces and important questions it obscures. Refined versions of the basic typology evolved accordingly: some adopting radical, liberal, Marxist and psychoanalytic categories (Elshtain 1981), others working with the categories of cultural, Freudian, existentialist, Marxist and radical

(Donovan 1985). By the late 1980s the list of categories had doubled – one popular text working with the categories of liberal, Marxist, radical mothering, radical sexuality, psychoanalytic, socialist, essentialist, and postmodern (Tong 1989).

Nonetheless, the inability of even such detailed typologies to capture adequately the range of positions emerging within feminist theory and practice became increasingly problematic, on both a theoretical and – perhaps more importantly – a political level. The absence of any direct consideration of issues of race and colour in these complex typologies was noted and extensively critiqued (Spelman 1988: 133–59). It has, says Haraway, 'become difficult to name one's feminism by a single adjective – or even to insist in every circumstance upon the noun. Consciousness of exclusion through naming is acute' (Haraway 1990: 196–7)

Some theorists, usually located within a postmodern camp, are critical of the construction of taxonomies per se and have rejoiced in the confusion of boundaries. The production of taxonomies, such critics argue, has the effect of presenting feminist debates as theoretical disputes between coherent ideological types persisting over time. Taxonomies are therefore an explanatory tool, but they also 'police deviation from official women's experience' (Haraway 1990: 198). Concern to avoid any such disciplinary constraints has led an increasing number of theorists to speak of feminisms in the plural and to accept, even celebrate, the 'disorderly polyphony' that constitutes them.

What becomes clear from these shifting and contested categorizations is not only the politically sensitive nature of the project of boundary definition, but also feminism's preoccupation with diversity and recognition of difference. For many who think of themselves as feminists, one of feminism's distinguishing features is its stress on the significance of personal experience, the moral and political importance of speaking from experience, and the obligation to recognize the distinctiveness of the experiences of others. Feminists, whatever their variety, have tended to assume that theoretical perspectives derive from and reflect personal experience. Attentiveness to the diversity within experience has therefore led to a commitment to fragmentation and multiplicity on the theoretical level also.

The problem of this approach is that the formation of any boundary, required to delimit a theoretical body of thought, is also a simultaneous act of assimilation and exclusion. As such it invites contestation. As a result the feminist concern to be sensitive to different voices within feminism has generated a concern to avoid the presentation of 'feminism' as a single unified body of thought, and to endorse subdivision and categorization within feminism. It has also led, at the same time and as a result of the same commitment, to a concern that the subdivisions are themselves exclusionary and assimilatory. Debates within feminist theory have therefore been intense, and certainly as numerous and time-consuming, as those between feminist and mainstream theories.

The debates and controversies within feminism have not, however, been static. There has been a marked shift in the type of categorizations deemed significant of late. Whereas the common categorizations of liberal, radical, Marxist and socialist focused attention on difference of political analysis and strategy, more recent debates within feminism have been more centrally preoccupied with different understandings of subjectivity and methodology. The inclusion, reversal, displacement schema that I have adopted in this book is intended to reflect this recent focus.

It will be apparent that the third strategy of displacement is pivotal in this schema. It highlights the mutual dependency of the strategies of inclusion and reversal and focuses attention on the need to deconstruct this particular dichotomy, which has been so central to feminist political theory. However, the status of this strategy in relation to the project of feminism and to the task of reconstructing political theory is simply not clear. There is a manifest concern among some theorists that to engage in a strategy of displacement alone is inadequate, as it provides no normative grounds for a strategy of political change.

One of the central issues facing contemporary gender theorists is the status of the strategy of displacement, both in relation to the other two strategies of inclusion and reversal, and in relation to the project of reconstruction. Is displacement antithetical both to inclusion and reversal, or is it better understood as a way of critically evaluating and augmenting each? It has become a matter of some political concern that displacement alone might not provide an adequate basis from which to engage in the process of reconceptualization. Reconceptualization is a utopian project; displacement is a deconstructive technique. It is the relation between these two that perhaps most neatly captures the focus of debate within current reflections on gender in political theory (see, for example, Hirschmann and Di Stefano 1996: 2–5, Benhabib, Butler, Cornell and Fraser 1995).

Advocates of displacement may argue that the feminist project entails only critique, creating uncertainty and challenging accepted meanings. Others have simply rejoiced in the contradictions and tensions of adopting and exploring all three strategies (Sylvester 1994: 66). Still others, more firmly wedded to a project of reconstruction, are concerned to locate such deconstructive strategies within a reconstructive agenda, to frame critique in utopia. Concern that to refuse to engage in a reconstructive task is to remain politically ineffective leads many to recommend the use of deconstruction as just one useful critical tool of analysis (Frazer and Lacey 1993: 171). Fraser argues against those who present different frames of feminist thinking as incompatible and argues instead for synthesis (Fraser 1995a: 60). And Ferguson too argues against the merits of being wholly 'enframed'. She shows perceptively how the strategies of reversal and displacement rely on one another: 'Genealogy keeps interpretation honest, and interpretation gives genealogy direction' (Ferguson 1993: 30). Each tempers the possible excesses of the other: both essentialism and inactivism are checked.

It may perhaps be possible, despite the theoretical tensions, to endorse both the genealogical and the interpretative frames and to pursue strategies of both reversal and displacement. The genealogical traces the heterogeneous discursive regimes that constitute particular subject positions, enabling one to transgress their operation. The interpretative perceives structural discrepancies in power accruing to distinct identifications, discerning shared experiences across subject positions and mapping affinities as the basis for collective action. Whether these two distinctive frames could also engage with a modified form of objectivity has, to date, received less attention. Yet this is now perhaps one of the more interesting questions facing theorists of gender in political theory.

The shift away from the strategy of inclusion, and its aspiration to impartiality and universalism, has been widely acknowledged. The strategies of reversal and displacement share a common rejection of the 'universal pretensions on political thought' (Phillips 1992), but offer very different alternative visions. It is the altercation between these two that has tended to predominate in recent debates within feminist political theory. Nonetheless, it should be noted that the strategy of inclusion, and its aspiration towards an ideal of universality, is not without its (cautious) advocates. Despite its rather unfashionable theoretical status, there are compelling reasons to reconsider the merits of impartiality, equality and justice as embodied in the strategy of inclusion. We should perhaps be cynical about a possible convergence between the other two strategies if the insights and ambitions of the strategy of inclusion are continually repressed. Whether resolution or ironic convergence is the aim, serious and sustained reflection on the possibilities for engagement between the three strategies is a second central task facing those seeking to theorize gender and politics.

The third and final underlying issue to which I want to draw attention concerns gender. The critique of dichotomous thinking invoked by a strategy of displacement has a paradoxical impact on feminist theory. It offers a way of moving beyond the apparently intractable opposition between equality and difference, inclusion and reversal. As such it might offer feminist political theorists a productive basis for engaging in a process of reconstructing the political. And yet it is not clear that such a reconstruction could continue to call itself 'feminist', if this entails an exclusive focus on the position and nature of women. The deconstruction of the male/female binary will itself be central to this strategic approach, and this has already had the effect of opening up a space for critical reflections on masculinities (plural) as well as femininities. In this context, theorizing gender and politics in the future will undoubtedly draw less specifically upon a body of feminist theory, which has in reality focused primarily on women, and may instead widen its horizons to include all theories of corporeal subjectivity. This will inevitably place the debates regarding strategies for reconceptualizing gender and politics in a new frame. The particular dynamic between inclusion, reversal and displacement that continues to preoccupy feminist political theorists may well have less relevance to those theorizing gender and politics from other perspectives. In other words, the two underlying issues which have provided the frame for this book, the relation between feminist theory and the study of politics and the relation between three distinct strategies within feminist theory, may themselves be eclipsed by a third issue which stands in need of more considered reflection than it has received to date, the relation between feminism and gender theory.

# References and Bibliography

Acklesberg, Martha and Shanley, Mary Lyndon 1996: Privacy, publicity and power: a feminist rethinking of the public–private distinction. In N. Hirschmann and C. Di Stefano (eds), 213–34.

Alcoff, Linda and Potter, Elizabeth (eds) 1993: *Feminist Epistemologies*. New York: Routledge.

Allen, Anita 1996: Privacy at home: the twofold problem. In N. Hirschmann and C. Di Stefano (eds), 193–212.

Allen, Judith 1990: Does feminism need a theory of the state? In S. Watson (ed.), *Playing the State: Australian feminist interventions*. London: Verso.

Andrews, Geoff (ed.) 1991: *Citizenship*. London: Lawrence & Wishart.

Antony, Louise and Witt, Charlotte (eds) 1993: *A Mind of One's Own: feminist essays on reason and objectivity*. Boulder, CO: Westview Press.

Arendt, Hannah 1958: *The Human Condition*. Chicago: University of Chicago Press.

Arendt, Hannah 1963: *On Revolution*. New York: Viking.

Arendt, Hannah 1969: *On Violence*. New York: Harcourt, Brace & World.

Aronowitz, S. 1988: Postmodernism and politics. In Andrew Ross (ed.), *Universal Abandon? The politics of postmodernism*. Minneapolis: University of Minnesota Press.

Atherton, Margaret 1993: Cartesian reason and gendered reason. In L. Antony and C. Witt (eds).

Bacchi, Carol 1990: *Same Difference: feminism and sexual difference*. Sydney: Allen & Unwin.

Baier, Annette 1987a: Hume: the women's moral theorist? In E. F. Kittay and D. T. Meyers (eds), *Women and Moral Theory*. Savage, MD: Rowman & Littlefield.

Baier, Annette 1987b: The need for more than justice. In *Canadian Journal of Philosophy*, 13, 14–56.

Baier, Annette 1997: Trust and antitrust. In D. T. Meyers (ed.), 605–29.

Banks, Olive 1986: *Faces of Feminism: a study of feminism as a social movement*. Oxford: Blackwell.

Baron, Marcia 1991: Impartiality and friendship. In *Ethics*, 101, 836–57.

Barrett, Michele 1992a: Words and things: materialism and method in contemporary feminist analysis. In M. Barrett and A. Phillips (eds), 201–17.

Barrett, Michele 1992b: *The Politics of Truth: from Marx to Foucault*. Cambridge: Polity Press.

Barrett, Michele and McIntosh, Mary 1982: *The Anti-social Family*. London: Verso/NLB.

Barrett, Michele and Phillips, Anne (eds) 1992: *Destabilizing Theory: contemporary feminist debates*. Cambridge: Polity Press.

Barry, Brian 1995: *Justice as Impartiality*. Oxford: Clarendon Press.

Bashevkin, S. (ed.) 1985: *Women and Politics in Western Europe*. London: Frank Cass.

Beckman, Peter, R. and D'Amico, Francine (eds) 1994: *Women, Gender and World Politics: perspectives, policies and prospects*. Westport, CT: Bergin & Garvey.

Benhabib, Seyla 1992: *Situating the Self: gender, community and postmodernism in contemporary ethics*. Cambridge: Polity Press.

Benhabib, Seyla (ed.) 1996: *Democracy and Difference: contesting the boundaries of the political*. Princeton, NJ: Princeton University Press.

Benhabib, Seyla and Cornell, Drucilla (eds) 1987: *Feminism as Critique: essays on the politics of gender in late-capitalist societies*. Cambridge: Polity Press.

Benhabib, Seyla, Butler, Judith, Cornell, Drucilla and Fraser, Nancy 1995: *Feminist Contentions: a philosophical exchange*. New York: Routledge.

Berlin, Isaiah 1962: Does political theory still exist? In P. Laslett and W. G. Runciman (eds), 1–33.

Bernstein, Richard 1976: *The Restructuring of Social and Political Theory*. Oxford: Blackwell.

Bernstein, Richard 1983: *Beyond Objectivism and Relativism*. Oxford: Blackwell.

Best, Steven and Kellner, Douglas 1991: *Postmodern Theory: critical interrogations*. London: Macmillan.

Bock, Gisela and James, Susan (eds) 1992: *Beyond Equality and Difference: citizenship, feminist politics and female subjectivity*. London: Routledge.

Boling, Patricia 1991: The democratic potential of mothering. In *Political Theory*, 19/4.

Bordo, Susan 1986: The Cartesian masculinization of thought. In *Signs*, 11, 439–56.

Bordo, Susan 1987: *The Flight to Objectivity: essays on Cartesianism and culture*. Albany: State University of New York Press.

Bordo, Susan and Jaggar, Alison (eds) 1989: *Gender/Body/Knowledge: feminist reconstructions of being and knowing*. New Brunswick, NJ: Rutgers University Press.

Bourque, Susan and Grossholtz, Jean 1998: Politics an unnatural practice: political science looks at female participation. In A. Phillips, *Feminism and Politics*. Oxford: Oxford University Press, 23–43.

Braidotti, Rosi 1991: *Patterns of Dissonance*. Cambridge: Polity Press.

Braidotti, Rosi 1994: *Nomadic Subjects: embodiment and sexual difference in contemporary feminist theory*. New York: Columbia University Press.

Braidotti, Rosi 1996: Cyberfeminism with a difference. In *New Formations*, no. 29. London: Lawrence & Wishart, 9–25.

Brittan, Arthur 1997: Masculinity and power. In C. Gould (ed.), 113–20.

Brod, Harry (ed.) 1987: *The Making of Masculinities: the new men's studies*. London: Allen & Unwin.

Brod, Harry and Kaufman, M. (eds) 1994: *Theorising Masculinities*. London: Sage.

Brown, Alice 1996: Women and politics in Scotland. In J. Lovenduski and P. Norris (eds), 28–42.

Brown, Wendy 1988: *Manhood and Politics: a feminist reading in political theory*. Totowa, NJ: Rowman & Littlefield.

Brown, Wendy 1995: *States of Injury: power and freedom in late modernity*. Princeton, NJ: Princeton University Press.

Bryson, Valerie 1992: *Feminist Political Theory: an introduction*. London: Macmillan.

Bubeck, Diemut 1995a: *Care, Gender and Justice*. Oxford: Clarendon Press.

Bubeck, Diemut 1995b: Thin, thick and feminist conceptions of citizenship. In *Contemporary Political Studies*, vol. 1 [Political Studies Association], 461–74.

Butler, Judith 1990: *Gender Trouble: feminism and the subversion of identity*. New York: Routledge.

Butler, Judith 1992: Contingent foundations: feminism and the question of postmodernism. In J. Butler and J. W. Scott (eds), 3–21.

Butler, Judith 1993: *Bodies that Matter: on the discursive limits of 'sex'*. London: Routledge.

Butler, Judith 1995: Contingent foundations. In S. Benhabib et al., 35–59.

Butler, Judith and Scott, Joan, W. (eds) 1992: *Feminists Theorize the Political*. New York and London: Routledge.

Carver, Terrell 1995: *Gender is Not a Synonym for Woman*. Boulder, CO: Lynne Rienner.

Castells, Manuel 1978: *City, Class and Power*. London: Macmillan.

Castells, Manual 1983: *The City and the Grass Roots*. London: Macmillan.

Chapman, Jenny 1993: *Politics, Feminism and the Reformation of Gender*. London: Routledge.

Chodorow, Nancy 1978: *The Reproduction of Mothering*. Berkeley: University of California Press.

Chodorow, Nancy 1989: *Feminism and Psychoanalytic Theory*. Cambridge: Polity Press.

Christian, Barbara 1997: The race for theory. In S. Kemp and J. Squires (eds), 69–78.

Code, Lorraine 1991: *What Can She Know?: feminist theory and the construction of knowledge*. Ithaca, NY: Cornell University Press.

Collins, Patricia Hill 1991: *Black Feminist Thought: knowledge, consciousness, and the politics of empowerment*. New York: Routledge.

Connell, Robert 1987: *Gender and Power.* Cambridge: Polity Press.

Connell, Robert 1995: *Masculinities.* Cambridge: Polity Press.

Connolly, William 1974: *The Terms of Political Discourse.* Oxford: Blackwell.

Connolly, William 1981: *Appearance and Reality in Politics.* Cambridge: Cambridge University Press.

Connolly, William 1988: *Political Theory and Modernity.* New York: Blackwell.

Connolly, William 1991: *Identity/Difference: democratic negotiations of political paradox.* Ithaca, NY: Cornell University Press.

Coole, Diana 1988: *Women in Political Theory: from ancient misogyny to contemporary feminism.* Brighton: Wheatsheaf.

Coole, Diana 1993: Constructing and deconstructing liberty: a feminist and poststructuralist analysis. *Political Studies*, 41, 83–95.

Coole, Diana 1996: Habermas and the question of alterity. In M. P. d'Entrèves and S. Benhabib (eds), *Habermas and the Unfinished Project of Modernity.* Cambridge: Polity Press.

Coole, Diana 1998: Master narratives and feminist subversions. In J. Good and I. Velody (eds), 107–26.

Cornell, Drucilla 1991: *Beyond Accommodation: ethical feminism, deconstruction, and the law.* New York: Routledge.

Cornell, Drucilla 1993: *Transformations: recollective imagination and sexual difference.* London: Routledge.

Cornell, Drucilla 1997: Gender hierarchy, equality and the possibility of democracy. In J. Dean (ed.), 210–22.

Crenshaw, Kimberle 1997: Intersectionality and identity politics. In M. L. Shanley and U. Narayan (eds), 178–94.

Dahlerup, Drude 1986: *The New Women's Movement.* London: Sage.

Dahlerup, Drude 1987: Confusing concepts – confusing reality: a theoretical discussion of the patriarchal state. In Anne Showstack-Sassoon (ed.), *Women and the State.* London: Hutchinson.

Daly, Mary 1987: *Gyn/Ecology.* London: Women's Press.

Dean, Jodi (ed.) 1997: *Feminism and the New Democracy: resiting the political.* London: Sage.

de Beauvoir, Simone 1997: The second sex. Reproduced in C. Gould (ed.), 3–15.

de Lauretis, Teresa 1984: *Alice Doesn't: feminism, semiotics, cinema.* Bloomington: Indiana University Press.

de Lauretis, Teresa (ed.) 1986: *Feminist Studies/Critical Studies.* Bloomington: Indiana University Press.

Delphy, Christine 1984: *Close to Home: a materialist analysis of women's oppression.* London: Hutchinson.

Derrida, Jacques 1988: The politics of friendship. In *Journal of Philosophy*, 80/2, 632–45.

Deutchman, Iva Ellen 1996: Feminist theory and the politics of empowerment. In Lois Lovelace Duke (ed.), *Women in Politics: outsiders or insiders?* Englewood Cliffs, NJ: Prentice-Hall, 4–16.

Dews, Peter (ed.) 1986: *Autonomy and Solidarity: interviews with Jürgen Habermas.* London: Verso.

Dews, Peter 1987: *Logics of Disintegration: post-structuralist thought and the claims of critical theory.* London: Verso.

Diamond, Irene and Hartsock, Nancy 1998: Beyond interests in politics: a comment on Virginia Sapiro's 'When are women's interests interesting?'. In A. Phillips (ed.), 193–203.

Diamond, Irene and Quinby, Lee (eds) 1982: *Feminism and Foucault: reflections on resistance.* Boston: Northeastern University Press.

Dietz, Mary 1985: Citizenship with a feminist face: the problem of maternal thinking. In *Political Theory*, 13/1.

Dietz, Mary 1991: On Arendt. In M. L. Shanley and C. Pateman (eds).

Dietz, Mary 1998: Context is all: feminism and theories of citizenship. In A. Phillips (ed.), *Feminism and Politics.* Oxford: Oxford University Press, 378–400.

Digby, Tom 1998: *Men Doing Feminism.* New York and London: Routledge.

Di Stefano, Christine 1990: Dilemmas of difference. In L. Nicholson (ed.), 63–83.

Di Stefano, Christine 1996: Autonomy in the light of difference. In N. Hirschmann and C. Di Stefano (eds), 95–116.

Donovan, Josephine 1985: *Feminist Theory.* New York: Continuum.

Dworkin, Andrea 1974. *Woman Hating.* New York: Dutton.

Easton, David 1953: *The Political System: an inquiry into the state of political science.* New York: Knopf.

Easton, David 1968: Political science. In *International Encyclopaedia of the Social Sciences*, 12, 282–98.

Eisenstein, Hester 1984: *Contemporary Feminist Thought.* London: Allen & Unwin.

Eisenstein, Zillah 1981: *The Radical Future of Liberal Feminism.* London: Longman.

Elshtain, Jean Bethke 1974: Moral woman and immoral man: a consideration of the public/private split and its political ramifications. In *Politics and Society*, no. 4.

Elshtain, Jean Bethke 1981: *Public Man, Private Woman: women in social and political thought.* Oxford: Martin Robertson.

Elshtain, Jean Bethke (ed.) 1982a: *The Family in Political Thought.* Brighton: Harvester.

Elshtain, Jean Bethke 1982b: Feminist discourse and its discontents: language, power and meanings. In *Signs*, 3/7, 603–21.

Elshtain, Jean Bethke 1990: *Power Trips and Other Journeys: essays in feminism as civic discourse.* Madison: University of Wisconsin Press.

Elshtain, Jean Bethke 1992a: The power and powerlessness of women. In G. Bock and S. James (eds), 110–25.

Elshtain, Jean Bethke 1992b: *Meditations in Modern Political Thought: masculine/feminine themes from Luther to Arendt.* University Park: Pennsylvania State University Press.

Elshtain, Jean Bethke 1995: *Democracy on Trial.* New York: Basic Books.

Elshtain, Jean Bethke 1998: Antigone's daughters. In A. Phillips (ed.), 363–77.

Enloe, Cynthia 1989: *Bananas, Beaches and Bases.* London: Pandora.

Enloe, Cynthia 1993: *The Morning After: sexual politics at the end of the Cold War.* Berkeley: University of California Press.

Etzioni, Amitai 1994: *The Spirit of Community: the reinvention of American society.* New York: Touchstone/Simon & Schuster.

Etzioni, Amitai 1997: *The New Golden Rule: community and morality in a democratic society.* London: Profile Books.

Evans, Judith 1995: *Feminist Theory Today: an introduction to second-wave feminism.* London: Sage.

Evans, Judith, Hills, Jill, Hunt, Karen, Meehan, Elizabeth, ten Tusscher, Tessa, Vogel, Ursula and Waylen, Georgina 1986: *Feminism and Political Theory.* London: Sage.

Evans, Mary 1997: In praise of theory: the case for women's studies. In S. Kemp and J. Squires (eds), 17–22.

Ferguson, Kathy 1984: *The Feminist Case Against Bureaucracy.* Philadelphia: Temple University Press.

Ferguson, Kathy 1993: *The Man Question: visions of subjectivity in feminist theory.* Berkeley: University of California Press.

Firestone, Shulamith and Koedt, Anne (eds) 1969: The manifesto of the redstockings. In *Notes from the Second Year.* New York: Radical Feminism.

Flanagan, Owen and Jackson, Kathryn 1990: Justice, care and gender: the Kohlberg–Gilligan debate revisited. In Cass Sunstein (ed.), *Feminism and Political Theory.* Chicago: University of Chicago Press, 37–52.

Flax, Jane 1987: Postmodern and gender relations in feminist theory. In *Signs*, 12/4, 621–43.

Flax, Jane 1990: *Thinking Fragments.* Berkeley: University of California Press.

Flax, Jane 1992: Beyond equality: gender, justice and difference. In G. Bock and S. James (eds), *Beyond Equality and Difference: citizenship, feminist politics and female subjectivity.* London: Routledge, 193–210.

Flax, Jane 1993: Women do theory. In Alison Jaggar and Paula Rothenberg (eds), *Feminist Frameworks: alternative theoretical accounts of the relations between women and men*, 3rd edn. New York: McGraw-Hill, 80–5.

Flax, Jane 1997: Postmodernism and gender relations in feminist theory. In S. Kemp and J. Squires (eds), 170–9.

Foucault, Michel 1978: *The History of Sexuality: an introduction*, trans. R. Hurley. Harmondsworth: Penguin.

Foucault, Michel 1980: *Power/Knowledge: selected interviews and other writings 1972–77*, ed. C. Gordon. Brighton: Harvester.

Foucault, Michel 1988: An aesthetics of existence. In *Politics, Philosophy, Culture: interviews and other writings, 1977–1984*, ed. L. Kritzman. London: Routledge.

Fraser, Nancy 1989: *Unruly Practices: power, discourse and gender in contemporary social theory.* Cambridge: Polity Press.

Fraser, Nancy 1995a: False antithesis. In S. Benhabib et al., 59–74.

Fraser, Nancy 1995b: Pragmatism, feminism and the linguistic turn. In S. Benhabib et al., 157–72.

Fraser, Nancy 1997a: *Justice Interruptus: critical reflections on the 'Postsocialist' condition.* New York: Routledge.

Fraser, Nancy 1997b: Equality, difference and democracy: recent feminist debates in the United States. In J. Dean (ed.), 98–110.

Fraser, Nancy and Nicholson, Linda 1990: Social criticism without philosophy: an encounter between feminism and postmodernism. In L. Nicholson (ed.), 19–38.

Frazer, Elizabeth and Lacey, Nicola 1993: *The Politics of Community: a feminist critique of the liberal-communitarian debate.* New York: Harvester Wheatsheaf.

Freeman, Jo 1975: *The Politics of Women's Liberation.* New York: Longman.

Fronow, Mary Margaret and Cook, Judith (eds) 1991: *Beyond Methodology: feminist scholarship as lived research.* Bloomington: Indiana University Press.

Fuss, Diana 1989: *Essentially Speaking: feminism, nature & difference.* London: Routledge.

Garry, Ann and Pearsall, Marilyn 1996: *Women, Knowledge and Reality: explorations in feminist philosophy.* New York: Routledge, Chapman & Hall.

Gatens, Moira 1991: *Feminism and Philosophy: perspectives on difference and equality.* Cambridge: Polity Press.

Gatens, Moira 1992: Power, bodies and difference. In M. Barrett and A. Phillips (eds), 120–37.

Giddens, Anthony 1968: 'Power' in the recent writings of Talcott Parsons. *Sociology*, 2, 257–72.

Giddens, Anthony 1998: A third way? *The Guardian*, 23 May, 2.

Gilligan, Carol 1982: *In a Different Voice: psychological theory and women's development.* Cambridge, MA: Harvard University Press.

Gilligan, Carol 1997: In a different voice: women's conceptions of self and of morality. In D. T. Meyers (ed.), 549–82.

Glendinning, Caroline 1990: Dependency and interdependency: the incomes of informal carers and the impact of social security. In *Journal of Social Policy*, 19/4, 167–97.

Good, James and Velody, Irving (eds) 1998: *The Politics of Postmodernity.* Cambridge: Cambridge University Press.

Gottlieb, Roger 1997: Mothering and the reproduction of power. In C. Gould (ed.), 41–8.

Gordon, Colin (ed.) 1980: *Power/Knowledge: selected interviews and other writings, 1972–1977.* Brighton: Harvester.

Gould, Carol (ed.) 1997: *Gender.* Atlantic Highlands, NJ: Humanities Press.

Grant, Judith 1993: *Fundamental Feminism: contesting the core concepts of feminist theory.* New York and London: Routledge.

Green, Karen 1995: *The Woman of Reason: feminism, humanism and political thought.* Cambridge, Polity Press.

Green, Phillip 1985: *Retrieving Democracy.* Totowa, NJ: Rowman & Allenheld.

Griffiths, Morwenna 1995: *Feminisms and the Self: the web of identity.* London: Routledge.

Griffiths, Morwenna and Whitford, Margaret (eds) 1988: *Feminist Perspectives in Philosophy.* Bloomington: Indiana University Press.

Grimshaw, Jean 1986: *Feminist Philosophers.* Brighton: Wheatsheaf.

Grimshaw, Jean 1988: Autonomy and identity in feminist thinking. In M. Griffiths and M. Whitford (eds).

Grimshaw, Jean 1993: Practices of freedom. In C. Ramazanoglu (ed.), 51–72.

Grosz, Elizabeth 1987: Conclusion: what is feminist theory? In C. Pateman and E. Grosz (eds).

Grosz, Elizabeth 1994a: Identity and difference: a response. In Paul James (ed.), *Critical Politics*. Melbourne: Arena Publications, 29–33.

Grosz, Elizabeth 1994b: *Volatile Bodies: toward a corporeal feminism*. Bloomington: Indiana University Press.

Grosz, Elizabeth 1995a: *Space, Time, and Perversion: essays on the politics of bodies*. New York: Routledge.

Grosz, Elizabeth 1995b: Psychoanalysis and the imaginary body. In Penny Florence and Dee Reynolds (eds), *Feminist Subjects, Multimedia: cultural methodologies*. Manchester: Manchester University Press.

Gunew, Sneja (ed.) 1990: *Feminist Knowledge: critique and construct*. London and New York: Routledge.

Gutmann, Amy 1992: *Multiculturalism and the Politics of 'Recognition'*. Princeton, NJ: Princeton University Press.

Habermas, Jürgen 1986: Interview. In P. Dews (ed.), *Autonomy and Solidarity: interviews with Jurgen Habermas*. London: Verso.

Habermas, Jürgen 1990: *Moral Consciousness and Communicative Action*, trans. Christian Lenhardt and Shierry Weber Nicholson. Cambridge, MA: MIT Press.

Habermas, Jürgen 1996a: Three normative models of democracy. In S. Benhabib (ed.), 21–30.

Habermas, Jürgen 1996b: Modernity: an unfinished project. In M. P. d'Entrèves and S. Benhabib (eds), *Habermas and the Unfinished Project of Modernity*. Cambridge: Polity Press.

Haraway, Donna 1990: A manifesto for cyborgs: science, technology and socialist feminism in the 1980s. In Linda Nicholson (ed.), *Feminism/Postmodernism*. London and New York: Routledge, 190–233.

Haraway, Donna 1991: 'Gender' for a Marxist dictionary: the sexual politics of a word. In Haraway, *Simians, Cyborgs and Women*. New York: Routledge.

Harding, Sandra (ed.) 1987: *Feminism and Methodology*. Bloomington: Indiana University Press.

Harding, Sandra 1991: *Whose Science? Whose Knowledge?: thinking from women's lives*. Ithaca, NY: Cornell University Press.

Harding, Sandra and Hintikka, Merrill B. (eds) 1983: *Discovering Reality: feminist perspectives on epistemology, metaphysics, methodology, and philosophy of science*. Dordrecht: Reidal.

Hartsock, Nancy 1983: *Money, Sex, and Power: toward a feminist historical materialism*. New York: Longman.

Hartsock, Nancy 1996: Community/sexuality/gender: rethinking power. In N. Hirschmann and C. Di Stefano (eds), 27–50.

Hartsock, Nancy 1997: The feminist standpoint: developing a ground for a specifically historical materialism. In S. Kemp and J. Squires (eds), 152–60.

Haug, Frigga 1995: The quota demand and feminist politics. In *New Left Review*, 209, 136–45.

Hawkesworth, Mary 1997: Confounding gender. In *Signs*, 22.

Hearn, Jeff 1999: A crisis in masculinity: new agendas for women? In S. Walby (ed.).

Hearn, Jeff and Morgan, David (eds) 1990: *Men, Masculinities and Social Theory*. London: Unwin & Hyman.

Hekman, Susan 1995: *Moral Voices, Moral Selves: Carol Gilligan and feminist moral theory*. University Park: Pennsylvania State University Press.

Held, David 1987: *Models of Democracy*. Cambridge: Polity Press.

Held, David 1989: *Political Theory and the Modern State*. Cambridge: Polity Press.

Held, David (ed.) 1991a: *Political Theory Today*. Cambridge: Polity Press.

Held, David 1991b: Editor's introduction. In Held (ed.), 1–22.

Held, David 1991c: Between state and civil society: citizenship. In G. Andrews (ed.), 19–25.

Held, Virginia 1985: Feminism and epistemology. In *Philosophy and Public Affairs*, 14, 296–307.

Held, Virginia 1993: *Feminist Morality: transforming culture, society and politics*. Chicago: University of Chicago Press.

Heller, Agnes 1991: The concept of the political revisited. In D. Held (ed.), 330–43.

Hernes, Helga Maria 1987: *Welfare State and Woman Power: essays in state feminism*. Oslo: Norwegian University Press.

Hill Collins, Patricia 1991: Learning from the outsider within. In Mary Margaret Fonow and Judith Cook (eds), *Beyond Methodology: feminist scholarship as lived research*. Bloomington: Indiana University Press.

Hill Collins, Patricia 1993: Toward an Afrocentric feminist epistemology. In A. Jaggar and P. Rothenberg (eds), 93–103.

Hirschmann, Nancy 1992: *Rethinking Obligation*. Ithaca, NY: Cornell University Press.

Hirschmann, Nancy and Di Stefano, Christine (eds) 1996: *Revisioning the Political: feminist reconstructions of traditional concepts in Western political theory*. Oxford: Westview Press.

Hirst, Paul and Thompson, G. 1996: *Globalization in Question*. Cambridge: Polity Press.

HMSO 1990: *Encouraging Citizenship: report of the commission on citizenship*.

Hollis, Martin 1970: Reason and ritual. In Brian Wilson (ed.), *Rationality*. Oxford: Oxford University Press.

Honig, Bonnie 1993: *Political Theory and the Displacement of Politics*. Ithaca, NY: Cornell University Press.

Honig, Bonnie 1996: Difference, dilemmas, and the politics of hope. In S. Benhabib (ed.), 257–77.

Honneth, Axel 1995: *The Struggle for Recognition*. Cambridge: Polity Press.

hooks, bell 1990: *Yearning: race, gender and cultural politics*. Boston: South End Press.

Hoskyns, Catherine 1996: *Integrating Gender: women, law and politics in the European Union*. London: Verso.

Irigaray, Luce 1985: *The Sex Which Is Not One*, trans. Catherine Porter. Ithaca, NY: Cornell University Press.

Isaac, J. 1987: Beyond the three faces of power: a realist critique. In *Polity*, 10, fall, 4–31.

Jaggar, Alison 1983: *Feminist Politics and Human Nature*. Brighton: Harvester.

Jaggar, Alison 1994: *Living with Contradictions: controversies in feminist social ethics*. Boulder, CO: Westview Press.

Jaggar, Alison 1997a: Love and knowledge: emotion in feminist epistemology. In S. Kemp and J. Squires (eds), 188–93 [originally pubd in *Inquiry*, 32 (1989), 151–76].

Jaggar, Alison 1997b: Human biology in feminist theory: sexual equality reconsidered. In C. Gould (ed.), 48–55.

Jaggar, Alison and Rothenberg, Paula (eds) 1993: *Feminist Frameworks: alternative theoretical accounts of the relations between women and men*, 3rd edn. New York: McGraw-Hill.

James, Paul (ed.) 1994: *Critical Politics*. Melbourne: Arena Publications.

James, Susan 1992: The good-enough citizen: female citizenship and independence. In G. Bock and S. James (eds), 48–65.

Johnson, Pauline 1988: Feminism and images of autonomy. In *Radical Philosophy*, summer.

Jónasdóttir, Anna G. 1988: On the concept of interest, women's interests and the limitations of interest theory. In K. B. Jones and A. G. Jónasdóttir (eds).

Jones, Kathleen 1990: Citizenship in a woman-friendly polity. In *Signs*, 15/4.

Jones, Kathleen B. 1993a: *Compassionate Authority: democracy and the representation of women*. London and New York: Routledge.

Jones, Kathleen B. 1993b: Configurations of citizenship: confederacies and feminism. Paper prepared for presentation at the European Consortium for Political Research, University of Leiden, April 2–8.

Jones, Kathleen B. 1997: The politics of responsibility and perspectives of violence against women. In J. Dean (ed.), 13–29.

Jones, Kathleen B. and Anna G. Jónasdóttir (eds) 1988: *The Political Interests of Gender: developing theory and research with a feminist face*. London: Sage.

Keller, Evelyn Fox 1983: Reflections on gender and science. In S. Harding and M. B. Hintikka (eds).

Keller, Evelyn Fox 1984: *Reflections on Gender and Science*. New Haven, CT: Yale University Press.

Kemp, Sandra and Squires, Judith (eds) 1997: *Feminisms*. Oxford: Oxford University Press.

Kiss, Elizabeth 1997: Alchemy or fool's gold? Assessing feminist doubts about rights. In M. L. Shanley and U. Narayan (eds), 1–24.

Kristeva, Julia 1980: Oscillation between power and denial. In Elaine Marks and Isabelle de Courtivron (eds), *New French Feminisms*. Amherst: University of Massachusetts Press.

Kristeva, Julia 1981: Women's time. In *Signs*, 13–35.

Kristeva, Julia 1993: *Nations Without Nationalism*. New York: Columbia University Press.

Kristeva, Julia 1997: Psychoanalysis and the polis. In S. Kemp and J. Squires (eds), 228–31.

Kritzman, L. (ed.) 1988: *Politics, Philosophy, Culture: interviews and other writings, 1977–1984*. London: Routledge.

Kymlicka, Will 1990: *Contemporary Political Philosophy: an introduction*. Oxford: Oxford University Press.

Kymlicka, Will 1994: *Multicultural Citizenship*. Oxford: Clarendon Press.

Landes, Joan 1995: The public and the private sphere: a feminist reconsideration. In J. Meehan (ed.), 91–116.

Larrabee, Mary Jeanne (ed.) 1993: *An Ethic of Care: feminist and interdisciplinary perspectives*. London and New York: Routledge.

Laslett, Peter (ed.) 1956: *Philosophy, Politics and Society*. Oxford: Blackwell.

Laslett, Peter and Runciman, W. G. (eds) 1962: *Philosophy, Politics and Society*, 2nd series. Oxford: Blackwell.

Leftwich, Adrian 1984a: On the politics of politics. In A. Leftwich (ed.), 1–18.

Leftwich, Adrian (ed.) 1984b: *What is Politics?* Oxford: Blackwell.

Leftwich, Adrian and Held, David 1984: A discipline of politics? In A. Leftwich (ed.), 139–61.

Levitas, Ruth 1999: *The Inclusive Society? Social exclusion and New Labour*. London: Macmillan.

Lister, Ruth 1990: *The Exclusive Society: citizenship and the poor*. London: Child Poverty Action Group.

Lister, Ruth 1997: *Citizenship: feminist perspectives*. London: Macmillan.

Lloyd, Genevieve 1984: *The Man of Reason: 'male' and 'female' in Western philosophy*. London: Methuen.

Lloyd, Genevieve 1993: Maleness, metaphor, and the 'crisis' of reason. In L. Antony and C. Witt (eds).

Longino, Helen 1993: Essential tensions – phase two: feminist, philosophical, and social studies of science. In L. Antony and C. Witt (eds), 257–73.

Lovenduski, Joni 1981: Toward the emasculation of political science. In Dale Spender (ed.), *Men's Studies Modified*. Oxford: Pergamon.

Lovenduski, Joni 1996: Sex, gender and British politics. In J. Lovenduski and P. Norris (eds), 1–16.

Lovenduski, Joni 1997: Gender politics: a breakthrough for women? In *Parliamentary Affairs*, 50/4, 708–19.

Lovenduski, Joni and Norris, Pippa 1993: *Gender and Party Politics*. London: Sage.

Lovenduski, Joni and Norris, Pippa 1995: *Political Recruitment: gender, race and class in the British parliament*. Cambridge: Cambridge University Press.

Lovenduski, Joni and Norris, Pippa (eds) 1996: *Women in Politics*. Oxford: Oxford University Press.

Lukes, Steven 1970: Some problems about rationality. In Brian Wilson (ed.), *Rationality*. Oxford: Oxford University Press.

Lukes, Steven 1973: *Individualism*. Oxford: Blackwell.

Lukes, Steven 1978: *Power: a radical view*. London: Macmillan.

MacInnes, John 1998: *The End of Masculinity*. Buckingham: Open University Press.

MacIntyre, Alasdair 1970: The idea of a social science. In Brian Wilson (ed.), *Rationality*. Oxford: Oxford University Press.

MacKinnon, Catharine 1982: Feminism, Marxism, method and the state. In *Signs*, 7/3, 515–44.

MacKinnon, Catharine (with Carol Gilligan et al.) 1985: Feminist discourse, moral values and the law – a conversation. In *Buffalo Law Review*, 34/1.

MacKinnon, Catharine 1987: *Feminism Unmodified: discourses on life and law*. Cambridge, MA: Harvard University Press.

MacKinnon, Catharine 1989: *Toward a Feminist Theory of the State*. Cambridge, MA: Harvard University Press.

McLean, Iain 1991: Forms of representation and systems of voting. In D. Held (ed.), 172–96.

McNay, Lois 1992: *Foucault and Feminism: power, gender and the self*. Cambridge, Polity Press.

McNay, Lois 1994: *Foucault*. Cambridge: Polity Press.

Mansbridge, Jane (ed.) 1990: *Beyond Self-interest*. Chicago: University of Chicago Press.

Marsh, Michael and Norris, Pippa 1997: Political representation in the European parliament. In *European Journal of Political Research*, 32, 153–64.

Marshall, T. H. 1950: *Citizenship and Social Class*. Cambridge: Cambridge University Press.

Martin, Biddy and Mohanty, Chandra 1986: Feminist politics. In T. de Lauretis (ed.).

Meehan, Elizabeth and Sevenhuijsen, S. 1991: *Equality Politics and Gender*. London: Sage.

Meehan, Johanna (ed.) 1995: *Feminists Read Habermas*. New York and London: Routledge.

Meyers, Diana Tietjens (ed.) 1997: *Feminist Social Thought: a reader*. New York and London: Routledge.

Mies, Maria 1983: Towards a methodology for feminist research. In G. Bowles and R. Duelli Klein (eds), *Theories of Women's Studies*. London: Routledge.

Mies, Maria and Shiva, Vandana (eds) 1993: *Ecofeminism*. London: Zed Books.

Miller, David 1993: The conceptions of citizenship. Paper presented to the Workshop on Citizenship and Pluralism at the ECPR Joint Sessions, Leiden, 2–7 April.

Miller, Jean Baker 1976: *Toward a New Psychology of Women*. Boston: Beacon Press.

Minow, Martha and Shanley, Mary Lyndon 1997: Revisioning the family: relational rights and responsibilities. In M. L. Shanley and U. Narayan (eds), 84–108.

Modood, Tariq 1996: Race in Britain and the politics of difference. In D. Archard (ed.), *Philosophy and Pluralism*. Cambridge: Cambridge University Press.

Moi, Toril 1997: Feminist, female, feminine. In S. Kemp and J. Squires (eds), 246–50.

Morgan, David 1992: *Discovering Men*. London: Routledge.

Mouffe, Chantal 1988: Hegemony and new political subjects. In Cary Nelson and Larry Grossberg (eds), *Marxism and the Interpretations of Culture*. Chicago: University of Chicago Press.

Mouffe, Chantal (ed.) 1992a: *Dimensions of Radical Democracy*. London: Verso.

Mouffe, Chantal 1992b: Feminism, citizenship and radical democratic politics. In J. Butler and J. W. Scott (eds), 369–84.

Mouffe, Chantal 1993: *The Return of the Political*. London: Verso.

Mouffe, Chantal 1996: Democracy, power and the 'political'. In S. Benhabib (ed.), 245–57.

Mouffe, Chantal and Laclau, Ernesto 1985: *Hegemony and Socialist Strategy*. London: Verso.

Mulgan, Geoff 1991: Citizens and responsibilities. In G. Andrews (ed.), 37–49.

Narayan, Uma 1997: Towards a feminist vision of citizenship: rethinking the implications of dignity, political participation, and nationality. In M. L. Shanley and U. Narayan (eds), 48–67.

Nash, Kate 1998: *Universal Difference: feminism and the liberal undecidability of 'women'*. London: Macmillan.

Nelson, Barbara 1984: Women's poverty and women's citizenship: some political consequences of economic marginality. In *Signs*, 10/2, 209–31.

Nicholson, Linda (ed.) 1990: *Feminism/Postmodernism*. New York: Routledge.

Noddings, Nel 1984: *Caring: a feminine approach to ethics*. Berkeley: University of California Press.

Norris, Pippa 1987: *Politics and Sexual Equality*. Brighton: Wheatsheaf.

Norris, Pippa 1996: Women politicians: transforming Westminster? In *Parliamentary Affairs*, 49/1, 89–102.

Norris, Pippa 1997: Representation and the democratic deficit. In *European Journal of Political Research*, 32/2, 273–82.

O'Brien, Mary 1983: *The Politics of Reproduction*. London: Routledge & Kegan Paul.

Okin, Susan Moller 1979: *Women in Western Political Thought*. Princeton, NJ: Princeton University Press.

Okin, Susan Moller 1989: *Gender, Justice and the Family*. New York: Basic Books.

Okin, Susan Moller 1991: Humanist liberalism. In Nancy Rosenblum (ed.), *Liberalism and the Moral Life*. Cambridge, MA: Harvard University Press, 39–53.

Okin, Susan Moller 1998: Gender, the public and the private. In A. Phillips (ed.), 116–41.

Outshoorn, Joyce 1994: Parity democracy. Paper presented at the Economic Consortium of Political Research, Leiden, April.

Parekh, Bhikhu 1991: British citizenship and cultural difference. In G. Andrews (ed.), 183–206.

Parsons, Talcott 1967: *Sociological Theory and Modern Society*. New York: Free Press, 297–354.

Pateman, Carole 1983: Feminist critiques of the public/private dichotomy. In S. Benn and G. Gaus (eds), *Public and Private in Social Life*. London: Croom Helm, 281–303.

Pateman, Carole 1988: *The Sexual Contract*. Cambridge: Polity Press.

Pateman, Carole 1989: *The Disorder of Women: democracy, feminism and political theory*. Cambridge: Polity Press.

Pateman, Carole 1992: Equality, difference, subordination: the politics of motherhood and women's citizenship. In G. Bock and S. James (eds), 17–32.

Pateman, Carole and Brennan, Teresa 1979: Mere auxiliaries to the commonwealth: women and the origins of liberalism. *Political Studies*, 27, 183–200.

Pateman, Carole and Grosz, Elizabeth (eds) 1987: *Feminist Challenges: social and political theory*. Boston: Northeastern University Press.

Petchesky, Rosalind 1984: *Abortion and Women's Choice: the state, sexuality and reproductive freedom*. New York: Longman.

Peterson, V. Spike (ed.) 1992: *Gendered States: feminist (re)visions of international relations theory*. Boulder, CO: Lynne Rienner.

Peterson, V. Spike and Runyan, Anne Sisson 1993: *Global Gender Issues*. Boulder, CO: Westview Press.

Phillips, Anne (ed.) 1987: *Feminism and Equality*. Oxford: Blackwell.

Phillips, Anne 1991a: *Engendering Democracy*. Cambridge: Polity Press.

Phillips, Anne 1991b: Citizenship and feminist politics. In G. Andrews (ed.), 76–90.

Phillips, Anne 1992: Universal pretensions in political thought. In M. Barrett and A. Phillips (eds), 10–30.

Phillips, Anne 1993: *Democracy and Difference*. Cambridge: Polity Press.

Phillips, Anne 1995: *The Politics of Presence*. Oxford: Clarendon Press.

Phillips Anne (ed.) 1998: *Feminism and Politics*. Oxford: Oxford University Press.

Pitkin, Hannah 1967: *The Concept of Representation*. Berkeley: University of California Press.

Plant, Raymond 1991: *Modern Political Thought*. Oxford: Blackwell.

Plant, Raymond 1998: Antimonies of modernist political thought: reasoning, context and community. In J. Good and I. Velody (eds), 76–106.

Popper, Karl 1977: *The Open Society and its Enemies*. London: Routledge.

Pringle, Rosemary and Watson, Sophie 1992: Women's interests and the poststructuralist state. In M. Barrett and A. Phillips (eds), 53–74.

Prokhovnik, Raia 1999: *Rational Woman*. London: Routledge.

Quinby, Lee 1997: Genealogical feminism: a politic way of looking. In J. Dean (ed.), 146–68.

Rabinow, Paul (ed.) 1984: *The Foucault Reader*. Harmondsworth: Penguin.

Ramazanoglu, Caroline (ed.) 1993: *Up Against Foucault: explorations of some tensions between Foucault and feminism*. London and New York: Routledge.

Randall, Vicky 1982: *Women and Politics*. London: Macmillan.

Rawls, John 1971: *A Theory of Justice*. Cambridge, MA: Harvard University Press.

Rawls, John 1985: Justice as fairness: political not metaphysical. In *Philosophy and Public Affairs*, 14, 223–51.

Rawls, John 1993: *Political Liberalism*. New York: Columbia University Press.

Redner, Harry 1994: *A New Science of Representation: towards an integrated theory of representation in science, politics and art*. Boulder, CO: Westview Press.

Rhode, Deborah 1992: The politics of paradigms: gender difference and gender disadvantage. In G. Bock and S. James (eds), 149–63.

Richards, Janet Radcliffe 1980: *The Sceptical Feminist.* Harmondsworth: Penguin.

Riley, Denise 1988: *Am I That Name? Feminism and the category of 'women' in history.* New York: Macmillan.

Riley, Denise 1997: Am I That Name? Extract repr. in S. Kemp and J. Squires (eds), 241–6.

Rinehart, Sue Tolleson 1992: *Gender Consciousness and Politics.* New York and London: Routledge.

Rosenblum, Nancy 1987: *Another Liberalism: Romanticism and the reconstruction of liberal thought.* Cambridge, MA: Harvard University Press.

Rosenblum, Nancy (ed.) 1991: *Liberalism and the Moral Life.* Cambridge, MA: Harvard University Press.

Rowbotham, Sheila, Segal, Lynne and Wainwright, Hilary 1979: *Beyond the Fragments: feminism and the making of socialism.* London: Merlin Press.

Rubin, Gayle 1975: The traffic in women: notes on the political economy of sex. In R. Reiter Rapp (ed.), *Toward an Anthropology of Women.* New York: Monthly Review Press.

Ruddick, Sara 1983: Maternal thinking. In J. Treblicot (ed.), *Mothering: essays in feminist theory.* Totowa, NJ: Rowman & Allanheld.

Ruddick, Sara 1989: *Maternal Thinking: towards a politics of peace.* Boston: Beacon Press.

Ruddick, Sara 1997: Maternal thinking. In C. Gould (ed.), 299–305.

Sandel, Michael 1982: *Liberalism and the Limits of Justice.* Cambridge: Cambridge University Press.

Sandel, Michael 1996: *Democracy's Discontent: America in search of a public philosophy.* Cambridge, MA: Harvard University Press.

Sapiro, Virginia 1983: *The Political Integration of Women: roles, socialization and politics.* Urbana: University of Illinois Press.

Sapiro, Virginia 1998a: Feminist studies and political science – and vice versa. In A. Phillips (ed.), 67–89.

Sapiro, Virginia 1998b: When are interests interesting? In A. Phillips (ed.), 161–93.

Scheman, Naomi 1993: *Engenderings: constructions of knowledge, authority and privilege.* New York and London: Routledge.

Scheman, Naomi 1997: Though this be method, yet there is madness in it: paranoia and liberal epistemology. In D. T. Meyers (ed.), 342–67.

Scobbie, Moira 1998: Nexus on-line discussion, May, <www.netnexus.org>.

Scott, Joan Wallach 1988: *Gender and the Politics of History.* New York: Columbia University Press.

Scott, Joan Wallach 1997: Deconstructing equality-versus-difference: or, the uses of poststructuralist theory for feminism. In D. T. Meyers (ed.), 757–71.

Sellers, Susan 1991: *Language and Sexual Difference.* London: Macmillan.

Segal, Lynne 1990: *Slow Motion: changing masculinities, changing men.* London: Virago.

Segal, Lynne 1994: *Straight Sex: the politics of pleasure.* London: Virago.

Seidler, Vic 1989: *Rediscovering Masculinity: reason, language and sexuality.* London: Routledge.

Seitz, Brian 1995: *The Trace of Political Representation.* Albany: State University of New York Press.

Sevenhuijsen, S. 1991: The morality of feminism. In *Hypatia*, 6/2, 173–91.

Shanley, Mary Lyndon and Narayan, Uma (eds) 1997: *Reconstructing Political Theory: feminist perspectives.* Cambridge: Polity Press.

Shanley, Mary Lyndon and Pateman, Carole (eds) 1991: *Feminist Interpretations and Political Theory.* Cambridge: Polity Press.

Shklar, Judith 1991: The liberalism of fear. In N. Rosenblum (ed.), 21–38.

Siltanen, Janet and Stanworth, Michelle (eds) 1984: *Women and the Public Sphere.* London: Hutchinson.

Skinner, Quentin 1988: Some problems in the analysis of political thought and action. In J. Tully (ed.), *Meaning and Context: Quentin Skinner and his critics.* Cambridge: Polity Press.

Smart, Carol 1989: *Feminism and the Power of the Law.* London: Routledge.

Soper, Kate 1990: Feminism, humanism, postmodernism. In Soper, *Troubled Pleasures.* London: Verso, 228–45 [extract in S. Kemp and J. Squires (eds), 1997, 286–92].

Spelman, Elizabeth 1988: *Inessential Woman: problems of exclusion in feminist thought.* Boston: Beacon Books.

Spelman, Elizabeth 1997a: Woman: the one and the many. In S. Kemp and J. Squires (eds), 235–6.

Spelman, Elizabeth 1997b: The heady political life of compassion. In M. L. Shanley and U. Narayan (eds), 128–44.

Spivak, Gayatri Chakravorty 1987: French feminism in an international frame. In Spivak, *In Other Worlds: essays in cultural politics.* New York: Methuen.

Squires, Judith (ed.) 1993: *Principle Positions: postmodernism and the rediscovery of value.* London: Lawrence & Wishart.

Squires, Judith 1994: Citizenship: androgynous or engendered participation? In *Swiss Annual Review of Political Science*, 34.

Squires, Judith 1996: Quotas for women: fair representation? In J. Lovenduski and P. Norris (eds), 73–90.

Stanley, Liz 1990a: Recovering women in history from feminist deconstructionism. In *Women's Studies International Forum*, 13/1–2, 151–7.

Stanley, Liz (ed.) 1990b: *Feminist Praxis: research, theory and epistemology in feminist sociology.* London: Routledge.

Stanley, Liz and Wise, Sue 1993: *Breaking Out Again: feminist ontology and epistemology.* London: Routledge.

Stephenson, Mary-Ann 1996: *Winning Women's Votes: the gender gap in voting patterns and priorities.* London: Fawcett.

Stetson, Dorothy McBride and Githens, Marianne (eds) 1996: *Abortion Politics: public policy in cross-cultural perspective.* New York: Routledge.

Stetson, Dorothy McBride and Mazur, Amy (eds) 1995: *Comparative State Feminism.* Newbury Park, CA: Sage.

Sunstein, Cass (ed.) 1990: *Feminism & Political Theory.* Chicago: University of Chicago Press.

Sylvester, Christine 1994: *Feminist Theory in International Relations in a Postmodern Era*. Cambridge: Cambridge University Press.

Taub, Nadine and Williams, Wendy 1986: Will equality require more than assimilation, accommodation or separation from the existing social structure? In *Rutgers Law Review*, 37, 825–44.

Taylor, Charles 1986: *Source of the Self: the making of modern identity*. Cambridge: Cambridge University Press.

Taylor Charles 1991: Cross-purposes: the liberal-communitarian debate. In N. Rosenblum (ed.), 159–82.

Taylor, Charles 1992: The politics of recognition. In A. Gutmann (ed.), 25–75.

Tickner, J. Ann 1992: *Gender in International Relations*. New York: Columbia University Press.

Tong, Rosemarie 1989: *Feminist Thought: a comprehensive introduction*. London: Unwin Hyman.

Tronto, Joan 1993: *Moral Boundaries: the political argument for an ethic of care*. New York: Routledge.

Tronto, Joan 1996: Care as a political concept. In N. Hirschmann and C. Di Stefano (eds), 139–56.

Voit, Rian 1992: Political representation and quotas: Hanna Pitkin's concept(s) of representation in the context of feminist politics. In *Acta Politica*, 27/4.

Voit, Rian 1998: *Feminism and Citizenship*. London: Sage.

Walby, Sylvia 1997: *Gender Transformations*. London: Routledge.

Walby, Sylvia (ed.) 1999: *New Agendas for Women*. London: Macmillan.

Walzer, Michael 1983: *Spheres of Justice*. New York: Basic Books.

Walzer, Michael 1992: Comment. In A. Gutmann (ed.), 99–104.

Watson, Sophie (ed.) 1990: *Playing the State: Australian feminist interventions*. London: Verso.

Waugh, Patricia 1997: Modernism, postmodernism, gender: the view from feminism. In S. Kemp and J. Squires (eds), 206–12.

Weldon, Thomas 1962: *States and Morals: a study in political conflict*. London: John Murray.

Whitford, Margaret 1991: *Luce Irigaray: philosophy in the feminine*. London: Routledge.

Whitworth, Sandra 1994: Feminist theories: from women to gender and world politics. In P. R. Beckman and F. D'Amico (eds), 75–88.

Wilkinson, Helen and Diplock, Shelagh 1996: *Soft Sell or Hard Politics: how can the parties best appeal to women?* London: Demos.

Williams, Wendy 1983: Equality's riddle: pregnancy and the equal treatment/special treatment debate. In *New York University Review of Law and Social Change*, 13, 325–80.

Wilson, Elizabeth 1997: Is transgression transgressive? In S. Kemp and J. Squires (eds), 368–70.

Winch, Peter 1958: *The Idea of a Social Science and its Relation to Philosophy*. London: Routledge & Kegan Paul.

Winch, Peter 1970: Understanding a primitive society. In Brian Wilson (ed.), *Rationality*. Oxford: Oxford University Press.

Wittig, Monique 1992: One is not born a woman. In Wittig, *The Straight Mind*. Hemel Hempstead: Harvester Wheatsheaf, 9–20.

Wolin, Sheldon 1961: *Politics and Vision*. London: Allen & Unwin.

Wright, Elizabeth 1989: Thoroughly postmodern feminist criticism. In Teresa Brennan (ed.), *Between Feminism and Psychoanalysis*. London: Routledge, 146–50.

Yeatman, Anna 1994a: The personal and the political: a feminist critique. In Paul James (ed.), *Critical Politics*. Melbourne: Arena Publications, 35–56.

Yeatman, Anna 1994b: *Postmodern Revisionings of the Political*. New York: Routledge.

Yeatman, Anna 1997: Feminism and power. In M. L. Shanley and U. Narayan (eds), 144–57.

Young, Iris Marion 1986: The ideal of community and the politics of difference. In *Social Theory and Practice*, 12/1.

Young, Iris Marion 1990a: *Justice and the Politics of Difference*. Princeton, NJ: Princeton University Press.

Young, Iris Marion 1990b: *Throwing Like a Girl and Other Essays in Feminist Philosophy and Social Theory*. Bloomington: Indiana University Press.

Young, Iris Marion 1996a: Communication and the other: beyond deliberative democracy. In S. Benhabib (ed.), 120–35.

Young, Iris Marion 1996b: Reflections on families in the age of Murphy Brown: on gender, justice and sexuality. In N. Hirschmann and C. Di Stefano (eds), 251–70.

Young, Iris Marion 1998: Polity and group difference: a critique of the ideal of universal citizenship. In A. Phillips (ed.), 401–29.

Young, Stacey 1997: *Changing the Wor(l)d: discourse, politics and the feminist movement*. London and New York: Routledge.

Yuval-Davis, Nira 1997: *Gender and Nation*. London: Sage.

Zaretsky, Eli 1982: The place of the family in the origins of the welfare state. In B. Thorne (ed.), *Rethinking the Family*. New York: Longman.

# Index